Goodbye, Tahrir Square

Coming of Age as a Jew of the Nile

Goodbye, Tahrir Square
Coming of Age as a Jew of the Nile

Elio Zarmati

CHERRY ORCHARD BOOKS

2024

LCCN: 2024948431

Copyright © Elio Zarmati, author, 2024

ISBN 9798887196657 hardback
ISBN 9798887196664 paperback
ISBN 9798887196671 ebook PDF
ISBN 9798887196688 epub

Book design by Lapiz Digital Services
Cover design by Ivan Grave

Published by Cherry Orchard Books,
an imprint of Academic Studies Press
1007 Chestnut Street
Newton, MA 02464
press@academicstudiespress.com
www.academicstudiespress.com

to my father
in memoriam

and

to Jenny
the light in my life

Contents

Prelude. Winter of 2011	xi
1. 1948	1
2. 1949	11
3. 1952	29
4. 1952-1955	45
5. 1955	63
6. 1956	81
7. Winter of 1957	105
8. Spring of 1957	119
9. Summer of 1957	137
10. Fall of 1958	173
11. Winter of 1958	203
12. Summer of 1959	221
13. Fall of 1959	271
14. Winter of 1959	287
15. Winter of 1960	311
16. Spring of 1960	341
Finale. Adieu	359

Adore ce que tu as brûlé, brûle ce que tu as adoré!

(Adore what you have burned, burn what you have adored!)
—*Saint Rémi, Bishop of Reims, Apostle of the Francs, 496 AD*

Si j'ai quitté l'Égypte, l'Égypte ne m'a jamais quitté. Quelquefois je pense que c'est seulement mon ombre qui est partie alors que moi je suis resté là-bas, seul, errant, comme durant ma jeunesse.

(Although I left Egypt, Egypt has never left me. / Sometimes I think that only my shadow has left / while I've remained there, alone, adrift, as I was in my youth.)
—*Tobie Nathan, Ce pays qui te ressemble, 2015*

Prelude

Winter of 2011

January 25, 2011. It's dawn in Los Angeles. I'm in the back seat of an airborne sedan, headlights piercing the foggy night, spiraling downward toward a large crowd assembled in a mammoth square. I shield my head with my hands, but nothing happens at first; then the car explodes into millions of particles that float in the air like lazy fireworks. My car seat, ejected from the pulverized car, is hovering in slow motion over the crowd. The square below is eerily familiar, but I can't place it.

When at last my ejection seat lands, a face in the crowd chants, "Ahlan wasahlan, ya'khouya!"—"Welcome, my brother!"—and the crowd echoes, "Ahlan wasahlan!"

The man in the crowd resembles my father, or rather the young man in the sepia photograph taken before I was born, but he's not my Papa. He smiles with mischief in his eyes.

"Who are you?" I ask him.

He taps me on the shoulder with one hand and touches my cheek with the other. "Ya salaam!" he exclaims in Arabic, then switches to Franco-Arabic, "Tu ne me reconnais pas, ya Loulou?"

I am dumbfounded. Since my mother died, no one calls me by that childhood nickname I hated.

"Sorry, I don't recognize you," I answer. "How do you know my name?"

A telephone rings in the distance. It's a faint old-style telephone bell ring, not the electronic ringtone of modern instruments. The rings get louder, but I don't respond. I don't want to break the spell of my father's doppelgänger presence. When, at last, the ringing stops, it's too late; gone is the doppelgänger, gone is the dream. As I reach for the notebook on my nightstand, the blasted telephone rings again, this time with the electronic notes of my bedroom cordless receiver. I pick it up.

"Are you watching the news?" I hear.

The voice on the telephone has a strong Middle Eastern accent, and before I can answer, he exclaims in Franco-Arabic, just like the man in my dream, "Ya salaam! Tu ne me reconnais pas?"

"Keep talking!" I say, stalling.

"Turn on the news! We'll talk later." A second or two after he hangs up, I recognize the voice. He's an old friend from my Egyptian childhood who now lives in Switzerland. We'd lost track of each other, but he'd recently come upon my name on the Internet, and we'd renewed our friendship after almost fifty years.

Fully awake now, I switch on the television set. On CNN, hordes of people are waving flags and chanting slogans, perhaps a million souls pressed against one another like so many canned sardines, inching toward a space that resembles the public square of my dream. The banners are in Arabic script. Is it another Palestinian Intifada? Another Tunisian uprising? Iraq, perhaps? Or Afghanistan? Before the newscaster identifies the event, an aerial shot reveals the entire square, and I'm jolted by a flash of recognition—the building on the left is the Museum of Antiquities on Tahrir Square, in the heart of Cairo. And I remember all too well the infamous Mogamma'a, the hideous government structure in which my father and I spent hours, sometimes days, awaiting an ever-elusive exit visa that would get us out of Egypt—forever.

An uprising in Egypt? Against the Mubarak regime's omnipotent military and police forces? I watch in disbelief and fascination as the police blast the crowd with water cannons and tear gas, and the demonstrators strike back with rocks, sticks, and an occasional Molotov cocktail. At the edge of the square, groups of protesters form a human chain in front of the museum, perhaps to defend it against looters.

Midan el-Tahrir, my old stomping ground. When I was a child, people still called the place by its old name, Midan el-Ismailia, even though the Egyptian revolution of 1919 had renamed it Tahrir Square, Liberation Square, in celebration of Egypt's independence from Britain. It was only after the second Egyptian revolution in 1952 that I heard people call it by its proper name. Was Tahrir Square hosting a third revolution?

No matter the name, the *midan* had been at the core of my boyhood in Cairo. During our last years in Cairo, my father and I had lived around the corner from the *midan*, in a hotel on the rue Champollion, and the *midan* was my gargantuan playpen. My mother lived with her new husband, his children, and their new son on the other side of the square, in a penthouse overlooking the Nile. My best friend lived a few blocks down the river, in the Garden City neighborhood. On my way toward many a destination, I had walked through Tahrir Square in joy and in distress, in exuberance and in abysmal misery.

As a child, the different translations of the Arabic word *midan* perplexed me—the French called it a *rond-point*, meaning a circle, the British a *square*, and in other languages it was *piazza*, *plaza*, or *platz*. In Arabic, a *midan* is an open space, an esplanade, a parade ground, a field, or an arena. Back in the fifties, Midan el-Tahrir was a huge oblong field with a large circle at its center, graced by a spectacular water fountain and gardens around which pulsated an infernal circle of traffic.

On one side of the *midan* lay the Nile Corniche along the majestic river and the Qasr-el-Nil Bridge guarded by two gigantic lions of stone at each entrance; on the other sides of the odd-shaped urban space were the Egyptian Antiquities Museum, several luxury hotels, a school campus, a church, a mosque, and beyond the ugly government structure, a smattering of belle epoque villas which housed royal families and embassies. Midan el-Tahrir was more than a geographical place; it was a magical dreamscape in which lives came together, often in joyful holiday celebrations, but sometimes in violent protest against kings and dictators.

In our early teens, my friends and I used to race our bicycles around Tahrir Square, braving the insane melee of cars, buses, motorcycles, donkeys, and horse-drawn carriages. The day before I left Cairo forever, I won a bet that I could ride my bike around the entire circle of Midan el-Tahrir without touching the handlebars. It was reckless, almost suicidal, but I knew I'd never see Tahrir Square again, and I wanted to bid it farewell with a little panache.

***

I am now watching the unfolding news on two screens, my laptop and the television. On the laptop, I go from one international newspaper to the next, and on the big screen, I zap from one broadcast to another. The televised news reminds me of the revolution of 1952. Midan el-Tahrir is now shrouded in clouds of smoke and tear gas. Some protesters attack a water cannon truck, others hurl rocks at the police and build barricades in the middle of the square. They all chant the same slogans. "Kefaya! Enough! Khalas! It's over!" I was never fluent in Arabic, and I haven't spoken it in decades, but an unexpected bit of atavistic knowledge, oozing out of deep recesses of my being, enables me to understand the chants of the protesters—"Erhal! Out! Emshi, ya Hosni! Go away, Hosni!"

I freeze the frame on a stunning shot of a lone man confronting a water cannon truck, not budging as the mammoth of steel rolls toward him. It is almost a carbon copy of the iconic video of the unknown rebel at Tiananmen Square standing in the path of a column of massive tanks. I unfreeze the frame. The Egyptian rebel stands his ground until the powerful jet of the water cannon propels him toward a group of policemen dressed like Darth Vader. Undeterred, the young man evades them, runs back toward the colossus and confronts the lethal muzzle once again.

Rioters have surrounded a building at the other end of Midan el-Tahrir and put it to the torch. A caption identifies it as the headquarters of the National Democratic Party, the party of Nasser, Sadat, and Mubarak. As the flames rise in the night, my gut hardens into a painful knot. It's a film I've seen before—Cairo burning. Six decades earlier. And now, the fire again.

There is something unreal, almost abstract, about these buildings burning on the screen. It's not as terrifying as it had been during the revolution I witnessed as a child. On the television screen, everything is muffled. The foul smell of fire and smoke is absent, and the palaver of anchors and reporters covers the screams of the crowds. I mute the sound and watch the riot in total silence—and I can now hear my father's anguished voice whispering once again, "C'est une révolte ou une révolution?" Is it a revolt or a revolution?

On that fateful day—January 26, 1952—Papa and I were standing on the top floor balcony of my grandmother's apartment, watching Cairo go up in flames. Six stories below, flatbed trucks were disgorging hordes of men wielding torches and sticks. Yelling anti-British and anti-Zionist slogans, the rioters were storming our neighborhood, leaving burning buildings in their wake. My favorite cinema, the Rivoli, a block away, was first; all I could see above the smoke and the flames was the blackened marquee that bore the name Clark Gable against the black and crimson skyline.

That day would be memorialized as Black Saturday, and that demonstration as one of the first salvos of the revolution that would overthrow King Farouk a few months later and establish a military dictatorship. And today, in a supreme twist of irony, it's the same dictatorship the people of Cairo are rising to abolish, after sixty years of absolute power. Will today's insurrection mark the beginning of true democracy in Egypt? Or will it be a flash in the pan, a revolution hijacked and relegated to the ash heap of history?

Almost sixty years ago, *my* revolution began with exalted hopes of liberation and justice and ended as a military coup. In its glorious beginning, it marked the end of the British Empire, the end of colonialism, geographic and cultural, the awakening of a new Arab identity and its apotheosis, the dream of Pan-Arabism. Inspired by Gamal Abdel Nasser, dominoes would fall throughout the Arab world, and monarchies would give way to revolutionary regimes with lofty aspirations. But total power eroded the noble ideals, and after a brief detour on the dance floor of democracy, Egypt joined the ranks of the celebrated revolutions—the French, the Russian, the Iranian, and so many others—that had begun with ideals of freedom and democracy and ended up spawning emperors, strongmen, and ayatollahs. Nasser, the beloved leader of the new Egypt, swiftly became a modern-day pharaoh, the uncontested king of the Arab world, and his sycophants in neighboring Arab countries became dictators of a lesser stature.

For us, Levantine Jews born and raised in Egypt, Nasser's military coup marked the end of an era that began four thousand years earlier, when Joseph of the many-colored coat was sold into slavery in pharaonic Egypt. In its effort to rally a country still reeling from its defeat in Palestine, the new regime was quick to equate Judaism with Zionism and make the Jews enemies in their native country. In a few months, large numbers of Jews would be expelled, their assets confiscated, and the remaining Jews would become pariahs. In the end, Egypt would be cleansed of its Jews, and all that would remain would be shuttered synagogues, desecrated cemeteries, and a few vestiges of the powerful Jewish culture that had flourished in the land since the early Iron Age.

***

February 11, 2011, eighteen days later. Paying little mind to my work deadlines—I'm writing the script for a documentary film—I'm still glued to the news on TV and my laptop. An announcement from the Mubarak regime is expected shortly. There are more than a million people in Midan el-Tahrir and on the adjacent Qasr-el-Nil Bridge awaiting the moment of truth.

The night before, the protesters had packed the square in anticipation of the dictator's resignation, and they had watched with mounting anger as the defiant dictator spoke of remaining in power until the end of his term. They had booed and waved their shoes to express their contempt for the strongman—whose tiny image, multiplied on giant television screens across Tahrir Square, no longer struck fear—and they'd kept chanting, "Revolution until Victory" and "We're not going away! He's leaving first!"

At long last, the dictator's grim-faced prime minister, Omar Suleiman, appears before the crowd. I brace for the worst—a declaration of civil war, a state of siege?—but the words are quick, stunning, and painless. Goliath has blinked. Pharaoh has deserted his throne. I listen in disbelief as

Suleiman adds that Hosni Mubarak has mandated the Armed Forces Supreme Council to run the state. As he utters his last words—"God is our protector and our rescuer!"—the crowd explodes with a million primal screams followed by loud honks, whistles, clapping hands, and the sound of *zaghareet*, the high-pitched ululations of joyful merrymaking, gushing out of a nation silenced for too long. It's a *hafla* of planetary dimensions, the mother of all celebrations, an exuberant affirmation of fraternity and hope. All that's missing is Om Kalthoum, the adored Egyptian singer, intoning a song while groups of men break out in a cane dance, in the way the popular Egyptian musicals of my childhood always ended.

I turn off the sound and watch the party in eerie silence. I am engulfed in bittersweet feelings of ambivalence. I love these people, I love what they've accomplished, and I want to celebrate with them, but I know I would not be welcome to partake in this most glorious day of their lives. We share a birthplace, but we're mortal enemies, the Capulets and the Montagues of the Middle East. As Arabs and Jews, we've been estranged for three generations. Sixty years of enmity, three wars, and rivers of blood separate us. We're enemies even though Egypt and Israel have had a peace treaty for some thirty years. If I showed up at their hafla wearing a Star of David, the older Egyptians would probably stone me to death in the public square. How would this younger, worldly, peace-hungry, and better educated generation welcome a Jew like me?

Most of the people on Midan el-Tahrir are too young to conceive of a world without hatred between Arabs and Jews. They do not know that there is such a thing as Egyptian Jews. As a peace activist, I've had countless conversations with young Arab men and women, American-born or refugees, and most of them look askance when I introduce myself as an Egyptian Jew. "There are no Jews in Egypt!" they affirm in disbelief. They find it hard to believe that, in the days of their grandfathers, nearly a million Jews lived in Arab countries, alongside Muslims and Christians, in a cobbled together and imperfect harmony, but with little or no bedlam and mayhem.

A roaming camera comes to rest on two youths in Midan el-Tahrir. The man sings and plays the oud, strumming its dozen strings in a plaintive melody of Arabian blues. He looks and even sounds like Bob Dylan circa 1967. Next to him, a lovely young woman holds a banner that says, "I dream of traveling from Casablanca to Beirut via Tel Aviv without a passport."

I freeze the frame and take in the couple. They're young, they're beautiful, and they're just discovering the power of their dreams. I once had the same dreams, but I've stopped believing peace will happen in my lifetime—or ever. Perhaps their generation will rekindle the hopes that our generation has given up; perhaps they will succeed where we have failed so utterly. *Insh'Allah!* God willing! If they can break the spell of the evil pharaoh in eighteen days, they can do anything.

***

On the news, a day later, Tahrir Square is empty of police and protesters. Street sweepers have replaced the tanks and the water cannons, and sanitation crews are scrubbing off the bloodstains and carting away the debris of the battlefield. I'm left with mixed feelings—sadness, relief, uncertainty, and the letdown from an emotional overdose of epic proportions.

In the first hours of the Tahrir Square demonstrations, I'd seen these protests as another episode of the Arab Spring that began in Tunisia earlier in the year. It mattered little that this potential revolution was taking place in my country of birth— I was no longer connected to it. My childhood in Egypt had ended abruptly some fifty years earlier, in the aftermath of the Suez war with France, Britain, and Israel. At the age of fourteen, I had escaped persecution by emigrating to France, and later to the United States, and I'd never looked back. Over the years, my memories of Egypt had blended into a dreamlike prehistory, like artifacts languishing in the remote edges of my consciousness, neither forgotten nor rejected, but stripped of emotion. It took a few days for the sounds and sights of Egypt to reawaken more dormant memories and emotions of me my long-buried childhood.

As I roam through news archives on the Internet, I come upon pictures and articles of the decade that altered the course of my early life—images of the end of an old world and the rise of a new order. I dwell on some pictures of British and French troops during the Suez war, and it triggers a distinct memory of my father on a night of blackout. At a distance, we could hear British jet fighters flying over the suburbs of Cairo, occasionally dropping batteries of bombs over faraway targets. My father was at my bedside, reading softly by dim candlelight the passage of Ecclesiastes that enumerated the seasons for everything under the Heavens. I can still hear Papa's musical voice saying, "A time to love and a time to hate, a time for war and a time for peace," like an incantation—and now I feel as though my father is in my room, speaking to me in the present. He tells me I can't keep the past in abeyance, and the time has come to confront it. A time to reopen the rusty sluice gates of remembrance and to allow old wounds to heal.

In an effort to jog my recollections, I search the Internet for pictures and maps of Cairo in the 1950s, and I forage for familiar haunts. Some are hard to find. The Cairo of my childhood had a poetic flair to it; its streets, alleyways, squares and bridges bore the names of kings and queens, pashas and sultans, goddesses and pharaohs. Most of them have been renamed to erase the traces of colonialism and the monarchy.

Today's Cairo is more prosaic; roadways and streets now bear the names of battles, political landmarks and dates of real or dubious victories. My Cairo, the vibrant cosmopolitan city where I came of age, that Cairo no longer exists, except perhaps in the vast memory banks of exile. Hence this attempt to retrieve a few echoes from the past before I run out of memory.

CHAPTER 1

1948

A few ethereal strands of memory culled from the fog of bygone times—a big house, the last on a cul-de-sac, hidden behind a tall iron gate and tall trees, and nestled below a tall hill upon which ran a rarely traveled railroad track. According to my father, that track had served the British forces during the war, but now it only served a lone train heading for an unknown destination every night at midnight.

The large house had been built or rebuilt by my mother's grandfather when he had moved from Haret el-Yahood, the Jewish Quarter in the heart of Old Cairo, to the posh area of Koubbeh, near King Farouk's palace. I'd never met my mother's parents. My maternal grandfather had died just before I was born, and my grandmother had followed him to the grave in short order. In those days, we all lived in the big house—my four maternal uncles and their wives and children on the ground floor, and my father, my mother and I on the smaller top floor. My fifth uncle was a college student in France. The servants and their children lived in a separate wing.

I have precious few memories of that period of my life—shadowy lines etched randomly on an otherwise blank canvas. The black Austin my father drove. The short burgundy-red cigarette holder he used to smoke strong perfumed Turkish cigarettes. Our playful rituals when he came home. He would blow the horn, and I would rush to jump into the Austin and sit on his lap, hands on the steering wheel as Papa drove to the end of the cul-de-sac, turned the car around and parked on the other side of the street as if he were readying for a quick getaway. I would bellow, "I want to drive! And smoke the red cigarette!" After a show of resistance he would give in, put the car in neutral, pull the hand brake, and gun the engine while I turned the wheel and chewed on his red cigarette holder for a few delicious minutes.

Of my mother, in those days, I remember mostly the luscious trail of perfume she left in her wake. She was beautiful, elegant, and she was often rushing to a party, a restaurant or a nightclub, always surrounded by admiring friends. She shone like a thousand lights, but sometimes it was a light without heat. Her professions of love were so excessive that it felt more like seduction than love. She seemed to desperately want to prove that she loved me more than my father did—and I hated it because I didn't like the pressure to choose between them.

The warmest memories of love and playfulness belong to my father, to my paternal grandmother, to my aunt Victoria, Tante Toto, whose infinite grace and kindness I cherished, and to the house staff who doted on me as if I were their child.

Tante Toto often looked after me when Maman was out and Papa at work. She liked to turn on the radio, lift me up and dance with me, singing along softly or whispering terms of endearment. She was the wife of my mother's brother Solomon, Oncle Moni, a shy and nervous man with a heavy mustache. He didn't seem to like our dances together. When Tante Toto held me in her arms, he would look at us in sadness or longing, or he would just turn away. I felt better when I was alone with Tante Toto.

It was a rowdy house, particularly at our Sunday breakfasts and lunches. My mother and her five brothers favored the *baladi* breakfast, the meal of the fellahin—*fûl-medammas*, made of crushed fava beans served with hard-boiled eggs, tahini, *ta'ameyas*, patties made of ground beans, and *e'aish baladi*, a coarse pocket bread. Lunch was often another national dish, the *molokheya*, a delicious stew of chopped mallow-leaves, cooked with a variety of spices and served with rice and chicken. The full complement of uncles, aunts and their broods sat around the L-shaped table. When they spoke of Oncle Mayer, the youngest brother who was a pharmacy student in Paris, they often lamented his marriage to Tante Florette, a Catholic Frenchwoman they believed to be antisemitic. My uncles Loufi and Jacques often engaged in loud arguments in French laced with Arabic invectives while their wives looked on. When the shouting went on for too long, Papa or Oncle Maurice would enter the fray and try to end the argument.

***

The house was maintained by a half-dozen servants. The women servants wore their traditional black robes as they cleaned the house or prepared the ingredients while the men did most of the cooking in their traditional loose-fitting, long-sleeved *galabeyas*. On festive occasions, the women worked in the kitchen, and the men served the meals, looking regal in their immaculate long white galabeyas with their red waistbands and red *tarbooshes*. My favorite was Osman, a tall and lean Nubian from Upper Egypt, on the Sudanese border. The three scars across his forehead—the markings of his tribe—gave him the fierce look of a warrior, but his wide smile and the twinkle in his eyes told a story of infinite kindness. I felt warm and safe in Osman's presence.

While my father was at work and my mother was out on the town, I would spend hours in the kitchen watching the women laugh and tease each other as they plucked chickens, cut vegetables, and crushed sesame in large pestles, filling the house with hearty and delicious smells. On laundry days they would gather on the roof, wash the clothes and linens in large buckets and spread them on clotheslines and racks; then they would apply henna to their hair, their eyebrows, and occasionally their nails. On occasions like birthdays and anniversaries, the henna ritual included adorning the back of their hands with graphic designs symbolizing joy, motherhood, serenity, and divine protection.

One afternoon, a man stopped me as I was going down the stairway. He was not one of the regular servants—probably a handyman because he wore a European-style khaki shirt and trousers instead of the traditional *galabeya*. He smiled and asked me, in a challenging tone, if I were a man.

"Of course I am a man. I'm three and a half years old," I exclaimed.

"You're not a man yet. I'll show you what it is to be a man!" he boasted.

Intrigued and slightly apprehensive, I watched him unbutton his pants and exhibit a large, hairy penis.

"Touch it!" he said. "Don't be afraid!"

"I'm not afraid!" I said. "But it's ugly!" I made a face and didn't move.

He sat on the stairway, pulled me toward him and rubbed his penis against my bare legs. I said I didn't like it, but he kept whispering, "It's good! I know you'll like it!" I waited a little longer, but I really hated the touch of his sticky flesh against mine, and I called out for Tante Toto. He retreated on the spot.

"Don't tell anybody!" he said in a tone that was at once apologetic, threatening and fearful, as he buttoned his pants. The fear he displayed told me that he'd done something wrong, something that deserved punishment, though I didn't understand the nature of the deed. "Don't tell anybody, ya khawaga!" he repeated, using the traditional honorific address for Europeans. He was almost begging.

I was stunned by his reaction. It was my first encounter with the barrier of fear and subservience that existed between European Egyptians and Arab Egyptians. How could a grown man be so fearful of a child? Goliath crumbling before a three-year old David? It made no sense, and I was torn between feeling sorry for him and reveling in the power I didn't know I had.

***

A vivid memory stands out in the fog of my third year. A piercing scream in the night, a deep burning sensation in my left eye, a time of total darkness—and the sudden realization that it is *my scream, my* pain, *my* darkness. A hazy feeling of panic, the movement of a car speeding through the night at a breakneck pace, its horn blasting madly and the angry blows of other cars honking back in counterpoint. Through my mostly closed eyelids, I could discern a kaleidoscope of incoming lights, then the blinding lights of a hospital lobby, followed by the quiet of a darkened room, and a man in white probing deeply into my eyes with a light pencil. And again total darkness.

Later, my father would tell me over and again how my mother, "irresponsible as usual," had mistakenly filled my eyewash cup with rubbing alcohol instead of the collyrium prescribed for an eye infection. "It's a miracle that she didn't blind you completely!"

The incident left me nearly blind in the left eye; from then on, it could only see blurred shapes and figures. For a long time, I had to do corrective therapy both at the ophthalmologist's and at home on my own. I would wear an eye patch on my right eye and use the left one to follow a moving penlight in the semi-darkness. Sometimes, I would move the right eye patch slightly to peek at myself. The black patch made me look like a pirate, and when I exercised by myself I would complete the look with a cape made of a blanket, a hat that went down to my ears, and a stick that made a fine sword. My fantasies made the ordeal a delightful adventure.

***

Of my father and my mother together, a lone memory endures—the day Papa and I left the Koubbeh house forever. I awakened from my afternoon nap with the sense that the earth was shaking. I got up, calling out for my father, but he didn't respond. I went to the living room and stood in the doorway. My father and my mother were yelling at one another. I couldn't make out the words, only that it was about the *walad*, the boy, and I wondered whether the *walad* was me or some other child. Papa opened a tube, threw two tablets of Alka Seltzer into a glass of water and waited for the medicine to dissolve. Maman yelled something. Papa looked at her with utter contempt and threw his glass against the wall. The shattering glass detonated in my ears like a crystalline explosion. I ran back to my room, climbed into bed and pretended to be asleep. A few minutes later, Papa came into my room with an empty suitcase and began to fill it with my clothes.

"Get up and get dressed!" he ordered.

"Where are we going?"

"Just get dressed!" he said impatiently as he helped me get into my clothes and tie my shoelaces.

He packed a suitcase, wrapped a few suits around his wooden valet hanger, and threw the lot in the back of the black Austin.

"Where are we going?" I asked again.

"We're going to Nona's," he answered.

Something was wrong. We saw Nona, my paternal grandmother, every Friday for the Sabbath and on the Jewish High Holidays, rarely on weekdays.

"But it's not Friday!" I exclaimed.

"We're going to spend a few days with her."

He started the car and stepped on the accelerator. The Austin roared away from the curb. Papa was uncharacteristically quiet. I kept asking him why we were going to Nona's. He didn't answer, but he gave me his cigarette holder as a pacifier. I sucked on it, wondering what Papa's new and unusual permissiveness meant. Had I suddenly become a grown-up? Could I smoke now? I didn't know whether to be happy or sad.

When we arrived at my grandmother's house, I was sent to the kitchen while Nona and my father sat in the living room, talking in hushed tones. Nona's two servants, Abdu and his wife Mayasoon, gave me milk and cookies before returning to their chores. They spoke in hushed tones in Arabic. I heard little of their conversation, but the words that kept recurring were *walad* and *maskeen*—the latter meaning "poor" in Arabic. As they kept looking at me, it became clear that the "poor boy" was *me*, and I couldn't fathom why they would feel so sorry for me.

***

My last memory of my maternal grandfather's house took place on a day I was visiting my mother. On the days we spent together, she would usually take me to a movie matinee or a puppet show, followed by the obligatory visit to Groppi's, the elegant teahouse where she met her friends in the afternoon. This time she had unexpectedly taken me directly to the Koubbeh house. I was surprised because Maman had insisted we go shopping for a gift since we were a few days short of my fourth birthday.

The house was eerily empty. My uncles and aunts were in Alexandria for the summer, along with all the servants save one, Ibrahim, who'd stayed with my mother.

Maman and I were in the upstairs bedroom, and she was holding me and kissing my nose and my cheeks, my arms, and my feet, calling me her treasure and the only one she had ever loved. It was delicious but so intense, so dramatic that I was a bit frightened and somewhat embarrassed. I was relieved when Maman got up, sat in front of the mirror and started the long and elaborate ritual of applying her makeup.

"What are you doing, Maman?" I asked.

"Je me fais une beauté," she answered, using a French expression that means both "putting on makeup" and "making myself beautiful." "Oncle Albert will be here soon."

"And Tante Marcelle?"

Albert and Marcelle were close friends of my parents. It was an Egyptian custom for the children to call their parents' close friends *Oncle* and *Tante*, Uncle and Auntie, even if they were not related.

"No. Just Oncle Albert."

"What about Tante Marcelle?"

"Tante Marcelle is in France for the summer," she said. "She won't be back for a while."

I had a sense of foreboding, but it was dispelled by the prospect of the outing.

"Where are we going?" I asked.

"Just for a drive, maybe go for ice cream," she answered, ill at ease. "We'll be back on time to take you back to your grandmother." A moment later, she said, "Go to the front gate and watch out for Oncle Albert's car. And tell him I won't be long."

I ran to the front gate and waited for the familiar blue Studebaker. An hour or so later, Oncle Albert hadn't arrived.

I rushed back to the bedroom, but my mother wasn't there. I went through all the rooms in the empty house, yelling "Maman!" at the top of my lungs. Ibrahim came out of the kitchen with a grin on his face.

"Ommak left a long time ago," he grinned. "With khawaga Albert."

"But I was out front! I didn't see his car!"

"He came through the back gate, and they drove away, far, very far away!" He seemed to think it was hilarious. I waited until Ibrahim was out of sight before bursting into tears.

I must have told my father about the incident, because I was never allowed to go back to the Koubbeh house or see Oncle Albert again. From then on, Maman would pick me up at Nona's apartment and take me to Groppi's, her favorite teahouse, or to the pictures or to her favorite shopping stores, but never again to her house. She didn't mention Oncle Albert again—not until much later when she would replace Tante Marcelle as Albert's wife.

It was the last time I saw my grandfather's house.

CHAPTER 2

1949

―――――

Nona lived on the top floor of a nineteenth-century French-style building on King Fuad I Avenue, a short walk from the Ezbekeyya Gardens. She had lived there for decades with Nono, my grandfather, and she had remained there after his death, even though the apartment was too big for a woman alone. When her children urged her to give up the apartment and come live with one of them, she refused adamantly—this is where her husband had died, and this is where she would die. When they insisted, Nona would remind them that it was not only her home, but also the home of Abdu, Mayasoon, and their many children who were born and raised in their rooms on the roof. Where would they go? What would happen to them? If anyone said another word, Nona would say, "Basta! Enough!" or she would close her eyes and appear to fall asleep in her armchair.

The apartment was divided into two parts—the austere, almost Spartan, living quarters and the reception rooms which were decorated with elegant furniture.

At the entrance, the front door opened onto a well-appointed foyer with leather chairs and a coffee table with mother-of-peal inlays. On one wall of the foyer, an imposing ornate set of double doors opened onto the formal dining room, with its long mahogany table, leather chairs, and a crystal chandelier. At the far end of the dining room, another set of double doors opened onto my favorite room—a wood-paneled room whose walls were covered with books bound in rich leather with gold-stamped spines.

It had been my grandfather's study, and long after his death it had remained a shrine to the departed patriarch, a sanctuary which we, Nona's grandchildren, were only permitted to enter on the important Jewish holidays when the connecting doors were opened to join the study and the dining room. It was as though my grandfather was part of the celebrations. Between festivities, the curtains were drawn, a heavy smell of mothballs and wood polish would permeate the air, and sneaking into either room was akin to violating the tomb of a pharaoh.

My room was next to the entrance foyer and the reception rooms. I loved that location because its proximity to the foyer allowed me to eavesdrop on the adults' conversations when I left my door ajar. Often after Shabbat diner, the grown-ups would send the children to the family room to play while they remained in the foyer to discuss the news of the week. More often than not, I would find a pretext to go to my room and listen to their conversations.

From the foyer by the front door, past my room, a long-tiled corridor led to a huge kitchen and pantry, and from there meandered on to Nona's imposing bedroom, whose door was always shut. At the epicenter of the apartment was the everyday dining room which doubled as a family room. Further down the hallway, smaller bedrooms were still identified by the names of Nona's four children, Victor, Léon, Rebecca, and Alfred, my father, the youngest of the brood. All the bedroom windows opened onto a large balcony overlooking the majestic King Fuad Avenue, flooding them with sunlight. There was a feeling of serenity and joy in the apartment whose nooks and crannies were an invitation to explore.

Nona was a gray-haired matriarch who radiated strength and spirituality. She was a severe, authoritarian, and rather rigid woman, although sometimes she would show kindness and understanding. When she was not working around the house, sewing, knitting, or supervising the servants, she retired to her room to read the Torah, pray and meditate. She spoke more languages than I knew existed: Greek, French, Italian, German, Arabic, Turkish and Ladino or Judeo-Spanish—the lingua franca of the Mediterranean Jewish communities, the Sephardic equivalent of Yiddish, a blend of ancient Spanish and Portuguese, with some French, Arabic and Hebrew thrown in. Our primary language was French, but Nona would switch to Ladino when she didn't want her grandchildren to understand. Of course, my cousins and I had learned Ladino by osmosis and understood almost everything or could easily guess the rest. Whatever language she spoke, Nona's sentences were often punctuated by one manifestation or another of God's will—"Dio mediante" or "Si Dieu veut" or "Insh'Allah."

Until Papa and I went to live with Nona, I had not spent much time with Nona alone. I always saw her every Friday for the Shabbat dinner and on the main Jewish holidays. Now, when Papa was at work, I spent my days with Nona, and I began to see hints of humor and playfulness under the mask of the strict disciplinarian she always affected to be because, as she often said, she thought my father was spoiling me rotten. She would also remind me that I was named after my grandfather, her husband, and that came with the obligation to be worthy of that honor.

When she spoke of Nono, it was always with infinite affection, respect and gratitude for his kindness, his vast culture, and his accomplishments. Sometimes she would close her eyes and fall silent, and I sensed that these moments were her way of pursuing the spiritual communion with him that his death had prematurely interrupted.

I liked my grandmother's cavernous apartment and the couple who'd served her for decades, Abdu and Mayasoon. They lived with their large brood in the servants' quarters on the roof of the building. The rooftop was forbidden territory because Nona feared I would hurt myself on the uneven surfaces of the asphalt, but I would sneak upstairs anyway and play with the children of the building's live-in servants.

I was shocked by their poverty. Most of the couples lived in one or two rooms with their children, sometimes ten or twelve of them. Our own servants, Abdu and Mayasoon, were more fortunate than the others; they shared three rooms with their eight children. Every year, when Mayasoon gave birth, a relative of hers was brought in from a distant village in Upper Egypt to replace her until she was well enough to resume work. Nona would give Mayasoon money, clothes, and our discarded toys for her brood.

Several months later, Mayasoon's belly would swell again, and Nona would scold her and tell her that she would die young if she kept giving birth every year, and Mayasoon always answered that it was the will of Allah. I could feel the strong bond that united Nona and Mayasoon, a bond of intimacy and respect which I sensed was forged by years of living together and raising their children.

Nona's absolute rule was that Abdu and Mayasoon were to be treated as family members, not as servants. She would eviscerate me, or any of my cousins, if we disrespected Abdu and Mayasoon in any way.

I spent many afternoons playing with Mayasoon's children. Some of our neighbors frowned upon it; they didn't approve of me playing with Arab children, perhaps because they feared their own children would follow suit. I overheard our downstairs neighbor complain about it to Nona when she came to pay her respects. My grandmother shrugged it off to the fact that I had no brothers and sisters, and added,

"There's no harm. After all, they're all the children of God." The neighbor fell silent. No one dared contradict the matriarch.

That same night Nona came into my room at bedtime. It was a rare event. Bedtime was the time for Papa and his stories. She startled me by saying she had seen me eavesdropping on her conversation with the neighbor and made me promise never to do it again. Then she said, "You heard what I said to her. You are all children of God." She fell silent for a long moment, and I knew she would talk about my grandfather. "Hijico mio,"—'my little boy' in Ladino—"Your Nono never tolerated any kind of discrimination. He was always on the side of the poor and the downtrodden. If he were alive, he would tell you that nobody is inferior to you, regardless of their education or circumstances. Or superior for that matter. God loves his children equally."

"Does it mean I can play with the boys on the rooftop?"

"Only if there are adults watching over you. I'll tell Mayasoon. And be careful not to hurt yourself on that broken asphalt!"

***

Both my grandmother and my father had a trove of stories about our family, and I never tired of hearing them, even the ones I'd heard many times before, because each retelling brought fresh details that made them even more interesting. I couldn't always follow the interlaced threads of the rich multicolored tapestry Papa and Nona were weaving before my eyes. Their stories went as far back as Spain, before the expulsion of its Jews in the fifteenth century, and afterward to Turkey and Italy and Greece and France, and even to Austria and beyond.

Nona and Papa had different storytelling ways. Nona's stories were understated and short on details while my father's were full of larger-than-life characters and epic events, but I recognized that they told the same story with endless variations—Jews fleeing hostile lands they'd once called home and rebuilding their lives elsewhere, sometimes more than once in their lifetime. Some of Papa's stories were so enthralling that, even at the age of five or six, I knew instinctively that these stories were embellished, and I wondered if they were legend or truth.

I had a soft spot for Nona's stories about growing up in Greece at the end of the nineteenth century, and I would keep begging for more tales. She was born Elena Cohen in the town of Vólos, in Thessaly, and grew up in Salonica, two cities of legends she wanted me to know—Vólos, built over the ancient city of Demetrias, the homeland of Jason and the Argonauts, and Salonica, named after Thessaloníki, the sister of Alexander the Great. From her stories of her early life, I gathered that she was a young child during what she called the Greco-Turkish war of 1897—violent times during which the Jewish communities suffered at the hands of both the Greeks and the Ottomans.

"When I was little," Nona said, "my father, your bisnono, said, 'Basta! Enough!' He sold everything, loaded a few belongings onto the back of a couple of donkeys and took us on a long journey from Salonica all the way back to our old city of Vólos—"

"On the donkeys?" I asked, incredulous.

"No, hijico mio, on foot behind the donkeys. My father, my mother and my eight brothers and sisters, your great-uncles and aunts, God bless their souls—"

I knew their names by heart. "Jacob, Abramino, Regina, Samuel, Fortunée, Esther, Eliah, and Moussa—"

"We walked through Thessalia—"

"There were no trains?" I asked.

"Of course there were trains, but your bisnono didn't want us to be noticed by the authorities. Once we were back in Vólos, we got on a boat to the Piraeus harbor, and from there onto another boat bound for Alexandria."

In Salonica, Nona's father, Yehuda Cohen, had been a prosperous rug merchant, and the family business had branches in three European cities. One of his brothers had married a Viennese Jewess and opened a Vienna branch of the family rug business, and another brother had fulfilled his life-long dream of living in Paris where he married a Frenchwoman of Polish origin. "They both married Ashkenazi women, but good women," Nona always said. I always wondered about the *but* she injected when she spoke of the Ashkenazi. Weren't they Jews like us? I didn't fully understand the differences between the several kinds of Jews that despised one another—the Ashkenazi Jews from Europe, the Sephardi Jews from Spain and Portugal, and the Mizrahi Jews from the Middle East, North Africa, and Asia who did not originate in the Iberian peninsula but practiced Sephardi Judaism.

Both the Ashkenazim and the Sephardim considered the other to be a breed apart. For the Sephardim, the Ashkenazi Jews were an odd kind of Jews, not quite goyim like Christians or Muslims but close. They didn't speak Ladino or Spanish, but an odd Germanic language called Yiddish, and their religious rituals were different. The Sephardim mocked them behind their backs, using derisive names like *shlekht* or the onomatopoeic *voos-vooss* that mimicked their guttural Germanic accents. In turn the Ashkenazim called the Sephardim *schwartzes*, which means black in Yiddish or German, a word they used equally to designate Oriental Jews and Arabs. "To them, we're not real Jews," Nona chuckled. "I guess they don't know or don't want to know that we, *Black Jews*, were fighting Roman oppression in Jerusalem, and that, along with Arabs in Spain, we were inventing new forms of algebra, mathematics, poetry and philosophy while they were illiterate peasants in the steppes of Russia."

When my great-grandfather decided it was time to leave Greece, he knew where to go. His brothers urged him to join them either in Vienna or Paris, but Yehuda Cohen didn't share his siblings' enthusiasm for Europe's enlightenment. He'd studied enough to know how fickle Europe was with its Jews. Its monarchs had welcomed Jews into their countries when they needed them, but had not hesitated to persecute them as they did in Greece and Turkey or even expel them generations later—England in the thirteenth century, France in the fourteenth, Germany, Poland, Italy and Spain through the fifteenth and later centuries. Who in 1899 could possibly foresee what Europe, in the twentieth century, had in store for its Jews? In his wisdom, Yehuda had concluded that there was only one place for a Jew to live and die: Palestine, the home of the Bible. It was just across the Mediterranean, still within the confines of the Ottoman Empire, but not at war like Greece and Turkey. Its large Jewish population was said to be living in relative peace with their Muslim and Christian neighbors.

But when their ship put in at Alexandria, Yehuda learned that famine and malaria were sweeping Palestine, and he thought it wiser to wait in Egypt for better times. Life in Palestine must've never gotten better because my great-grandfather remained in Egypt for the rest of his life, praying that his children would one day enter the Promised Land that, like Moses, he had been denied.

In her late teenage years—it was hard to imagine Nona as such a young woman—Elena met a dashing young Jewish-Italian bank clerk known as Eliahu Zarmati in Hebrew, Elio in Italian, Elia in Greek, and Elie in French. His father or perhaps his grandfather had come to Egypt from the Tuscan city of Livorno, which had been a haven for the Jews after their expulsion from Spain. There was another family legend that claimed that my great-great grandfather had been a Turkish or Palestinian Jew who had migrated to Egypt and gotten an Italian passport by deception. Since the archives of the Jewish community of Livorno had been lost in a fire, many Jews found witnesses to testify they were born in Livorno and became instant Italian citizens—and as Jews were not eligible for Egyptian citizenship, the Italian birth certificate was a coveted commodity.

Neither legend said how Eliahu had acquired the linguistic skills and the encyclopedic culture that so dazzled the young Greek-Jewish girl he wanted to marry.

"If Nona was Greek and Nono was Italian," I asked my father, "how come they spoke French together?"

"They spoke Ladino among themselves, but the new educated Egyptian elite—Jews, Muslims and Christians alike—studied and spoke French. It was the language of the Century of Enlightenment, the language of diplomacy, and it was the herald of a new age of universal progress." All over the Middle East, the French educational system was the crucible in which Arab Muslims, Jews and Christians of all denominations and nationalities—Greeks, Armenians, Copts from all the countries of the Mediterranean basin and even Eastern Europe—came together and forged a common identity as cosmopolitan Levantines. Nona would sometimes tell Papa that he was speaking above my intellectual grasp, but I insisted that I understood everything. It wasn't entirely true, but I knew that whatever was obscure today would be clarified in further conversations, and I loved to listen to my father extemporize.

From the first day of their courtship to their last day together, my grandparents continued to speak Ladino with one another, but they spoke French with their children, and over time French superseded Ladino as the primary language of daily life.

As a nod to their new identity, Elio and Elena Gallicized their names to Elie and Hélène Zarmati. In short order, they produced four children: Victor, Léon, Rebecca and my father, Alfred. Nono rose to become the manager of the bank for which he worked, but his real life was devoted to the study of history and literature. He subscribed to numerous French and Italian publications, and every Sunday the poor or illiterate Jews from the neighborhood flocked to his house to listen to him read the news from Europe. Although the Dreyfus Affair that had divided France for a generation had ended years earlier, the neighbors never tired of the saga of Captain Alfred Dreyfus, from his first conviction to his reinstatement in the French Army. Such was my grandfather's passion that he named my father Alfred after Captain Dreyfus.

Even after my grandparents left the Jewish neighborhood and moved to the King Fuad Avenue apartment in the European part of Cairo, Nono continued to go to the old neighborhood to spread the news from the many French and Arab publications he received, read and write letters for the illiterate, and give money to the poor and advice to the rich.

I never met my grandfather. He died at the young age of fifty-nine, before I was born. Following the tradition of naming a first-born after a grandparent, alive or dead, I was registered as Elie at the French hospital where I was born, Elio at the Italian consulate of Cairo, and Eliahu at our synagogue. In keeping with a family tradition, I was given the androgynous nickname of Loulou. Since an older cousin had also been named after my grandfather and nicknamed Loulou, he became Le grand Loulou while I was saddled with Le petit Loulou—which quickly became le petit méchant loup, the Small Bad Wolf.

***

Life at Nona's was punctuated by the Sabbath and the Jewish holidays. On those days, at the earliest hour, the servants opened the doors and windows of the reception rooms to let in the fresh air. They polished the silverware and set the dining room table. In the evening the crystal chandelier would glow, lit by Abdu since no Jew was allowed to touch fire or light on Shabbat, and the clan would gather around Nona's huge table.

The immediate family—Papa's brother Oncle Léon, his wife Tante Marie, and their three daughters; his sister Tante Rebecca, her husband Oncle Maurice, and their three daughters—was often joined by second and third cousins and other guests. After the prayers, Nona never failed to say a blessing for the absent members of the clan who had gone to Palestine before a portion of it became the state of Israel—Oncle Victor, his wife Judith, their children, Elie and Annie, and Rebecca's son from her first marriage, Felix.

The prayers always ended with the Mourner's kaddish for our family members in France and Austria who had died in a place called "The Camps" during the Nazi regime. When I asked Papa about it, he just said it was a bad place that no longer existed. The final words were the traditional, "Next Year in Jerusalem!" which sounded like an inaccessible dream. I wondered why we didn't just go there. According to Papa, Jerusalem was only eight hundred kilometers away, just a long train ride in the days before Egypt's war with Israel.

Every few weeks, at the Shabbat dinner, Oncle Léon would read Oncle Victor's latest letter from Israel. Since there was no mail service between Egypt and Israel, the letters were routed through Tante Jeanne in Italy. In every letter, Victor urged Nona and his brothers and sister to join him in Israel. Since it was hazardous to mention Israel, they used a euphemism in its stead—Israel became 'chez nous,' which means 'our home' in French. Neither Nona nor her other children felt that we would ever need to flee to Israel, but they admired Victor, Judith, their children and Felix for fulfilling Yehuda Cohen's dream—rebuilding the land of the Bible.

We all feared for our family in Israel. The threat of a second war between Israel and a new alliance of Arab countries loomed large, and our kin would be called to arms. Even my cousin Annie. Women served alongside men in the new Jewish state's military.

I loved the Shabbat gatherings and the High Holidays, especially Passover. My cousins would usually spend the whole day at Nona's, and the seven of us would help Nona and the servants prepare for the evening festivities. Every minute of the day was full of anticipation. Live chickens roamed the kitchen until a rabbi came and slaughtered them in accordance with the kosher ritual. Mayasoon would burn their feathers on the stove to make plucking them easier, and Abdu would cook them. Once again, the regular silverware was put away and the silver holiday set would be brought out and rubbed until it shone brightly.

Shortly after sunset Papa and Oncle Léon would come home from the synagogue, and we would sit around the huge dining room table and begin the prayers, punctuated by Oncle Léon's painstaking explanation of each part of the interminable ritual. Sometimes one of the youngest children, Simone, Viva or I, couldn't suppress outbursts of laughter, and Nona would silence us with a severe look. By the time dinner was served, we'd all be starved nearly to death, but Nona wouldn't have allowed anyone to skip a single sentence in the prayer book.

Every year during the Seder, I was struck by the absurdity of celebrating the exodus from Egypt while we were *still* in Egypt. Had the Exodus really existed? If Jews had really reached the Promised Land, why did they return to the land of slavery? Between the Exodus and now, little seemed to have changed. There was still a pharaoh; his name was King Farouk, and his armies had fought the Jews in the same Sinai desert. There was now a new Moses; his name was David Ben Gurion, and he had led the Hebrews to independence in their ancestral lands.

Nona had little patience with my incessant questions, and she would bark an imperious, "God has His reasons. When He decides that the time is right, He will take us back to Jerusalem." If I insisted, she would shake a piercing finger at me and sternly say, "Basta!"

When my cousins went home, I would feel lonely and sneak into my grandfather's forbidden study. Ignoring Nona's interdiction, I would open one of my grandfather's books. Some of them had drawings, and I would look at them for hours in an attempt to decipher the mysteries contained in the books they illustrated. Even the smell of paper and ink was an invitation to a magical journey. There was comfort and peace in the books, even if I couldn't read them—yet.

When Nona caught me coming out of my grandfather's library, she gave me a hard look and sent me to my room. I was so upset that I told Abdu that I was sick and couldn't join Nona for dinner. She came to my room and sat on a chair by my bed. "It's not your first time sneaking into Nono's room, is it?" My face must have registered shock and fear, but she wasn't as angry as she looked. "You thought I hadn't noticed, did you?" I looked down. Nona bent over and tapped me on the forehead. "If I catch you again, I'll spank you until your backside is as red as a monkey's. You're too young for these books! They are rare editions, and I don't want you to damage them. But someday, when you're older and wiser, I'll give them to you."

It wasn't the reaction I'd expected, and I could only mumble a weak thank you. Nona put her hand on my forehead and blessed me. "You're his spitting image, son portrait craché! You bear his name, you have the same eyes, the same intelligence, the same inquisitive mind. He would have been proud of you." She raised her hand and shook it in a threatening way, "But he was too kind, like your father. I'm not, so behave!"

***

It took me a long time before I understood that the "few days" at Nona's meant forever. The word "divorce" began to creep up in conversations between my father, his siblings and Nona, always in hushed tones as though it was a shameful word. All I knew was that nothing would ever be the same. The word "custody" also came up in the obscure conversations, and I learned that "negotiations" were taking place between my father and my mother to determine my fate.

And at long last I was told of the verdict—Papa would be my guardian and we would live with Nona. I would be allowed to spend Saturdays with my mother. I didn't mind the new rules. Papa seemed to be much calmer now than he had been with Maman, and one day a week with my mother seemed fine. All I would miss from the Koubbeh house was dancing with Tante Toto, and that made me very sad.

In practice, the arrangement was not as smooth and peaceful as I'd hoped it would be. In the eyes of my paternal family, I ceased to have a mother, and she lost her first name. Every arrangement with *her* was handled by Oncle Léon. After my weekly visit with Maman, Papa or Nona would ask, "Where did *she* take you this time?" When she called on the telephone, Nona would call me with visible reluctance. "*She's* calling you!"

The telephone was an imposing black contraption hung on the wall in the middle of the long corridor that separated the formal reception area from the rest of the apartment, perched high above a dark oak chair immaculately waxed and shined. I would run down the hall, and Nona would hand me the receiver as though she were getting rid of a soiled rag. If the call exceeded two or three minutes, Nona would gesture impatiently from the other side of the hallway. "The telephone is only for emergencies and to make appointments," she would say. "It's not for chitchat. You say hello, make your arrangements, say goodbye and basta! Save the chitchat for when you see *her*!"

For her part, my mother displayed the same dislike for Nona and for my father. She went on endlessly about how they had mistreated her during her years of marriage and how they would only let her see me one day a week since the divorce. I didn't dare say that her recriminations were spoiling that only day I had with her. I would just shut my eyes and pretend not to hear them.

Yet, in spite of the feud between my father and my mother, I felt safe, protected and happy much of the time. My father and I spent a lot of time together. On days without school, he often took me along when he went to work at Dorville, his haberdashery on Soliman Pasha Street. Located in the prestigious commercial artery of the capital, his store was frequented primarily by British officers and by the Egyptian elite of all faiths. The elegant store smelled of leather and musky colognes, and its glass counters shone with cufflinks, tie clasps and other male adornments. I liked to sit with the tailors in the huge backroom, watching them work, and I was especially fond of Mahmoud, the chief tailor. He seemed to enjoy showing me his vast collection of needles and bobbins, and the infinity of stitches he could do with the big Singer machine he ran like a one-man band, using alternatively the hand crank, the foot pedal or the electric switch.

On Sundays Papa took me to the Pyramids, where we rode horses or camels before having lunch at the Mena House, or he would rent a felucca and we'd sail on the Nile for a few hours. Papa sang melodious songs or recited poems and entire passages from the plays of the French trinity of Classics—Racine, Corneille, and Molière. At night, I wouldn't go to sleep until he'd read a few verses of one of my favorite plays or told me more stories about the gods of Mount Olympus or the Trojan war or Ulysses's return to Ithaca. There was no end to my father's passion for literature, language and history, a fervent love imparted to him by his own father, and he was now passing it on to me with humor and lightheartedness.

Sometimes, Nona would come into the bedroom and tell my father in Ladino that he was spoiling me rotten—which had become her motto. Papa would answer something about needing to be both mother and father to the *little one*. I never let on that I understood enough Ladino to get the gist of their conversation. What did Papa mean when he said he needed to be *mother* and *father* to me? I didn't feel I was missing anything, and I liked the way things were. Papa was as much a playmate as a father and teacher. He didn't speak to me as though I were a baby, the way many parents I knew spoke to their children, except perhaps when he scolded me for misbehaving. Although he pretended to complain about my incessant questions and nicknamed me Señor Why, he always asked for my opinion on the poems and plays he'd read to me. If the poems were written in complex or ancient French, he would clarify their meaning, and even when their substance eluded me, the music of the words and their different tonalities would transport me into magical worlds. Long before I could understand the intricacies of seventeenth-century French, I could recite entire passages of the classic plays from Molière to Shakespeare—the latter in French translation, until I could learn enough English to read it.

"One more verse, Papa, just one, and I'll go to sleep, Promis, juré, craché! Cross my heart and hope to die!"

He always gave in and recited a few more passages from one of the classical plays. Corneille's *Le Cid* was my favorite. No matter how often I heard them, the poet's stanzas never lost their magic.

CHAPTER 3

1952

———

On a Saturday morning in the winter of 1952, I was playing in my room when I heard a cacophony of screaming voices and car horns ringing from the street. I joined Nona, Abdu, and Mayasoon on the dining room balcony and looked down on Fuad Avenue. A procession of flatbed trucks full of men yelling and chanting anti-British slogans was heading toward the Cairo Opera. Throngs of demonstrators, some in galabeyas, others in Western garb, followed the trucks on foot, waving torches, jerrycans, and ragtag flags. At the far end of the avenue, flames and thick smoke rose from burning buildings, a gigantic bonfire that turned the sky crimson.

Papa, home from his haberdashery, yelled, "Quick! Inside! Don't let them see you!"

"What's happening, Alfred?" asked Nona. "What do these people want?"

"They scream anti-British slogans, but they're actually burning down any European building without distinction," he said. "The store is OK, but for how long?"

"They burn homes too?" cried Nona.

"Houses, apartment buildings, restaurants, stores, everything! I just saw the Shepheard's Hotel go up in flames! They're looting and beating anyone who looks European!"

"That's the Rivoli building!" exclaimed Abdu. "Humma maganeen! They're crazy! I'm going down to see what's going on!"

"Be careful, Abdu!" Nona and Mayasoon cried in unison.

"Is it a revolt or a revolution?" Papa muttered. He repeated the question several times, in a tone of increasing anguish. He seemed to be whispering to someone only he could see. Regaining his composure, he said, "I have to check on my staff at the store. I'll be back in no time."

Nona went to her room and began to pray. I slipped out onto the balcony, crouching to make myself less visible, and watched from high above the city in flames, thinking how much it looked like one of the scenes from *Quo Vadis* in which Emperor Nero plays the lyre and sings as he watches Rome burn down. I'd seen the film a few weeks earlier at the Rivoli Cinema, the very theater that was now burning before my eyes, and I half-expected Peter Ustinov to show up on the rooftop with his lyre. As I watched the blaze that was my neighborhood, it was clear that this was happening in real life, *our* life, not in a movie; all along the avenue *real* people were putting *real* torches to *real* buildings, and *real* men and women were pouring out of their burning dwellings and running for their lives. I wondered how long it would take the mob to reach our building and put us all to the torch. I hoped I'd die first rather than see the people I loved go up in flames.

As the mob came closer, the servants of the building, headed by Mayasoon and Abdu, assembled outside the front door. I watched them tangle with the swarm of incendiary men. Even from the height of the eighth floor I could hear the fracas of the struggle. "Emshi! Yalla! Emshi!" they yelled. "Go away! There are no Ingilisi in this building!" There was a lot of shoving and screaming, but ultimately the arsonists moved on.

For the rest of the day, every time Papa went back to the burning streets to check on Dorville and the store staff, I had hellish visions of Papa and his family of employees being torched by the mob. Every time he came back home, I would ask, "Do you still have to go back?" and the invariable answer was, "It's a man's duty to protect his family, and my staff is also family." He would give me a hug and say, "Don't worry, the crowd is burning down buildings, not killing people." I wasn't sure I could believe him.

We spent hours listening to the radio in the living room. I loved the imposing RCA-Victor console radio with its half-round dial scale that lit up in orange, green and red, and the speaker that crackled and hissed as Papa navigated the tuner between the shortwave and the broadcast bands. There was magic in the machinery that brought home the sounds from such faraway places as Britain, France or Russia with the same clarity as those coming from Cairo itself. As Papa moved the dial in search of a clear station, I could see in my mind's eye the high-pitched sounds traveling through space from these faraway places all the way to our living-room.

Throughout the day neighbors stopped by to get our news and give us theirs. They talked about their sons and daughters and brothers and sisters caught in the maelstrom, and they shared their fears and their questions. Who was behind these riots? The Muslim Brotherhood? The communists? The British? The king himself? Everyone had a different opinion.

When Papa came back home later in the afternoon, he announced that the protesters had occupied Tahrir Square, the old Midan Ismailia. "The square is packed with thousands and thousands of people! And on the way back, I saw with my own eyes several policemen in uniform helping the mob burn down stores on Soliman Pasha! The army is nowhere to be seen!"

"They can't let them stay there," said Nona. "Not with the Museum on Midan Ismailia!"

A wave of cold sweat ran through me. My mother's apartment overlooked the Nile, a stone's throw from the Museum of Antiquities on Midan el-Tahrir, and I wondered if her building was still standing. She had called on the telephone earlier in the day, just as the riots had started, and promised to call me back in the afternoon, but she hadn't.

"Our line was busy, but your mother spoke with Oncle Léon," Papa said as though he'd read my thoughts. "She's in the Koubbeh house with her brothers." It was the first time I'd heard him talk about Maman without distaste or contempt; I was sad that it had taken the burning of Cairo for it to happen.

An announcer on the BBC said that the Egyptian Army, which had remained on the sidelines for most of the day, was now moving to defend the king's palace and British property, but only after Great Britain's ambassador had threatened to dispatch the British troops stationed at the Suez Canal to Cairo. Toward the end of the day, the army proclaimed a state of emergency and restored order. By then, much of the city of Ismailia, on the west bank of the Suez Canal, had been reduced to smoldering rubble.

Papa went out once again to check on his store and came back with the news that Dorville had been spared. The entire staff had stood their ground in front of the store. Mahmoud said he was the owner of the business and challenged the mob to burn him and his staff along with his store. The mob backed off and turned its ire against the British Turf Club nearby.

All through the night, Papa and Nona listened to the radio. I was sent to my room, but I couldn't sleep. I opened the door and tried to understand what the voices on the radio were saying. Papa kept switching from one station to the next, listening to broadcasts in French and in English. They were reciting the endless tally of the burned-down buildings of the day like a litany—so many people had died, so many had been injured, so many businesses and homes destroyed. It seemed that all the familiar places where my mother took me on her visitation Saturdays had gone down in flames—Groppi's, the tea room and pastry shop where we often went after a movie, Maman's favorite department stores, the elegant hotels where we went for lunch, and two of my favorite cinemas. Would there be any place left to go on Maman's Saturdays?

The next morning, I woke up to the sound of tanks and armored cars driving up Fuad Avenue. Papa was on the telephone talking to Oncle Léon. "Be careful, Léon. They've proclaimed martial law. That means they can shoot anyone on sight," said Papa. "This is not a minor revolt. It's the beginning of a revolution. Mark my words, the days of the monarchy are numbered. Maybe Victor was right. Maybe our days in this country are numbered too."

***

After the riots ended, the atmosphere remained heavy with fear and apprehension. At the next Shabbat dinner, the customary laughter and banter gave way to discussions of the Cairo fire, now known as Black Saturday. Over and again, I heard the question that seemed to have no answer, "Was it a revolt or a revolution?"

Revolution! The word evoked images of guillotines and regicide, decapitated aristocrats and Napoleonic victories. Since I was an infant, Papa had fed me stories of the French revolution and Napoleon's glorious battles, although what Papa glorified the most was not the Emperor's military triumphs but his Code Napoléon, the civil code that established freedom of religion and granted the Jews civil rights and citizenship. Papa worshipped the holy trinity of

Liberty, Equality and Fraternity proclaimed by the French revolution.

I liked the word *revolution*. It was a word of many colors—it gave a name to the violent madness of the rioting mobs, it reeked of anger, fire and death, but it also held a promise of change, purpose, nobility and even grandeur.

"Papa, will they behead King Farouk like the French did Louis XVI?"

"I don't think so! Maybe the riots will cause King Farouk to treat his people better and prevent a national tragedy. If he doesn't learn why people hate his regime, this revolt will become a revolution. Either way, it's not good for us."

Winter gave way to summer, and the anxiety in the city remained palpable. Louder voices rose, accusing the king of being pro-British and blaming him and his cronies for Egypt's defeat in the Palestine War of 1948. A power struggle between the monarchy and the military heightened the tensions. The king appointed several prime ministers to form new governments and dismissed them in short order. The country was paralyzed.

On a July morning, all the radio stations in all languages delivered a momentous message—a former officer of the Royal Army, Anwar El Sadat, announced that the Free Officers, a group he called the Blessed Movement, had deposed the king whose corruption was destroying Egypt. A new revolutionary regime led by General Muhammad Naguib was now in charge. Throughout the day one heard the message rebroadcast in Arabic, and in the European languages most spoken in cosmopolitan Egypt—French, English, Italian and Greek.

"Muhammad Naguib is an honorable man, but not his cohorts," said Papa. "And Gamal Abdel Nasser, that mamzer, was a pro-Nazi Green Shirt—and that Sadat is an a'aragoz, a puppet, who was also a Green Shirt and a Muslim Brother, jailed by the British for being a German spy! The man runs with the hare and hunts with the hounds! If they're the leaders the revolution has to offer, God help us all!"

To our relief, the new regime did not behead the king. The new leader of Egypt, Muhammad Naguib, dispatched King Farouk and his family to exile aboard his royal yacht, the *Mahroussa*, with all the money and jewelry he could carry and a dignified ceremony. I admired General Naguib's gallantry and generosity.

At home, the family gathered more often than before the revolution. Tante Rebecca and Oncle Léon would come and talk with Nona and Papa before going home to their spouses and children. I would stand out of sight in the hallway and listen to them as they attempted to decipher the future. The new leaders of Egypt, General Mohammed Naguib and Colonel Gamal Abdel Nasser, were both heroes of the 1948 war against Israel. The radio broadcasts were filled with anti-Jewish rants by the new regime—but since the Arabic language used the word *Yahood* for Jews and Israelis alike, the lack of distinction increased the sense of jeopardy of the entire Jewish community. What should we do? Join Oncle Victor in Israel before it was too late? Stay and wait out the storm? The dearth of answers filled them, and me, with anxiety and fear. How was it possible for our whole lives to be turned upside down overnight?

General Naguib tried to reassure the Jewish community by coming to our synagogue on Yom Kippur and embracing our Grand Rabbi, Haim Nahum Effendi. I was standing in the third row of the synagogue, and I could see General Naguib's face as he addressed the congregation. He did not fit the image of the Jew-hating power-hungry revolutionary men who thundered against the Jews on the radio waves. He was a soft-spoken, kind-looking man wearing a uniform that made him look like a character out of *The Prisoner of Zenda*. But as he spoke his reassuring words, my eyes were drawn to a young officer who stood beside him. The intensity of his gaze scared me. The hatred that emanated from his jet-black eyes told me that the forces set in motion by the revolution were irreversible and fraught with danger.

Even though I was not quite seven years old, I had an instinctive understanding of the forces at play. I'd heard the gossip about the excessive lifestyle of the king, the corruption of his entourage, and the increasing poverty of the masses. I understood the reasons for their hatred of King Farouk. Papa had often expressed anger and contempt at the behavior of the monarch. Once the handsome boy-king who had raised great hopes when he rose to the throne, Farouk had ended up as a repulsive fat tyrant, known for the corruption of his court and for his unbridled debauchery. Stories abounded of Farouk summoning his cronies' wives or sisters to the royal bedroom and of kidnapping female tourists who caught his eye. One of Papa's cousins, who had served as one of the king's attorneys and been rewarded with the title of *Bey*, had countless stories about Farouk's rich courtiers who extorted astronomical sums to grant business contracts or social favors. In Papa's store, I'd seen the way the Arab aristocrats treated the tailors and the servants who served them refreshments and cigarettes. They yelled at them, insulted them and even slapped them. From the back room where I played, I had observed my father's efforts to protect his staff without losing his clients altogether, and the infinite kindness in his voice as he comforted them after these instances, although he knew it did little to wash away their wounds. The British were no better. They ignored the form of humanity they deemed inferior and called *wogs*, *niggers*, and *gyppos*. Even though their presence in Egypt had diminished, the remaining Brits continued to behave with harsh arrogance. I couldn't bear to see the humiliation these brave men—my father's staff, my second family—had to endure, and I understood the revolution and hoped it would end the long suffering of the Egyptian people.

What made no sense to me was the dark side of this good revolution—the sudden persecution of local Jews for a conflict that took place between Jews and Arabs in Palestine, another country. "If I understand," I asked, "the United Nations voted to partition Palestine into a Jewish nation and an Arab nation, and Israel was created. What happened to the Arab nation in this deal?"

"The Arab countries neighboring Palestine rejected the UN decision and went to war to prevent the founding of a Jewish state." Papa said. "Egypt, Syria, Transjordan, Iraq, Lebanon, Saudi Arabia, and Yemen. They lost, and Israel came to exist three years after you were born."

"So there was never an Arab state in Palestine?"

"After the Arab defeat, Transjordan—which means 'across the Jordan River'—annexed the West bank of the river and changed its name to Jordan, and Egypt occupied Gaza, leaving no land to build a Palestinian state. And all the Arabs of Palestine got was refugee camps and promises that they would get their state after the next war with Israel."

The unfairness of the Palestinian Arabs' condition shocked me. If indeed there was another war between Israel and the Arabs, what would happen to these Arab refugees? Or, if Israel lost the war, what would happen to the Jews of all the Arab nations who, like my cousins, had made their home in Israel?

Noticing my distress, my father took my hand. "Your guess is as good as mine, hijico mio. All we can do is pray. But remember this—nobody ever wins a war. Jews and Arabs bleed the same red blood, mourn and bury their dead in similar ways, and everybody loses. In the 1948 war, the Palestinian Arabs lost their lives, their homes, their jobs, and their dignity—and the victors achieved statehood, but they also lost lives, homes, and many sacred Jewish shrines, including the Wailing Wall, and the jewel of Jewish knowledge, the Hebrew University at Mount Scopus."

Before I could say another word, Papa silenced me by putting his index over my lips. "No more! If I had a piaster for every question you ask, I'd be richer than King Farouk!"

***

A short few months after the revolution, a measure of normalcy returned to our lives. Many of the restaurants, cinemas, and shops burned down on Black Saturday were now rebuilt, and my routine resumed in its cruel polarity—Saturdays with my mother at Groppi's Café, a brand-new replica of its pre-blaze self, and Sundays with my father sailing feluccas, going to the open-air cinemas and riding horses or camels under the Great Pyramids.

The Giza Plateau and its majestic pyramids were my second home. I found solace in their serene might. They were impervious to riots, fires and revolutions, divorces, treachery and cruelty, and their timelessness was reassuring. Yet the revolution had changed everything beneath them. The tourists no longer came. I'd never had much love for the busloads of visitors of different colors and creeds, snapping pictures of one another standing next to the camels and their dragomen—their noise violated the repose of the pharaohs buried within their ancient stones and disturbed the reverie of the mighty Sphinx. But now there was an eerie silence, and the dragomen looked desperate. I was torn between crying for their loss of livelihood and rejoicing for the pesky photo-shooters' absence.

Since my earliest childhood, my father had told and retold the story of each of the three pyramids and the pharaohs for whom they were built. I knew their names in the language of

Ancient Egypt and in their Greek transliteration, which were far apart. Why were the Greeks compelled to change the name Khufu to Cheops, Khafre to Chephren and Menkaure to Mykerinos? Papa took pride in the fact that Khufu was one of the Seven Wonders of the World and ridiculed the notion that Jewish slaves built them. An avid reader of archeological reviews, Papa had sided with the historians who believed the Giza Pyramids predated Jewish slavery and Moses's exodus by a thousand years.

"It's not a settled matter. Archeology is not an exact science. It keeps evolving with every new discovery of ruins or artifacts, and with the interpretations of scientists and historians. Maybe in twenty or fifty years, after many more discoveries, we'll be able to distinguish between myth and truth."

"So, the Bible may be wrong?"

"The Bible was written by men, not by God. Men make mistakes. They narrated events that happened centuries earlier. The times or locations of these events may sometimes be inaccurate, but they captured the spirit that makes the Bible so relevant for eternity."

Papa also loved to repeat Napoleon Bonaparte's words to his troops when they first laid eyes on the Pyramids, "Soldiers, from the top of these pyramids, forty centuries look upon you!"

"So? What's so great about it?"

"It was a cry of admiration and humility. Bonaparte was expressing humility and reverence for a civilization that built wonders that lived on for forty-thousand years—comparing it to France whose existence as a nation was a tiny fraction of that time," Papa said. "Napoleon was a man of vision. When he set out to conquer Egypt, he came with an army of scientists along with his soldiers. He knew that knowledge was as potent a weapon as the sword." Papa remained quiet for a moment, then added, "When he gave citizen rights to the Jews, Napoleon was condemned by the Orthodox Church as the Antichrist and the Enemy of God. No other rulers had ever done so much for us for little or no benefit. I can only imagine what this man could have built if he hadn't waged war so many times!"

We went to lunch at the Mena House. It was late afternoon, and our favorite table was available. It was at the foot of the Great Pyramid, a spot that always took my breath away. Looking at the top of the monument, Papa said, "Today, it's forty-one and a half centuries looking upon you. Do you know how many generations that would be?"

"What's a generation?" I asked.

"A generation runs from the time it takes newborns to grow old enough to have children of their own. My parents are one generation, I'm the second generation, you're the third generation, and your children will be the fourth," he explained. I grimaced at the mention of *my* children which made Papa laugh.

"Now if we say there are only three generations per century, how many generations in forty-one and a half centuries?" he asked. Papa enjoyed these challenges. He was an ace at mental mathematics, which I hated. My mind was racing to do the math, but I lost my count and ventured a random number, "A hundred generations, many more?"

"It's actually a hundred twenty-five generations, more or less. When Nona is gone, and I'm gone, and you're gone, and your children's grandchildren and their children's grandchildren are gone, the Sphinx will still be here looking at the rising sun."

Papa's words moved me. It was my first glimpse into mortality, my father's and mine. I felt in the core of my being the wonder of eternity that stood before my eyes. Entire civilizations had lived and died, pharaohs and slaves, kings and prophets, scribes and warriors but, century after century, the world had endured and would endure until the end of time. A disquieting and reassuring revelation that made the presence of God almost palpable.

***

Shortly after that day at the Pyramids, the meaning of mortality was brought closer to home. One morning I woke up to the sound of people chanting and wailing. I got up and stepped out of my bedroom into a nightmare. The holiday rooms were wide open. A dozen rabbis, enshrouded in their shawls, were praying aloud. The rabbis were mumbling their prayers without looking at each other, each one an island of grief and gloom. No member of the family was present.

Terrified, I ran to my grandmother's room. Behind her closed door I could hear her sobbing and moaning like a wounded animal. I was in a state of sheer panic when Papa and Oncle Léon came home. They had gone to the synagogue to pray for Oncle Victor who had died of a heart attack in the country whose name was never spoken. The news had been relayed by Tante Jeanne who lived in Milan.

Since Egypt and Israel had no direct communications, the mail between the two countries was rerouted via intermediaries in Europe. Letters took months to arrive, and the government's censors further delayed their delivery. When they arrived at last, in envelopes marked with the large red "CENSORED" in three languages, many words or entire paragraphs were covered with thick black ink. The letters were full of euphemistic code devised to avoid direct mention of country, city, or religion. Israel became our neighborhood or chez nous—'our home' in French. References to Jewish matters were disguised under their Christian equivalent—communion for Bar Mitzvah, church for synagogue, and High Priest for rabbi, and so on, and sometimes the terms were so obscure that we had to guess their meaning. But, happy or sad, hopeful or desperate, the mail from Europe was always a momentous event.

The scarce information in Tante Jeanne's letter brought home the meaning of the war with Israel. It meant that our kin could die a few hundred miles away from us, but we couldn't go to their funeral and comfort their spouses and children. It meant a death without a body to bury, a death mourned in secret because it had happened in a place deemed nonexistant.

Oncle Victor's death at the age of forty-six robbed us all of our family life. Nona never recovered from the shock of losing her eldest son. She hardly ever left her room; her days and nights were spent crying and reading the Bible. The Sabbath dinners were no longer the joyous celebrations they had once been. There was now a sad and heavy silence in Nona's presence, and when she retired all the grownups talked about was the revolution, the speeches of the Free Officers, and whether there would be another war between Egypt and Israel.

When summer came, Papa enrolled me in Madame Victoria's camp in the resort of Ras-el-Bar. "It's where the Mediterranean Sea and the Nile meet. You'll like it."

"I don't want to go! I don't care about where the stupid Nile and the stupid Mediterranean meet!" I yelled.

"You must, my boy. Nona is still in mourning. She can't take care of you right now. This is just for the summer! You'll be back before your birthday. I don't want you to be around death and mourning all day long!"

"I don't need anybody to take care of me! I can take care of myself! I'm not going to your stupid summer camp!" I cried.

A day or two later Papa packed a bag of my clothes, pulled me into the Austin and drove to Bab el-Hadid, Cairo's central railway station. There were two dozen boys of various ages bidding their parents goodbye while a few counselors looked on. I started to cry and begged Papa to take me home. "You'll see! You'll like summer camp. You'll never want to come home, I promise you," Papa insisted.

The train whistled. I howled. A counselor dragged me kicking and screaming onto the train. As the train left the station, I looked at my father standing on the platform, looking distraught and sad, and I cried harder because I knew deep in my heart that I was leaving my childhood behind.

CHAPTER 4

1952-1955

Nothing had prepared me for an inflexible environment in which every hour of the day was planned. Accustomed as I was to the solitude of an only child, I couldn't adjust to sharing a dorm with a dozen noisy boys, or to being compelled to eat foods I didn't like, and to take part in boring social games and sing idiotic songs. My first days at Madame Victoria's summer camp felt like one long dark passage between purgatory and hell. Only I didn't know what sins I was expiating. My only reprieve was father's visits every other weekend.

The summer camp was located on the peninsula of Ras-el-Bar where the waters of the Damietta branch of the Nile flow into the Mediterranean Sea. The peninsula counted few permanent buildings; most of the summer huts and bungalows were built of papyrus and dry reeds, and they were erected every year for the summer vacationers. In the fall they would be dismantled before the confluence of the waters from the river and from the sea would submerge Ras-el-Bar. It would have been a fun place were it not for the rigid discipline imposed by the camp's formidable directress.

Mme Victoria was a short, very thin woman of indistinct age with a commanding presence. She wore severe dark-colored dresses, no makeup or jewelry, and her hair was rolled into a tight bun. She seldom smiled or laughed, at least in her students' presence, and she was quick to dispense orders in a low but imperious voice. She ran her army of tutors, instructors and servants with an iron hand while her husband Dr. Václav Novak, a retired concert pianist, taught a few music classes and spent much of his time playing Chopin on the grand piano in the foyer. He was a kindly man who seemed to live in a cloud of music and only came down to earth to dote on the couple's son, a handsome and quick-witted devil named Renzo who was about my age.

Throughout the summer, I struggled to cope with the loss of my precious freedom. It affected me, body and mind. I was frequently afflicted with bouts of flu, rashes, boils and queasiness. Muttering about my "bad blood," Mme Victoria would dab the boils on my arms and legs with iodine tincture, then cover them with Mercurochrome. It made me look like an albino leopard with red spots. Much to my relief, Mme Victoria barred me from joining the others in the usual activities for fear of contagion. I spent my days on the beach away from the other kids, my red Mercurochrome spots covered by a large towel, reading comic books or daydreaming of escaping to faraway islands.

Miraculously my symptoms would diminish or go away when my father came up to Ras-el-Bar for a weekend. We would go on long walks up and down the peninsula. I loved the spot where the Nile and the Mediterranean came together to form a wide salty torrent. I loved to walk barefoot in the water, my feet sinking into the soft red clay of the Nile. I loved sitting on the bow of the fast feluccas sailing towards the sun, listening to my father recite poems or sing, although the sentimentality of his songs embarrassed me when there were other passengers on board. For a few hours I would forget Mme Victoria, the death of Oncle Victor and Nona's grief and be a child again, but come sunset reality would return with a vengeance—Papa would take me back to camp, and I would cry and beg him to take me back to Cairo. Papa couldn't understand my tantrums. "At your age, I would have liked to go to such a fine summer camp!" he would say, and I would answer, "Yeah, a summer *prison* camp!"

As the summer drew to a close, I had an intuition that I wouldn't go home again. Not for good anyway. Papa's frequent assertions that Nona was still unwell, and his numerous conversations with Mme Victoria hinted at his intention to enroll me in her boarding school near Cairo.

The last days of summer bore out my intuition. After ten quiet days at Nona's, during which I rarely saw her, we packed my things and headed south along the Nile toward the small suburban town of Maadi. I knew it well. It was where Tante Rebecca, Oncle Maurice and my three cousins lived—and it was also home to Tante Aïda, my mother's best friend.

Maadi was a lush, green, quiet city with wide residential streets lined with rows of palm trees. It smelled of fresh-cut grass and chlorophyll. Unlike some areas of Cairo, there were no beggars and no donkeys or camels on the streets. Most of Maadi's stately mansions belonged to diplomats and to well-off Egyptians of all extractions—Arabs, Greeks, Italians, Armenians and Jews. Most of them congregated at the country club which had an Olympic-size swimming pool, tennis courts and a golf course in which armies of white-clad caddies tended to the golfers' clubs and bags. The boarding school, lodged in a sprawling house in the heart of Maadi, was home to the children of the cosmopolitan elite of Cairo for whom a French education was de rigueur.

***

The curriculum at Mme Victoria's establishment did not differ much from the grade school's at the French lycée, except that there were fewer students. The tighter scrutiny from the teachers made me feel claustrophobic, and the classes' pace was far too slow. I missed my family's fast-paced conversations around the Shabbat table. I would learn much more on those evenings than in weeks at school.

On Saturdays and Sundays, the gates would open, and big shiny cars would roll up to the front porch. Mme Victoria would greet her students' parents, often with scathing comments about their offsprings' schoolwork or behavior before letting them go with the offending child.

Saturdays were Maman's day. Around ten o'clock, her blue Studebaker would roll in and whisk me away. It was driven by Aa'm Mustafa, the aging club-footed chauffeur who had served my maternal family for two generations, and calling him *Aa'm*, Arabic for uncle, was a sign of both affection and respect. I loved Aa'm Mustafa. His calm and quiet demeanor was warm and reassuring. He reminded me of safer times before our world was turned upside down. I missed him when he was away visiting family in his native village in the Fayyoum Oasis. The younger driver from Oncle Albert's office who would then replace him, Tarek, made me uneasy; I could see his gaze in the rearview mirror, the way he looked at my mother with contempt and naked desire all at once, and I could feel his resentment of our wealth and privilege. I could understand it. My mother's expensive car, her jewelry, dresses and perfumes were an unabashed display of arrogant riches that often embarrassed me, but the hatred and envy I saw in Tarek's eyes were frightening.

On these Saturday visits, Maman and I would have lunch at one of her favorite spots, then we would spend time shopping for books I wanted and needed, and for clothes I neither wanted nor needed, and then we would catch a film. I had a marked preference for French art films such as *Casque d'or* and *Fanfan la Tulipe* while my mother favored the Egyptian highbrow dramas starring actors like Omar Sharif and Faten Hamama. Maman said they rivaled the best of European cinema. The rest of the Egyptian film industry consisted of dime-a-dozen corny musical comedies and melodramas. I didn't like these films, but I wanted to see them now and again because I enjoyed the reactions of the audiences. They would clap and cheer or insult the actors on the screen and sometimes erupt in dance along the aisles. In those dark rooms, I felt a deep connection to the soul of Egypt.

Going to the cinema was the best way to enjoy time with my mother because it avoided the awkward conversations, or rather the monologues, in which Maman would complain at great length about how much *they*—my evil father and grandmother—were depriving her of my daily presence.

Everything about my mother and her second marriage was shrouded in ambiguity and mystery. Fragments of overheard conversations within the family unveiled a dark world of shadows and whispers, and it was all opaquely linked to the end of Albert's marriage with Marcelle. And now my mother was Albert's second wife and was raising his two children, Simone and Sidney, who were forbidden to see their mother just as I was forbidden to see my stepfather or my step-siblings. When I asked Papa what was wrong with seeing Albert or his children, he always answered with a cryptic, "You're not old enough to understand." I didn't think it was a satisfactory answer, but that was as far as I could get.

On Sundays Papa would come in his beat-up old Austin. After listening to Mme Victoria's litany of complaints about my work, my lack of discipline and my insolence, Papa would promise to have a serious chat with me, and off we went. His "serious" chats consisted of a few minutes of admonishment followed by my pledge to behave, and the fun day would begin. Sometimes we would go to Cairo to visit Nona, or we would spend the day at the Pyramids riding camels or horses as the mood struck. We often went to the Museum of Antiquities on Tahrir Square or to film matinées. Other times we'd stay in Maadi and visit Tante Rebecca and Oncle Maurice. My uncle worked at the Coca-Cola Company and often brought home wonderful toys, among them big yellow plastic trucks emblazoned with the brand's looped cursive red signature. Since my female cousins had no use for the toy trucks, I ended up with a large collection of them in my empty room at Nona's.

I was far more at ease in my paternal family's less ostentatious environment. But for good or evil I was the son of a rich woman and a man of modest means, caught between their two worlds, an awkward situation with which I grappled every weekend. On Saturdays I rode in the back seat of a shiny chauffeur-driven American car, and on Sundays I sat in the passenger seat of a beat-up but valiant old Austin. One day my mother would take me to her elegant restaurants and teahouses where I ate refined pastries, and the next my father and I would go to less-expensive restaurants or patronize the street vendors who sold peasant food in donkey-drawn carriages along the Nile. I enjoyed both worlds but not in equal measure. I was partial to the simpler lifestyle, but I felt guilty in either environment because each parent made feel as though enjoying one meant rejecting the other.

The tug of war between my father and my mother was far beyond wealth or the lack of it. Everything about them was in opposition. My mother's family was Egyptian first, and European second; my father's was the reverse. They were both native francophones, but at home my paternal family's second language was Ladino while my mother's was Arabic. Maman liked to boast that her family's presence in Egypt dated back to pharaonic times, unlike my father's which was a few generations out of the ghettos of southern Europe. He looked down upon her as a *baladi* Jew, the daughter of less-educated nouveau-riche provincial Jews, and she had no love lost for those she called the snobbish *soi-disant* Europeans. Since I was out of the cradle, Papa had hammered into me our family's high spiritual and philosophical ideals in opposition to the materialistic values of my maternal family.

"My family's just as good as your father's family if not better." She'd say that her father hadn't gone to college, but he hadn't been an uneducated man; through his street-smart wisdom he had risen out of poverty and been a generous member of his community. Maman's uncle Simon graduated from the Sorbonne and had been a respected scholar and anti-Nazi activist, and another uncle Eliahu Mani was a Supreme Court judge in Israel. "He was a more important jurist than your uncle Victor, may he rest in peace," my mother liked to say. "He was a *judge* in Israel's Supreme Court!"

Where and how in the world, I wondered, could such a pair have met, fallen in love or even liked each other enough to marry and have a child?

***

Many a Saturday with my mother was spent with my mother's best friend Aïda Gabr whose house, by an odd coincidence, sat kitty-corner from the boarding school. Following the Egyptian custom, the family's near and dear were addressed as aunt and uncle, except for of Khadr Gabr, Tante Aïda's husband. As a sign of respect, everyone addressed him as Khadr Bey, his aristocratic title—Bey meant "Lord" in Turkish—even though the revolution had rendered the aristocratic titles obsolete.

Unlike most other aristocrats, Tante Aïda and Khadr Bey had close ties to the new regime by a fortuitous twist of fate. Their daughter Magda had married a low-echelon army officer, Hussein el-Shafei, who became a member of the Free

Officers movement that overthrew King Farouk. He was aboard the royal yacht when General Naguib, the new ruler of Egypt, had given the deposed monarch a last salute before sending him off to a dignified exile. Magda and Hussein still lived in a wing of Tante Aïda's house, and the only change Hussein's ascendancy to power had brought to Tante Aïda's life was the armed guards at the gates.

I felt at home in Tante Aïda's house. I liked her humor, her kindness, and her cookies. I liked her children, Magda, Magged and Malek. Even though they were older than I was, they treated me like a peer. The only time I felt a distance separating us was when Magda's husband, Hussein el-Shafei, came home in his military garb. In civilian clothes, he was Uncle Hussein, a kind gentleman who revered my mother, but when I saw him in his military uniform, I remembered he was the man who made fiery speeches on the radio, calling for the allied Arab troops to throw every Jew in the sea. How could the two Husseins inhabit the same body?

When my father heard of my visits to Tante Aïda, he tried to put an end to them. "El-Shafei and his lot are Muslim Brothers! These fanatics are our enemies!" he said. If Hussein was a Muslim Brother, he showed no sign of it. As for Tante Aïda, she was just as gentle and loving as she had been before the revolution, she told the same funny jokes and baked the same cookies. Was she to be punished because her son-in-law was a revolutionary officer?

I continued to visit Tante Aïda whenever Maman took me there; I just stopped telling my father about it. I was learning that lies, whether by omission or by commission, were a key to my survival in the war between my parents. It wasn't hard to make up stories that would give both parents the impression I was on their side.

When I went to Nona's after a day with my mother, I would hide the things she'd bought me to avoid Nona's disapproving remarks. "She's spoiling you rotten. No wonder you're such a difficult child," she'd say. Nona was right, but I didn't mind being spoiled once a week. Likewise, my mother's comments about Papa and Nona were always bitterly critical. Sometimes I wished that Mayasoon and Abdu would adopt me. I'd grow up on the roof with all my Arab brothers and sisters. They were not torn between two warring clans and they could freely love both of their parents without guilt and lies. But the fantasy didn't carry far. I was well aware that the servants were illiterate, and I couldn't imagine a life without books.

Yet in the scorched battlefield of my life between two intractable parents, there were fleeting moments of respite and even joy—evening sailings on a felucca with my father, long drives along the banks of the Nile with my mother—luminous moments that shone like small patches of bright multicolored flowers growing in the desert.

One such moment stands out among others. During one of our drives along the Nile Corniche, my eyes were drawn to a ramshackle *a'arabeya hantoor*, a horse-drawn carriage, driven by an old *aarbagi*. He had only one tooth in his mouth, but he smiled as though he were the happiest man on earth. Maman noticed my interest and, unexpectedly, ordered Aa'm Mustafa to stop the car and hail the carriage.

We rode along the banks of the Nile, Aa'm Mustafa in the Studebaker gliding behind the *hantoor* like a silent vigil. We watched the feluccas sail down the Nile as the sun made its descent over the minarets of Cairo on both banks of the river. My mother didn't talk at all. She just held me tight. There was no tension in the air. It was as though an invisible mask had been dropped. The woman beside me was not the victim of all the injustices of the world, and I was not her irritated audience. She was just my mother. I savored the rare moment. I wished that magical connection would never end, and I sensed that Maman did too.

When the Studebaker dropped me off on King Fuad Avenue, I was engulfed in a cloud of sadness. For the first time in memory, I wanted to cry for my mother. But the tears stopped at the edge of my eyes. They told me that we still had miles to go.

***

Early in my second year at Mme Victoria's, my mother stopped coming on Saturdays. Tante Toto came in her stead and told me that my mother was at a health resort in Helwan-les-Bains for a cure of sulphur springs with Dr. David Glanz. "He's the most famous doctor for her condition," said Tante Toto. "While Maman's is not well, I will take you out on Saturdays, and when her health improves, we'll go visit her in the hospital."

"What's wrong with her?" I asked.

"She's just not well and Dr. Glanz wants her to have total rest for a few weeks. It's nothing to worry about."

Every Saturday, Tante Toto told me that Maman would prolong her cure for a week or two. I grew concerned and asked, "Is she going to die?"

Tante Toto smiled and said, "No. It's *not* that kind of illness. It's just a difficult time for your mother. In a few weeks, she'll come back with a surprise for you."

"What surprise?"

"It's not a surprise if I tell you, silly!" She flashed a mysterious smile. "Be patient. She will tell you herself."

We never got to visit Maman in Helwan. Her health remained precarious. A few weeks later, Tante Toto told me Maman was now at the French hospital in Cairo and was expected to be released any day.

"She's cured?" I asked.

Tante Toto laughed heartily and said, "You could say that, but she's not fully recovered yet. She was going to tell you the surprise herself, but now that they're keeping her longer, she doesn't want you to hear it from someone else—"

Time had eroded my interest in Maman's "surprise," but I feigned curiosity for Tante Toto's sake. "Hear what?" I asked.

"Last Saturday," Tante Toto said, "your mother gave birth to a baby boy! Your baby brother's name is Sami, and he's adorable."

"*Is that* my surprise?" I asked, then realizing how bad it sounded I changed my tone. "Good!"

Tante Toto went on, telling me about Maman's difficult pregnancy and added that I'd enjoy having a new baby brother. I cringed at the combination of *baby* and *brother*. I didn't want to be anybody's brother. The baby belonged to my mother's *other* life, a life I barely knew and didn't care to know. We lived in two separate and distinct worlds, and my mother stepped into mine once a week. A brother just made things more complicated because he belonged on the other side. On my side, I was an only child, and I wanted it to stay that way.

***

Every quarter, Mme Victoria awarded three prizes for academic excellence: gold, silver and bronze medals engraved with the student's name. The gold medal always went to her son Renzo and I received the silver. Renzo was a brilliant kid who deserved the gold medal much of the time, but not all the time. Our grades were close enough for the final scores to go either way, but the teachers' assessments never varied. I suspected that, given the choice of rewarding their bosses' son or the rebellious boy who thumbed his nose at them, they would swing the pendulum in favor of Renzo. I took it in stride because I liked Renzo. He was the only boy with whom I could have any kind of intellectual discussion, and getting the gold medal didn't mean that much to me. I cared even less for the silver medal, but it made my family happy, and that was good.

Now and then, a bully and his cronies would take exception to the fact that I spent my free time reading my comic books instead of participating in ball games. They called me a *khawal*, a faggot, which is one the most vulgar insults in the Arabic language, and one of them would pick a fight. I would take up the gauntlet and fight for no good reason other than to be left alone. Win or lose, there would be peace for a week or two, then another bully would challenge me. Good fists were the key to survival in boarding school, and I was blessed with decent ones. But I hated to fight, even when I won.

After some tough fights, Mme Victoria would summon us to her office, and she would scold us all. She always refused to accept self-defense as my reason for fighting back, and she seemed to be frequently irritated with me. It seemed that something in my personality rubbed her the wrong way, and she often castigated me for being "a bad element who gets in trouble with everybody." Her constant denigration led me to open rebellion.

As time went by, I became gradually more arrogant, impertinent, and rude with my teachers; and more withdrawn and unfriendly with my classmates. My life felt like a train speeding toward a collision, and I couldn't find the brakes to stop it or slow it down.

***

Summer break put a temporary pause to my misery. Papa must have sensed that I had reached a breaking point because it only took a few tantrums to convince him to let me spend the summer at home rather than return to Mme Victoria's Ras-el-Bar summer camp.

At home in Cairo Nona seemed to be in better health. She had resumed a few of her social activities, albeit in slow motion and without gusto. The death of her eldest son seemed to have destroyed her spirits, and I felt I had to tiptoe around her sometimes, but we got along. We would read in silence, Nona her eternal Bible, and I the new books one or the other of my parents had bought me for the summer.

Papa and I spent many weekends in Alexandria, a city I came to love with passion. We also drove a few times to El Alamein, the site of a decisive battle between the British and the Nazis during the Second World War.

As we visited the cemeteries of the fallen soldiers, Papa would describe in vivid details the two battles that pitted Bernard Montgomery's Commonwealth Forces against Rommel's Afrika Korps and its Italian allies and say, "Churchill wrote, 'Before Alamein we never had a victory. After Alamein, we never had a defeat.' He was right. If Monty hadn't won at El Alamein, the Nazis would have occupied Alexandria and Cairo and Tripoli! And only God knows what would have happened us all!"

"You mean concentration camps like in Europe?"

"Possibly. But the British won, so it's water under the bridge," said Papa, visibly trying to avoid that subject. He didn't need to protect me from the horrible facts of the second world war. I'd known for a long time that "The Camps" were more than bad places where people died, as Papa once told me. Spying on family conversations, and reading some British World War II picture books, I'd learned that many of the camps had been killing fields in which the Nazis had exterminated millions of European Jews. I'd always thought it odd that so many of Nona's European relatives had suddenly vanished from the face of the earth—and now I knew they had reduced to ashes in Hitler's death camps.

At the close of summer, it was plain that my hopes of staying in Cairo for the school year and having a *normal* life—living at home and going to day school like *normal* kids—were just wishful thinking. Nona was still too unwell to look after me, and Papa was too busy at work, so on a September day, right after my birthday, I returned to Maadi with the heaviest of hearts.

Nature was in its last bloom of the season, and its exuberant beauty only compounded my feelings of loneliness and confinement. I felt as though I were floating in the air without anchor or purpose, and I wondered if putting an end to my life would be an act of courage or cowardice. I began to ruminate about the best way to kill oneself.

A gun was beyond my reach, and I rejected any violent form of self-immolation. The trail of blood it would leave would be too hurtful for my family. A simple vanishing act would be in better taste. I would let myself die by starvation in the desert, far beyond the Great Pyramids, far from human life. In time my remains would blow away at the whim of the *khamsin*, the powerful sandstorms that could last fifty-odd days and blow away any trace of my ten years on earth.

The obstacle to my plan was that I didn't have any money to pay for the train fare to the Cairo central station, but I took my chances and sneaked out of school. At the station, I gathered up some courage and approached a kind-looking woman. I told her I'd lost my train ticket to Cairo and assured her that my father would reimburse her tenfold if she would advance me the fare money. She nodded and told me to wait while she bought my ticket. A few minutes later, an old *shawish*, a policeman, came up to me and asked for my name and address. I refused to answer.

"Ya khawaga," he said. "If you don't tell me where you live, all I can do is put you in jail. Do you want to break your mother's heart? Or humiliate your father?"

I said I had no mother and no father. He took me to a room behind the ticket booth. "Do you have an uncle or an aunt?"

I said no. He shook his head and gave me a sorry look. "In that case, it's time for prison. But I have to tell you, the caracol is no place for a khawaga. It's full of thieves and beggars. They'll eat you alive."

The shawish drew such a frightening picture of the jail and its population that I wavered and blurted out Tante Aïda's name. The policeman threw me a glance of disbelief and made me repeat her name and asked for her telephone number. Maman had made me memorize it in case of emergency.

"35244," I said.

The shawish let out a whistle and dialed. He looked at me in disbelief when the number I'd given him reached the Gabr residence. He waited patiently for Tante Aïda to come to the phone, fawned on her for several minutes, and said he'd be honored to escort me to her house without delay.

As we walked away from the train station, I felt the weight of the policeman's glance and the unspoken questions it carried. How could a khawaga of European origin be related to the mother-in-law of an illustrious hero of the revolution? Why would anyone run away from such a fine life? What was wrong with this boy?

On the way to Tante Aïda's house, the old *shawish* boasted of having served as a security guard during some of Hussein el-Shafei's parties, and having seen the likes of General Naguib, Colonel Nasser, Anwar el-Sadat and other military luminaries up close. "Aïda Hanem," he said, using her Turkish aristocratic title, "is always kind and generous with us, the common folk who guard them, Allah bless her!"

Tante Aïda came to the door, listened politely to the *shawish*'s tales about saving me from the worst dangers, thanked him and slipped him a large backsheesh. True to tradition, the *shawish* refused three times, then he gleefully pocketed the money, thanked her profusely and departed.

Tante Aïda fed me cookies and lemonade, listened to my list of woes, and said, "The bad times will pass, as all things pass. Be strong. And don't worry, I won't say a word to your mother. It'll kill her. She's still recovering from her difficult pregnancy."

She took me across the street and had a long talk with Mme Victoria while I waited outside the office. When she emerged, she was smiling. She hugged me tight and whispered in my ear, "Courage, mon petit!"

Mme Victoria ordered me into her office. "Don't do this again! Ever! Nobody ever ran away from my school. I promised Madame Aïda that I won't call your father, and I won't this time. It's for your mother's peace of mind, but I'll watch you like a hawk. First sign of misbehavior and you're out!"

A telephone ring interrupted her litany of threats. While she talked to the parent of another kid in trouble, I went to the window and looked at the gardener who tended to Mme Victoria's flowers. The roses were so red and the grass so green that I felt pangs of pain. The red flowers reminded me of a silly French love song my father had been singing all summer long. It was about a man loving a beautiful woman in a wheat field, only to find her later lying on the ground with three drops of blood on her white blouse in the shape of a red poppy. The woman had been killed by a jealous rival. Mesmerized by the red roses, I forgot about Mme Victoria and began to hum silently my father's favorite song: "La première fois que je l'ai vue / Elle dormait a moitié-nue / Dans la lumière de l'été / Au beau milieu d'un champ de blé."

Suddenly, I heard a shriek, "Basta!" Mme Victoria was standing behind me, and she was screaming, "How dare you sing such filth in my presence?"

I realized that my "silent" humming hadn't been so silent, and I turned beet red.

The song had played on the radio for the entire summer, and I'd not heard of anyone minding its mildly salacious lyrics: "The first time I saw her / she was asleep, half-naked / in the summer light / in the middle of a wheat field..."

"Such filth!" Mme Victoria repeated. "A bad element, you are! Un mauvais élément! You have no morals! No decency! Mark my words: you'll always bring tears and shame to your family! I'm calling your father after all!"

She ordered me to stay in my dormitory until my father came for me. Before leaving her office, I smiled at the red roses and thanked them for my good fortune. I was going home and my heart was singing.

CHAPTER 5

1955

At long last, home! I was both happy and apprehensive. This time, my return to the Fuad Avenue apartment was permanent, and it filled me anxiety. It had been nearly three years since Oncle Victor's death, but there was still an aura of darkness around Nona. She was still dressed in mourning and her salt-and-pepper hair had turned pure white. She now had a painful medical condition that inflated her legs almost to the size of a pachyderm's and made her walking painful and slow. Papa explained that Nona's ailment, called elephantiasis, was propagated by mosquitoes and other insects carrying parasites. There was no cure, just treatment to contain the disease and ease her pain. Shunning a wheelchair, her legs wrapped in compression bandages, she used a cane to shuffle from her room to the kitchen or the dining area, mumbling prayers or talking to her beloved departed in hushed tones while she moved. At mealtimes, she made efforts to pay attention to me, but her focus had not fully returned to the world of the living.

After Shabbat night, Nona would retire early, and Papa, Oncle Léon, and Tante Rebecca would often discuss what to do with me for the upcoming school year. If I left my bedroom door ajar, I could eavesdrop on their conversations, and I often did. They thought that keeping me home was too much of a burden for Nona, and Papa should consider another boarding school in Cairo or Alexandria. I was furious. Why didn't they mind their own business?

The family discussions often extended to my behavior and my father's parenting skills. Tante Rebecca and Oncle Léon believed that my rebellious streak was encouraged by my father's excessive permissiveness. "Children need discipline and boundaries, not unlimited freedom. You spoil him rotten! It's understandable since the boy doesn't have a mother, but there are limits!"

The boy has a mother, I wanted to interject. A Saturday mother, perhaps, but a mother. I didn't want a full-time mother fussing over me. As for my father's "permissiveness" and my "unlimited freedom," how permissive and free were the years I spent locked up in a prison masquerading as a boarding school? I was tired of being the only "problem child" among Nona's nine grandchildren. Again, why didn't they mind their own business?

To my surprise, Nona intervened. "Basta cosí!" she yelled. "Send the boy to the same school his cousins attend, and his father and I will take care of him. I'm well enough now!"

At long last, the stars had switched to my side. I hadn't expected that Nona would forgo her need for solitude for my sake, and I was full of gratitude and anticipation for the following year.

I spent the remaining weeks of the summer reading and rereading my picture books. My favorite French friends were Tintin and Captain Haddock, Milou and Spirou. They were closely followed by my new American acquaintances whose names all ended with the letters "m-a-n"—Batman, Superman, and Wonder Woman. I also loved the more serious British comics about the battles of Europe and the London Blitz. They were educational more than entertaining, but I loved learning about recent history and its winners and losers.

I realized I was outgrowing the books with pictures, and I was ready for *real* books.

From my earliest days, the closed doors of my grandfather's study had been an irresistible magnet, not only because it was forbidden territory, but because Nona had made it a hallowed sanctuary. Wide double doors connected the study to the formal dining room, which Nona opened only for the Jewish holidays. Only Mayasoon and Abdu went in to maintain the perfect cleanliness of Nono's kingdom.

I liked to sneak into the sanctuary. It smelled of pungent furniture polish, insecticide and mothballs. I could feel Nono's strong presence in the darkened study. I imagined he'd retired for a nap and would soon return. I would sit at his desk and gaze at his portrait, hung high on the wall. Encased in a mahogany frame inlaid with mother-of-pearl motifs, the portrait showed a kind-looking man in the prime of life. Behind his round glasses, his eyes were full of sparkling intelligence, infinite curiosity and earnest empathy. On both sides of his desk, the walls were covered with shelves laden with gold-stamped, leather-bound volumes. A spotless glass cabinet sheltered the books that my father had said were rare editions.

On one shelf stood a large sepia photograph of my grandparents—Nona already an imposing matron sitting in an armchair, and Nono standing by her side, looking frail and lost in his thoughts. In smaller frames, the portraits of their four children bore the date 1927 under the photographer's tiny signature. It was fun to see my father and his siblings as they looked a quarter-century earlier. Victor was a mirror image of his bookworm father in a smart but conservative suit; Léon looked like a determined athlete looking for a ball to hit; Rebecca, dressed and coiffed like a modern woman of the early century; and my father, the runt of the litter, dressed to the nines, beaming with energy and joie de vivre, his hand nonchalantly patting a furry dog perched on a high chair, striking the pose of a Romantic poet.

Several shelves were dedicated to the novels of Alexandre Dumas, Victor Hugo and Emile Zola. Among them, *The Count of Monte Cristo* beckoned. I had vague memories of the story from its picture-book edition at a bookstore, but I'd shunned it in favor of Dumas's musketeers. Not without flutters of guilt and sacrilege, I opened *The Count of Monte Cristo*. The elegant print was so intimidating that I quickly shut the book and put it back on its shelf. I leaned back and looked at Nono's portrait. I wished I could ask him all the questions in my mind—Where do I begin? Which of these books should I read, and in what order?

The portrait remained silent, but I could swear I'd seen a flicker of encouragement in Nono's benevolent eyes. Gingerly I opened the book again and flipped the pages, admiring the illustrations that separated the chapters. On the frontispiece, a sketch of an imposing Alexandre Dumas was inviting the reader to enter his world of adventure. I took the plunge and read the first lines: "On the twenty-fourth of February in the year 1810, the lookout at Notre-Dame de la Garde signaled the three-master, the Pharaon, from Smyrna, Trieste, and Naples."

The words set my imagination ablaze. I read a few more pages. The words spoke to me in a better way than any picture. I was there, inside the ship, inside the story. I could see the vessel entering the harbor. I could feel the anticipation of the sailors' homecoming, the hustle and bustle of the port of Marseille. I knew that Edmond Dantès, the main protagonist, would become my hero, my friend. I was home. It was difficult to stop, but I knew Nona would be looking for me and I'd be in dire straits. Before putting the book back in its place, I flipped to the last page and read the last line of the book: "Darling," replied Valentine, "has not the Count just told us that all human wisdom is summed up in two words—'Wait and hope?'"

I was filled with wonder. An entire world existed between the first and the last page of this book—so many stories, so many people, so many adventures—and I couldn't wait to enter it. Skimming the book, I noticed allusions to Napoleon and political events that were beyond my knowledge. Reading the entire book seemed to be an impossible undertaking, but I knew I was embarking on a journey that would change my life forever. Part scared to death, part chomping at the bit, I was good and ready!

***

Most Saturdays, my mother would take me on a shopping spree or to the movies or to the *a'aragoz*, a puppet show, but we seldom missed the ritual afternoons at Groppi's. It was a Mecca of beauty, elegance and sensuality, and Maman was among its brightest jewels. With her raven hair and full lips, she looked like a movie star, and I was proud to be at her side. I enjoyed her chats with the other lovely women who came to our table to exchange gossip and pleasantries. When they bent down to plant lipstick-staining kisses on my cheeks, their perfume made me deliciously dizzy. But I dreaded the moment they would leave me alone with my mother. Her mask of lightness and joy would drop and reveal a dark face of misery and pain.

It would begin with a litany of monologues I'd heard in all their variations—how my father and Nona had ruined Maman's life by separating her from her beloved son. "Your father promised me I would have custody of you as soon as I remarried," she intoned. "You'd live with your grandmother *only* while I was single and wasn't able to give you a good home. A Belgian *millionaire* proposed; he was a very nice man; you would have liked him very much. He wanted to take us to Brussels with him. But your father said he'd never let his son leave Egypt, so I didn't marry the Belgian millionaire—"

After the andante came the allegro of sacrifices. A rich jeweler would succeed the Belgian millionaire, followed by a rich surgeon, succeeded by a rich industrialist. I wasn't surprised that my mother would attract so many suitors—I could see the way men looked at her—but if their wealth was important, why did she marry my father? He was neither rich nor aspiring to be. It was all so mysterious!

"Your father made a solemn promise, before the rabbi, to give me custody when I had a stable home for you. Custody of you was my only condition to agree to the divorce! They took advantage of me because my health and my spirits weren't good in those days!"

The tempo would rise to staccato impetuoso. "I only married Oncle Albert to give you a proper home with us and his children as brother and sister. Right after the wedding ceremony, I called your uncle Léon and said, 'I have a home for my son, I want him back with me as promised!' Léon hemmed and hawed before putting the knife to my heart by admitting your father was reconsidering—meaning he changed his mind!"

A waiter would bring a pot of hot cocoa and a plate of pastries. Maman would stop until the waiter served our orders and left before bursting into tears. "I married again *only* because I wanted you to live with me! I would never, never have gotten married otherwise! Once was enough!"

I would take a bite of my chocolate éclair and wait for the tempo furioso. "I love you more than your father or your grandmother ever will! You came from my flesh—not theirs! I almost *died* giving birth to you, but it was worth it!" She choked. "And they say they're raising you! Well, my son, I want you to know that I'm always involved in your upbringing, even though you don't live with me. I paid for your schools and your school supplies and your summer camps. Your father never made money. He couldn't afford Mme Victoria's without my help. You don't know how expensive that school was! I buy all your clothes and your books. They look down on my father's money, call us nouveau riche, but if it weren't for me, you'd be playing on the streets like an Arab child!"

"*Mother*! I play with Arab children on Nona's rooftop!" I said. "So what?"

"My darling, you must stop calling me "Mother." We're not in the court of Louis the Fourteenth!" She laughed and went on to disparage my father's origins by mimicking European manners she thought were pretentious.

The negative talk about my father was exhausting. It was as though I had two mothers in one body—one, a vulnerable woman full of guilt, anger, and self-pity, and the other a powerful, elegant, and self-assured woman whose magnetism could seduce the devil himself. I knew that she felt guilty for abandoning me and feared that I would abandon her in return. That made me keenly aware of the power I held over my mother, and it filled me with understanding and compassion for her suffering. In time I learned to use wit and humor to deflect her torrential grievances and make our time together less unpleasant.

***

When my mother was out of sorts, she often turned to the occult, and we would pay a visit to her psychic seer, Abu Labib. He lived on a street that bordered the Khan el Khalili souk. We would leave the car near the mosque, bypass the souk, walk to the end of an unpaved alleyway and enter the courtyard of a small house. A pair of eyes would appear in the small opening in the door, and a young and pretty maid would let us into the darkened house.

The one-eyed seer was old. His glass eye was larger than his good eye, and he always wore the same bluish *galabeya* and white headgear. He sat on the floor of a darkened room, legs crossed under a large copper tray resting on low Bedouin trestles. Maman would kneel next to him, kiss his hand and inquire about his health in Arabic. When she settled by his side, Abu Labib would clap his hands and call, "Aïsha!"

The girl servant would bring a tray of sweets and a *kanaka* of Turkish coffee. She was an adolescent, a child with a womanly body whose breasts were bursting out of her cotton dress. When she bent down to pour the coffee, I could see the fullness of her breasts, and a strange and delicious emotion would run through my body. She filled Maman's demitasse to the brim, but she'd only pour a half-cup for me, just enough for Abu Labib to read the coffee grounds. Maman would empty her cup, twirl it three times to spread the grounds on the walls of the cup, and turn it over, letting the heavy coffee grounds drip into the saucer. She'd urge me on to do the same, quickly, before the grounds could dry up at the bottom of the upright cup. Sometimes when I picked up my cup, I'd make a false move and knock my demitasse over, just for the thrill of watching Aïsha's breasts shake as she vigorously wiped off the soiled copper table.

Abu Labib would take Maman's cup and examine it, bringing it close to his lone seeing eye. The coffee grounds had dried and formed odd shapes around the bottom and sides of the cup. Abu Labib would study the entwined curls, twists and loops of the grounds. After several minutes of deadly silence, he would ask Maman a question or two and scrutinize the dry grounds again before announcing his findings. His predictions were sometimes ominous, sometimes light and happy. Maman would bombard him with anxious queries, and he would elaborate at length on each one.

When Maman's reading was over, Abu Labib would look into my cup and interpret my future. I didn't understand everything he said, and I wasn't all that interested. Maman did all the talking. I pretended to listen, but my mind was still on Aïsha.

After a long interlude of unctuous professions of love and gratitude, Maman would drop a bundle of banknotes on the coffee table and kiss the old man's hand again. The young maid would escort us to the courtyard and refuse to take the banknote Maman was handing her. Maman would slip the money in the girl's bosom and tell her to buy something nice for herself. After a few more *salaams*, Aïsha would open the gate and usher us out onto the alleyway.

***

After the visit to Abu Labib came the ritual visit to the Khan el Khalili, the mother of all souks, a world of its own that contained all the treasures of Cairo, Damascus, and Baghdad. Surrounded by a multitude of mosques and minarets, the Khan el Khalili was a patchwork of bazaars spanning several streets and alleyways. Maman's reading with Abu Labib often buoyed her spirits and inspired her to embark on a shopping spree. I often asked her what she did with all the things she bought, and her usual answer was, "There's always a birthday, an anniversary, a birth, a death—God forbid!—and other occasions when a gift is de rigueur." It made sense in a fashion, but it seemed excessive and wasteful. She would close the subject by making a circular gesture to encompass the entire souk, "Besides, these poor devils need to make a living!"

In each of the bazaars in the Khan el Khalili, Maman had a favorite shop or two. There was an established ritual that varied only with the age of the merchant. The older the man, the longer the expression of respect and appreciation; the very old rated a kiss of the hand.

Maman's merchants welcomed her like they would the Queen of Sheba. They would proffer profuse expressions of gratitude for the honor she was bestowing upon their modest stall. Maman would respond in kind, saying how happy she was to see them in good health and prosperity. Boy servants rushed to fetch chairs and trays of refreshments and pastries. She would accept a Coca-Cola for me and a cup of mint tea for herself. After a sip or two, she would let out a sigh of contentment and business would begin. If she had a specific item in mind, the owner always responded with, "A'la ei'ni wa rassi! Upon my eye and my head," moving his hand twice from his eyes to his headgear as a promise to meet her wishes. He would then present his finest, expanding effusively on the quality of the craftsmanship, and if Maman showed interest, the ritual bargaining session would begin.

"Ya balash! For nothing!" the vendor would say, swearing that he wasn't making a piaster of profit and that his only gain was the honor of serving her. Invariably, they'd reach a deal, money changed hands, and Maman would slip her purchase in her purse and walk to the next vendor.

The ritual was repeated from souk to souk. At the Souk al Siyagh, the Goldsmiths' Bazaar, my mother's favorite was the store of Hadj Bashir Al Masri. Upon entering the store, Maman always went to Hadj Bashir and kissed his hand. He would put his other hand over her head and whisper a blessing, then touch my hair with an incantation before enquiring about her family. As she spoke of her other son, her stepchildren and her husband, I had to resist the temptation to say that I was not a part of *that* family—I was the alien son.

Even though the hand-kissing was a traditional sign of respect for the elderly, I found it too subservient and a little embarrassing, but not with Hadj Bashir. The man had an aura of holiness that moved me in profound ways. The title of Hadj meant that he had made the *hadj*, the pilgrimage to Mecca, and everyone knew that Hadj Bashir had circled the Kaaba many times during his long life. The impairments of old age and ailments didn't deter Hadj Bashir from coming to the store he'd owned since the previous century. He sat on a throne-like chair richly upholstered with Persian tapestry, received visitors or just took naps. His sons, Nabil and Mounir, ran the business and came to him only for his advice.

Hadj Bashir's stalls gleamed with gold and silver bracelets, earrings and chains. Maman always bought one or two pieces of jewelry without the customary bargaining; she knew she'd get a good discount without requesting it. After paying for her purchases and dropping them in her bottomless handbag, Maman always complimented Nabil or Mounir for their jewelry's perfection. They always responded with small gifts for me and for the rest of her family.

The second favorite was Waleed's stall at Souk al Attarin, the market for oils and perfumes. The air was filled with overpowering fragrances of exotic essences and mysterious creams. My mother believed they enhanced beauty and health, and she always bought a variety of vials and bottles of all colors. Next was Hamid's stand in the Souk al Nahassin, the Coppersmiths' Bazaar. It was a paradise of glowing copper and brass trays, glimmering pots and pans, and an infinite variety of cigarette cases, spice containers and water pipes. Maman was always in need of kanakas, the stove-top conical pots made to prepare coffee, and small pots she used to burn incense. If she needed fabrics, her only destination would be Abu Zaki's shop at the Souk Ghoureya, a bazaar of shiny textiles and embroideries. Maman would pick up the cloth, caress it, smell it, and lift it to gauge its weight. "There's always a dress to make, a curtain to replace, a chair or a sofa to reupholster," she would say.

My own favorites among the alleys laden with antiquities, fake and real, were the leather shops where the saddles and ottomans spoke of travel and adventure. The blended smells of leather and aromatic spices were intoxicating, and the wealth of carpets and rugs, belly dancing attires and Bedouin costumes made me dream of faraway journeys on camels and flying carpets. Every stall was as beckoning as Ali Baba's cave, any man might be one of his forty thieves, any of the veiled women might be Scheherazade, and the stories they could tell would fill tens of thousands of Arabian nights.

***

More often than not, upon leaving the souk, Maman and I would make the pilgrimage to the temple that her father had built in Haret el-Yahood. It meant literally the "Alley of the Jews" but it was actually an entire Jewish district whose hundreds of narrow streets and alleyways seemed to have missed the passage of time since its medieval beginnings.

The Jews of the old quarter were said to be the descendants of the Jewish slaves who'd stayed behind when Moses led the exodus out of Egypt. They had survived the Arab conquest, the invasion of the Ottomans, the French occupation, the British protectorate, and now the end of the last monarchy. Many of them were Karaite Jews. I never understood the differences that separated them from us, Rabbinic Jews, other than that they rejected some interpretations of the Torah. They spoke a smattering of Arabic and Hebrew, wore *galabeyas* and *tarbooshes* rather than occidental clothes, and they seemed to be as poor as their poorest Arabs neighbors.

Looking at my mother, beautiful, elegant, sophisticated, perfumed and bejeweled, it was hard to believe that her father could have come from such a wretched place—that he had walked the streets and alleys of Haret el-Yahood, peddling his wares, eking out a living until, as Maman liked to say, the Lord had smiled upon him. When the time came to move away from the ghetto and into the wealthy neighborhood of Koubbeh, Felix Mani left in body but not in spirit. A part of him always remained there, in the tiny temple—more talmudic school than synagogue—he'd commissioned as an offering to the Lord.

The old *shamash*, the guardian of the temple, always treated us like visiting royalty. My mother accepted his respects and reminisced with him about my grandfather, whom the *shamash* called Felix Pasha with great flourish and genuine affection. Then the *shamash* intoned a prayer and blessed us both. My mother kissed his hand respectfully and handed him a bulging envelope.

As we walked through the medieval alleys toward my mother's car, I would try to sort out the mixed feelings of pride and shame that always engulfed me when we came to the Alley of the Jews. While I was proud of my maternal grandfather's accomplishments, I felt shame at the very existence of Cairo's Jewish ghetto. It harkened back to an era when Egypt's rulers confined their Jewish subjects to their own quarters and made them wear a piece of yellow clothing, just like their European counterparts. In recent decades, the Jews had not been oppressed, but the buildings and streets of Haret el-Yahood still exuded the stench of centuries of servitude, ignorance and poverty. It was a stain that time hadn't rubbed out, a permanent blemish on the Jewish soul. It was hard to imagine my mother growing up in the slums my grandfather had escaped through hard work and by the grace of God.

I was aware that my feelings were shaped by my European education, and I was ashamed of being ashamed, but I knew Haret el-Yahood would forever be a reminder of painful atavistic memories in my mind. I was also aware that a new breed of Egyptian rulers was ushering in a new era of oppression for the Jews of Egypt.

It was quite a relief to see the blue Studebaker awaiting us at the end of the lace of narrow alleyways, Aa'm Mustafa at the wheel. It was the magic carpet that would fly us back to the modern world.

***

Since I could only read *The Count of Monte Cristo* in Nono's study, it took me weeks to get to the last page. I had to skip the numerous political asides that I didn't understand. The main hero, the characters around him and their stories were far more interesting than any of my picture book heroes. I could identify with Edmond Dantès. Like him, I'd been torn away from my life and incarcerated. Like him, I'd longed for freedom and liberation, and I'd dreamed of the day my real life would take flight.

Having honed my skills with *Monte Cristo*, the following book, *The Three Musketeers*, was an easy read. Later that summer, I began to tackle Victor Hugo's *Les Misérables*. It turned out to be the hardest book of all. It contained more digressions than the other books, more long and tedious dissertations on religion or politics before the story resumed its course. Some characters would disappear and reappear under fake names, which made the threads of the intertwined stories difficult to follow. I persevered because I was under the spell of Valjean and Cosette and Javert and the others, but it was an arduous task.

When I put the book down, my head was reeling from the whirlwind of emotions, feelings and thoughts that *Les Misérables* had unleashed, just as *Monte Cristo* had before it. Blasphemy of blasphemies, I thought the books of Dumas and

Hugo were more exciting than the Bible, and they were written by people of flesh and blood, not by invisible prophets in the ether.

I longed to learn more about the people behind the books. Were they gods, demigods or mere men?

***

A thirty-minute walk separated home from the lycée. Papa would often give me a ride in the morning, but I walked back home every day, except for most Fridays. On that day, Oncle Léon would come to school, and my cousins and I would pile in his Plymouth and drive to Nona's for the Shabbat celebration.

I enjoyed walking home. Halfway to Nona's, a small detour would take me to the Bab-el-Louk *souk*, a large bazaar. My cousins and I were not allowed to enter the souk without an adult chaperone. Nona called it a den of disease and contagion, and I didn't disagree with her—but the souk beckoned like a mirage, and I could rarely resist the temptation to roam its forbidden alleyways.

The Bab-el-Louk souk lacked the refined stalls of the Khan el Khalili. It was a bazaar for ordinary people. Its distinctive smell—a mixture of rotting food, camel dung and human excrement—mingled with the hearty smells emanating from street carts or hole-in-the wall storefront kitchens. Pastry bakers melted sugar, honey and rosewater for their confections while bread bakers never stopped loading their clay ovens with loaves of *e'aish baladi*, the coarse peasant bread that was a meal unto itself. Cooks roasted *dora*, fresh ears of corn on the cob, or deep-fried *ta'ameya*, the round patties made of fava beans, while fanning sizzling skewers of lamb and chicken kebobs on their charcoal grills. In the outer alleys, Bedouins peddled their wares, their camels still covered with desert dust. Veiled women furtively minded their babies, their goats, their chickens and their donkeys while half-naked older boys played football with watermelon rinds. Old men sat at tables on the sidewalk, drinking coffee, smoking their *sheesha*, their water pipes filled with perfumed tobacco, laughing and joshing one another while they played dominoes or *shesh-besh*, a version of backgammon, slamming their pieces on their wooden boards with visible relish.

I always felt at home in the souk. Even though I was European by language and culture, I had a visceral bond with Egypt and its people that seemed to emanate from a time that long predated my birth. I often felt torn between my French, my Egyptian, and my Jewish cultures. And, to complicate matters, both of my Arab and French cultures had a long history of persecuting Jews. It was as though my heart was a pendulum that swung in all directions asking me if I belong somewhere or nowhere. Either answer would have been correct. It was all I could do to bring the pendulum to a halt and allow the void to heal my wounds.

In the spring, another tragedy hit our family—the unexpected and woefully premature death of Oncle Maurice. After the initial period of mourning, Tante Rebecca closed her house in Maadi and came to live at Nona's with her three daughters, Myra, Lena and Viva. They took over the bedrooms overlooking the avenue, and I had to share my bedroom with my father.

It took me time to adapt to the new changes. I loved my cousins and enjoyed their company, but I missed being alone. Myra was sixteen, she had a boyfriend and went to parties with other teenagers. Lena was thirteen, a gentle and friendly soul who kept to herself, but she could show tough teeth when she was hurt. When I once thoughtlessly said I missed the privacy I'd had before they moved in, she shot back, "You think we enjoy being here? If my father was still alive, we'd be living in our house instead of being here with a stupid kid like you!" The sadness in her eyes filled me with remorse, but kind Lena forgave me long before I forgave myself.

Viva, my junior by six months, ran through the rooms in the house like a live tornado. Since it disturbed Nona, I was tasked with keeping her busy. After school, we cavorted on the roof with Mayasoon's kids, played games and bickered all the time. We sneaked together into Nono's study, and it was all I could do to keep her quiet and let me read.

In the early fall, my older cousin Hélène was ready to attend medical school in France. Oncle Léon would accompany her to Paris to get her settled before classes began. I had pangs of envy.

"Your turn will come soon," said Lena who never missed a beat. "After mine, of course!"

At the Shabbat dinner preceding their departure, as he said goodbye, Oncle Léon shook my hand and asked, "How old are you now?"

"Eleven. Well, soon."

"You're a big boy now. Your father and you are the only two men left in Cairo while I'm away. That means your job is to protect and take care of the women in the family."

I was about to ask why the women and girls, all strong and capable, needed the care of men, but before I could utter a word, I was hit by a petrifying premonition that this was the last time we'd all be together.

CHAPTER 6

1956

In the fall of 1956, I went back to my old lycée, full of excitement and anticipation, eager to start the elective study of Latin and Greek. My father had paved the way with his bedtime readings of the classic French dramas based on Greco-Roman mythology or the Trojan Wars and the wanderings of Odysseus. For once, I was ready and even happy to go to school.

Latin classes were an unmitigated source of joy. I was learning or rediscovering familiar phrases and mottoes from those stories—carpe diem; veni, vidi, vici; *alea iacta est*; and my favorite, *Et tu, Brute?* I also enjoyed the usual classes, literature, history, and geography, in ways I never did before. Yet many dissonances gave me pause, primarily in history classes. The textbooks' frequent references to "our ancestors, the Gauls" and to "our" Catholic kings, emperors and saints were alienating. My ancestors were not Gauls, and there were no Christian kings or saints in my heritage. When we studied the numerous Crusades aimed at conquering the Holy Land from the Muslim Infidels in the name of the Cross, my ancestors were on the enemy side of the Mediterranean. While Christians and their Muslim foes called each other infidels, they both considered the Jews to be the lowest breed of Infidels.

Who were my ancestors? Where did we belong? When I asked my father, he would remind me to read about our glorious history in the Bible. It was not much of an answer. I'd read or heard enough to know that the glory of the Jews had ended in the ashes of the Second Temple of Jerusalem.

"What since—?" I asked.

"There's a Spanish word that describes it well: *desdichado*. It means disinherited, destitute, miserable, unfortunate, wretched." said Papa. "What we'd done in the past twenty centuries is to survive. Rebuild. We contributed to the world of philosophy, literature, science and the arts, and we won Nobel Prizes and high rewards." He winked, "And, these days, Jews are working on reclaiming the ancestral lands of our people."

These answers were not sufficient to help me understand my nebulous identity. Most of the people in the world could define their identity in one word—French, American, German, Brazilian or New Zealander, or two hyphenated words like Franco-Russian—but not me. There was no single word, or string of words, to capture the identity of an Egyptian Jew of Italian, Greek, Turkish ancestry, whose roots stretched back to medieval Spain.

Born in Egypt, but not an Egyptian citizen since Egypt denied citizenship to its Jews, even those who'd remained after Moses's exodus. *Italian* by citizenship because an ancestor had hailed from Tuscany generations ago. *French* by education, because France had colonized much of Africa by spreading her culture. The only solid element in my life was that I was *Jewish* by heritage and tradition, and that too was uncomfortable because I loved the history of my people, but had little or no affinity with the religious aspects of Judaism.

Failing to define myself by geography, I looked at other characteristics to search for clues to my identity, and I found the element that touched the deepest recesses of my heart was my language. My first language. My great love. Without it, I would be nothing; with it, I existed. Since birth I'd sucked at the breast of French poetry and literature. I had a natural understanding of the French language, its rhythms, its intricacies, its lyrical powers, its infinite subtleties and its delicate beauties. Despite the absence of roots in France's culture—there was nothing Gallic in my heritage—I, a Middle Eastern Jew, felt French at the core of my being. Because the vagaries of persecutions, expulsions and migrations inherent to the Jewish condition had made French my native language. And because writers named Corneille, Racine, Molière, Dumas and Hugo had opened the royal path of French literature before my eyes. My true home was my language. Everything else was an accident or a mistake of History.

***

I loved being back at the French Lycée, which I had attended before Oncle Victor's death. Unlike the boarding school, the lycée admitted boys *and* girls, albeit in separate sections. A small building housing the Chemistry and Physics Laboratories divided the genders into two distinct areas. The windows on both sides of that building gave plenty of opportunity for boys and girls to see one another, and even exchange notes at recess. Outside the front doors, boys and girls were free to congregate without supervision.

My cousins Viviane and Simone also attended my lycée, and now that Tante Rebecca had moved in with us, her three daughters, Myra, Lena, and Viva, were also enrolled in the same school. Only I, among the six children, was deemed to be a potential troublemaker, and Nona had charged my oldest cousins with the task of keeping me on the straight and narrow. Luckily, the girls had neither the time nor the will to bother with me, and I was left to my own devices.

The first days at the boys' lycée were lonely. Some faces were somewhat familiar, probably kids from elementary school, but no true friend—although the loneliness was mitigated by the joy of being free again.

When I first met Jean-Patrick Lombroso, it was dislike at first sight. He was popular, handsome, rich, and elegant, all of which reinforced my feelings of complete social inadequacy. Even the fact that everyone called him by his initials, JP—pronounced *Jee-Pé* in French—was an irritant. He had a rather distant attitude with his classmates, except for his small group of friends, but he surprised me by approaching me and being cordial. I realized that my aloofness was nothing but petty jealousy, and I broke the ice by responding in kind. We found that we had in common an insatiable curiosity, a predilection for provocative ideas, an allergy to small talk and a visceral inability to suffer fools. The foundation was laid for our improbable friendship.

In time, I got to know JP's friends. The group was as diverse as Egypt itself, and surprisingly I felt at ease with them. Besides JP, the motley crew included Gil, Momo, two Isaacs and me. We couldn't be more different in personality, looks and creed. Gil, Gilbert Choukri, was film-star handsome, bright but painfully shy; Momo, Mohammed Abdel Moneim, was brilliant and possessed a devilish sense of humor; Isaac Chedid, nicknamed Ike, witty and gregarious, and Isaac Moreno, called Coco, who was an incomparable athlete. Together, the six of us almost represented the full spectrum of cosmopolitan Egypt. Gil was Catholic; Momo was Muslim; Coco half-Coptic and half-Protestant; and JP, Ike and I were Jewish. On the social scale, JP, Gil and Momo had prosperous parents; the family of both Isaacs had little means, and their boys attended the lycée on scholarships; and I, the son of a wealthy mother and a father of modest means, sat in the middle.

We usually gathered at JP's vast apartment in Garden City, an upscale Cairo neighborhood. JP's mother kept an open house for her son's friends. She was kind, light-hearted, and very funny—a sunny personality that was the opposite of my mother's dramatic persona. Refreshments and cookies always at the ready, Mrs. Lombroso often said she'd be delighted if we all moved in permanently. JP's father looked uncomfortable with us, the younger generation, but he made a valiant effort to emulate his wife's hospitality. I envied the ease with which JP's parents seemed to care for one another, and the love and strength they gave their son.

Having been a loner all my life, it was odd for me to be a part of a group. I didn't know how to reconcile my conflicting needs for aloneness and companionship. It took me a long time to learn to balance the imperious demands of the two sides of my psyche.

The boys and I engaged in heated discussions, even arguments, about a multitude of topics ranging from girls and movies to books and gadgets, and sometimes politics. The political discussions, based on information gleaned from parental conversations and movie theater newsreels, were attempts to decipher the news as well as debate its meaning. So much of it existed on a cloud way above our heads, but I loved flexing my brain muscles with intelligent people.

There was no shortage of gadgets and doohickeys at JP's. A tourism magnate, JP's father took frequent trips to Europe, America and Asia, and always returned with a treasure trove of electronic gizmos and other gifts. There I saw my first transistor radio, my first 45-rpm single record and my first 33-rpm long-playing album. At home, Papa played his collection of scratchy 78-rpm records on a huge RCA-Victor machine emblazoned with a brass dog listening to a large conical speaker. It looked ancient compared to JP's latest gift from Munich, a tiny battery-operated record player that could play both 45s and 33s and fit in a coat pocket. On that contraption and similar ones, we discovered the strange new sounds from America called *rock 'n' roll*.

In what seemed like the blink of an eyelid, the artists we knew and loved—Edith Piaf, Yves Montand and Frank Sinatra among others—were rendered old-fashioned, evicted by the likes of Bill Haley and the Comets, Elvis Presley, Peggy Lee, Paul Anka and the Platters. With their galvanizing rhythms and idiotic lyrics, they were ushering the dawn of a new all-American world order.

***

On an early November day, the shrill sound of sirens resounded throughout the schoolyard. It took me a while to realize that it was not a drill or a fire alarm. The deafening sirens echoed throughout the neighborhood, far beyond the confines of the school. All hell was breaking loose in the schoolyard; the principal's voice came on the school speakers, summoned the main teachers to his office and ordered the supervisors to assemble the pupils in the courtyard.

We waited with bated breath while the alarm sirens seemed to get louder—until the principal, flanked by a few teachers, appeared on the balcony overlooking the schoolyard. He announced that the school was closing because of the current political events, and our parents would come and collect us as soon as they could. In the meantime, he urged us to stay calm.

What political events? He didn't say. Another revolution? Really?

Papa came to fetch us in Oncle Léon's Plymouth. He sat next to the driver, listening to the radio on an Arabic station. As my five cousins and I piled in, Papa hushed us and turned up the volume. On the airwaves, the familiar voice of Gamal

Abdel Nasser—who had replaced General Naguib as the Raïs, the leader of Egypt—was thundering over the din of a galvanized crowd. That was familiar fare on the airwaves since the revolution, but this time the blaring alarm sirens made every word sound ominous. The speech of the Raïs was more fiery than usual, and the same words kept recurring—*imperialism, colonialism, Zionism, England, Suez Canal, France, and Israel.* Nasser repeated the word nationalization and war several times over the cheers and chants of what sounded like a huge crowd. I did not know the meaning of the word *nationalization.*

"What's happening?" all of us asked my father.

Papa didn't answer. The anxiety I could read on his face as he listened to the radio heightened my sense of foreboding. He listened a bit longer and said that Israel, France and Britain were at war with Egypt because Nasser had nationalized the Suez Canal. I asked what that meant, but he shooed me away with one word, "Later."

At home, Nona, Tante Rebecca and Tante Marie were listening to a French broadcast. It told of combat between the Egyptian armies and Israeli forces in the Sinai Peninsula, of British and French warplanes bombing Port Said, and all of them parachuting troops over the banks of the Suez Canal. And again the word *nationalization*, which I gathered meant that Nasser had seized the Suez Canal which was owned by Britain and France. The broadcast was a mishmash of declarations about colonialism and imperialism, the breach of treaties and the actions of the United Nations. Although I'd witnessed the burning of Cairo during the revolution, all I knew about war was the battlefields of the movies, and I now realized that it also took place in family rooms in which the old and the young assembled with anxiety and fear. Our anxieties and fears were about Felix, Tante Rebecca's son, Elie, Oncle Victor's son, and Annie who was old enough to be drafted in the Israeli forces. Were they among the troops fighting in the Sinai?

The family was sinking into a quicksand of confusion, uncertainty and inner conflict. It was as though the disparate elements of our hearts and minds were fighting one another in an excruciating inner civil war—Egypt, the country of our birth, against Israel, the land of our religion, France, the core of our culture, and Britain, the kingdom that had saved us from the Nazis at the gates of El Alamein.

"Nom d'un chien! Il est complètement fou, cet homme!" thundered Tante Rebecca, in a smattering of French, Arabic and English. "Howwa mag'noon! He is crazy! Did he think he could nationalize the Canal without starting a war?"

"Dio mio!" Nona cried. "Are we really at war?"

Oncle Léon was still in France, and Tante Marie worried 'they' wouldn't allow him to return to Egypt. "Qu'est-ce que nous allons faire sans Léon? How will we manage without Léon?"

"We'll be all right," my father echoed over and again. "There will be a ceasefire. Nobody wants a war."

"Come on, little brother!" said Tante Rebecca. "We *are* at war! The French and the British have already bombed Port Said! They'll be bombing Cairo very soon!"

"And the Israelis in the Sinai!" echoed Tante Marie. "Why did they get into this mess? You'll see! They'll blame it all on the Jews!"

"Israel had to intervene! That mamzer Nasser blockaded the Strait of Tiran. It's an act of war!" said Tante Rebecca.

"What's the Strait of Tiran?" I asked Papa.

"Not now!" he answered.

During the first days of the war, swarms of Arabs rode in army flatbeds, shouting anti-English, anti-French and anti-Zionist slogans. It was like the revolution all over again—only this time there was a greater sense of danger, or perhaps I was now old enough to recognize danger. Blackout orders came through the airwaves. We covered our windows with thick sheets of dark blue cardboard and kept the curtains drawn day and night. If a single ray of light shone through a window at night, the people out on the street would yell, throw stones at the culprit's windows and call the police. Powerful sirens blared throughout the days, and we could hear the faint rumble of bombs falling and exploding, first over distant neighborhoods, then at closer range. At night, airplanes flew in and dropped bombs over the far suburbs of Cairo, then flew away under a barrage of fire that crisscrossed the dark skies like thunderbolts, fleetingly illuminating an eerie skyline of mosques, citadels and minarets.

The trusty BBC and French radio broadcasts kept us abreast of the progress of the war. They told a different story than the broadcasts of the Arab radio stations. The European radio news reported that the Israeli troops had stopped at the edge of the Suez Canal, and English and French paratroopers had occupied Port Said and the Canal Zone. On the Egyptian stations, reporters described the progress of Egypt's armed forces as they were occupying Tel Aviv and Jerusalem. Some of them would add fine details of the bloodbath inflicted by the forces of Allah upon the Infidels.

"Al-Bahr al-Ahmar, the Red Sea, is a darker hue of red for all the thousands of Jews we have decapitated and thrown into the water," an announcer proclaimed with relish. "In no time, we will cleanse the Holy Land of the Zionist Infidels and, insh'Allah, restore the glory of Islam over Palestine!"

The hatred in the newscaster's words sent shivers down my spine. Papa cursed in multiple languages before switching to another station. "Kazzab, ebn el kalb! Menteur, fils de chien! Lying son of a bitch!"

Twice a day, and sometimes more often, Abdu ran down to the newsstand around the corner to buy the special editions of the Egyptian newspapers in Arabic, English and French which were renewed every few hours. Papa translated the headlines of the two Arabic dailies, *Al Ahram* and *Al Akhbar* for Nona and my aunts. I would hurry to look at the headlines of the three French-language dailies, *Le Progrès Egyptien*, *La Bourse Egyptienne*, and *Le Journal d'Egypte* before everyone else. And, when Papa was done with the English-language daily, *The Egyptian Gazette*, I would work on my English skills by painstakingly deciphering its headlines.

With every broadcast and every overheard family conversation, new names and expressions were entering my consciousness—*tripartite attack, Guy Mollet, Anthony Eden, Ben-Gurion, Eisenhower, Dulles, Sharm-el-Sheikh, Aqaba*, and a sea of others. The headlines and the illustrations of the Arab press horrified me. There were maps with captions showing the advance of the Arab forces into Israel, cartoons of Jews drowning in the Mediterranean and Egyptians planes strafing English and French troops, and photographs of soldiers waving the Egyptian flag.

How could Papa be so sure they were lies and fabrications? In the mad kaleidoscope of war, how could he know who was whom and what was what?

In Papa's book, the BBC broadcasters always told the whole truth, the French most of the time but not all the time, and the Arabs were lying dogs. "Propaganda! That's what the Arab press is about! Lies and propaganda!" Papa's voice boomed, full of anger and contempt. "We've lived with the Arabs long enough to know that they believe what Pharaoh wants them to believe! And that pharaoh, Nasser, is cunning, very cunning. C'est un malin, celui-là!"

"Eisenhower should have given him the Aswan goddamn dam!" said Tante Rebecca. "If he had, Nasser would have kept his dirty fingers off the Suez Canal!"

"What's a goddamn dam?" I asked.

"Quiet!" yelled Papa before turning to Tante Rebecca. "It might have stopped him, but I doubt it. He's aligned with the

Soviets since they sold him all these weapons, and they want his help to get the other Arab leaders into their orbit!"

"I still think Eisenhower should have given him his goddamn dam!" Tante Rebecca repeated, blowing a thick stack of smoke from her Belmont cigarette.

"What's a goddamn dam?" I asked again.

"Later!"

***

Since the outbreak of war, Nona's telephone rang incessantly as friends and family called to share their news rather than visit in person as they usually did. Nona became more tolerant of the contraption and even allowed the children to answer it.

My mother called every day, sometimes even twice a day.

"Don't talk too long!" admonished Nona. "There may be an emergency,"

I was just as eager to keep the calls brief. The conversations with Maman varied little.

"Did the bombs scare you last night?" she would ask.

"No, Maman, I wasn't scared. I was fine. I *am* fine."

She would tell me how much she missed me, how she hated the awful war that kept us apart. If my father would allow her to visit me, even for a few minutes, she'd be at my doorstep in no time, no matter how unsafe the streets.

Then came the tears. I'd let her sob for a long moment, then say, "Sorry, Maman, but I can't talk too long. There may be an emergency." She would cry louder and say that she loved me.

"Me too," I would answer in a whisper if Papa or Nona were within earshot.

The war of nations didn't put an end to the war within my heart. I tried hard not to offend Papa or Nona by expressing overt love for my mother. They assumed that I despised my mother as much as they did, and I was too cowardly to contradict them. In truth, I had conflicting emotions about my mother. Her expressions of love were so dramatic that I sometimes doubted their sincerity, and yet I felt drawn to her in a powerful visceral way that I couldn't ignore.

"One more minute, ya rohi," Maman would beg. "Is your father talking about leaving Egypt?" She used terms of endearment—ya rohi, my soul, ya albi, my heart, or ya habibi, my loved one—so often that sometimes I wondered if she'd forgotten my real first name.

"No, Maman. So far, only Tante Marie is packing her valises," I said to reassure her.

She would cry again. "I'll burn the boukhour tonight and pray that God will not separate us again. I couldn't bear it, ya rohi."

After she hung up, I would remember my mother at the Koubbeh house, engaged in the *boukhour* ceremony—the ancient ritual that dispelled negative energy—before praying to the gods and goddesses of pharaonic times. Hunched over the stove, Maman would throw the *boukhour*, a resin-like ball of incense, into the blackened frying pan she only used for that purpose, and she would mutter prayers in a mishmash of Arabic, French and unintelligible tongues. As the foul-smelling *boukhour* burned, Maman would take a sheet of translucent onionskin paper and write in small cursive letters a litany of pleas, supplications and grievances. She would then cut each plea into a narrow strip, and toss each single strip over the burning gum, fanning the flame with one hand, all the while inhaling the thick black smoke that rose from the pan and imploring the goddess Hathor to grant her prayers.

Before the flames died down, Maman would add frankincense to replace the foul smell with a sweet one, before putting the blackened pan away. She would kiss the many talismans she wore on a gold bracelet and linger on her favorites—a hand of

Fatima to ward off the evil eye, and a medallion of amber and gold depicting my mother's favorite goddess, Hathor. She was the goddess of beauty, motherhood and joy, and she held a golden ankh, the hieroglyphic key to eternal life. Her crown was made of an amber-colored sun disc lodged between the horns of a cow, the symbol of fertility.

Maman swore that Hathor would someday grant her fondest wish—to return me to her care forever.

But neither the goddess Hathor nor the high priests of Ancient Egypt could stop the wheels that were spinning a little faster every day on the broadcast news. In Britain and France, there were anti-war rallies and talks of governments falling, and even Papa's great war hero, Winston Churchill, criticized the "tripartite" attack. Papa's other hero, Ike Eisenhower, and two politicians named Dulles were sparring with two Russians named Khrushchev and Bulganin who threatened to enter the war on Egypt's side. Leaders of less prominent countries cajoled, threatened and implored the parties to stop the fighting and warned of the apocalyptic consequences of another world war. It unnerved me to know that our fate was in the hands of leaders in places like the Élysée Palace, 10 Downing Street, the White House and the Kremlin. What did these warlords know about us? Did they see us as anything other than pawns on their planetary chess games?

***

The chess games ended as abruptly as they had started. The United Nations voted a resolution calling for a ceasefire and the withdrawal of British, French, and Israeli armed forces from Egypt—and both the USA and the USSR turned off their killing machines. A nuclear war would not take place this time. The Suez war was over.

After the United Nations' vote for a ceasefire and the withdrawal of all troops from Egypt, jubilant crowds descended on the streets of Cairo, acclaiming Gamal Abdel Nasser for his tremendous victory against the forces of imperialism, colonialism, and Zionism. "Long live Nasser!" they chanted. "Down with Eden!" and "Down with Mollet" they intoned, cursing both the British and the French prime ministers. A tidal wave of humanity engulfed Midan el-Tahrir. Loudspeakers played and replayed the Raïs's thunderous victory speech in which he proclaimed December 23—the day the UN had set for the last French and British troops to evacuate the Canal Zone—as Victory Day forevermore.

December 23 of 1956 was also my father's forty-sixth birthday. "Nice birthday gift, Mr. Nasser," Papa mumbled. We were standing on the balcony overlooking Fuad Avenue, our usual observation spot. Down below, convoys of honking flatbed military trucks, full of soldiers waving to the adoring multitudes, were rolling along the broad thoroughfare toward Tahrir Square.

"Look at them!" muttered Tante Rebecca. "The Egyptian military was on its knees, all their Soviet tanks and airplanes were destroyed, and they had lost the war when Eisenhower made the UN call for the ceasefire—and now they're celebrating the goddamn ceasefire as a victory!"

"Eisenhower had no choice!" Papa said. "Khrushchev was ready to push the button!"

"It's shameful! Don't the Americans understand that giving Nasser his sham victory meant anointing him king of all the Arabs?" she exclaimed.

"This is the end of the road for us," said Papa. "In five, ten, twenty years, not a single Jew will be left in Egypt!"

***

The aftermath of the ceasefire was more frightening than the war itself. Nasser's government expelled all French and British nationals and revoked the citizenship of Jews who'd been naturalized after 1900, rendering them stateless. Without transit papers, the Jews of Egypt couldn't find refuge outside of Egypt—and remaining in Egypt had become hazardous.

Day after day, visitors and telephone callers brought the news of friends and relatives being arrested, accused of espionage in favor of "the Zionist entity," interrogated, and sometimes tortured. The wealthier would be forced to sign over their property to the state in trade for "no-return" exit visas. It was such a commonplace story that I soon knew the names of the prisons near Cairo like Abu Zaabal and Les Barrages which held both Jews and Muslim Brothers. With the flurry of expulsions, I also knew the names of the passenger liners that took the Jewish refugees out of Egypt—the *Esperia* bound for Genoa, the *Enotria* bound for Naples, and both the *Misri* and the *Nefertiti* for Marseille.

At bedtime, I couldn't help but ask, "Nasser—is he like Hitler? Will he put us in camps?"

Papa sat on the edge of the bed and took me in his arms. "No, hijico mio. You have nothing to fear. Nasser is no friend of the Jews, but he's not a madman like Hitler. He puts Jews in prison, but he doesn't kill them. And, unlike the Jews of Europe, we have the choice to leave Egypt! Most of us at least"

"Leave to go to France?" I asked.

"Or anywhere—or maybe join the family in Israel?"

"France is where I want to go if we leave Egypt." I said. "I don't want to speak Hebrew all the time."

"I understand. I have a preference for France too—if they'll accept us as refugees."

"Why did Oncle Victor decide to live in Israel?"

"He felt it was the only safe place for Jews to live, despite the wars with the Arabs. My brother had predicted what's happening now. In '45, days after you were born, there was violence against the Jews in Cairo. A great many Egyptians had rooted for the Nazis during the war and took their frustrations out on the Jews. In 1945, the right-wing Young Egypt Party and the Muslim Brotherhood had organized violent rallies in the Jewish quarters. Synagogues, Jewish hospitals and homes were ransacked and burned, killing a dozen Jews and injuring hundreds. Victor saw it as a sign and moved to Israel with his family. At the same time Félix, my sister Rebecca's son, was beaten senseless at the University of Cairo by a band of Muslim Brothers students. They took the writing on the wall very seriously."

"You think we should have gone too?" I asked.

"Yes, I wish I'd listened to my older brother," Papa said after a long hesitation. "Years ago, Victor had warned me that in Egypt, no matter how well we do, we'd always be dhimmis. Not full citizens. Never full citizens."

"What's a 'dhimmi'?" I asked.

"That's for another day. Briefly, a 'dhimmi' is a non-Muslim in a Muslim country, tolerated, even protected, but still an infidel, still an inferior."

"Is that still true?"

"Yes and no. The dhimmi laws fell out of practice after the first Egyptian revolution, but they were never abrogated." Before I could ask another question, Papa blocked my lips with his index finger. "Basta così! Bedtime!"

***

Around Christmas, Tante Marie and her daughters Viviane and Simone arrived at Nona's house with their suitcases for their last days in Cairo. In a letter mailed via Italy, Oncle Léon, barred from returning to Egypt after the war, had sent clear instructions for Marie to leave everything behind and join him in Paris with the girls. They would be the first batch out of Egypt.

One evening at dinner, we said our goodbyes to Tante Marie, Viviane, and Simone. The next morning when I woke up, they were gone. In one swoop, an entire branch of our family tree was cut out.

Nona, Tante Rebecca and her daughters would leave a few weeks later. Oncle Léon would meet them at the Genoa harbor and Nona would live in Paris with his reunited family. Rebecca would sail with her daughters to Haifa and reunite with her son Félix. Nona wanted to live in Israel, but she was too frail to start a new life in an unknown environment. Perhaps later, when Tante Rebecca was settled, but not now.

Papa decided to stay in Cairo a little longer. He wanted to liquidate some family assets and smuggle money out of Egypt, so we wouldn't be destitute in our first days of exile. Nona, Tante Rebecca, and Tante Marie tried to dissuade him by insisting that the dangers far outweighed the benefits, but Papa was adamant. He knew a reliable "passeur," a Copt who'd saved many Jewish families from total destitution by moving their money to Swiss banks. He was expensive but honest, unlike the many other middlemen who stole the money and ran.

I felt in my bones that remaining in Egypt after the family had left would be disastrous—but a boy of eleven had no voice in the chorus. At night, I seldom found sleep. Half comatose, I'd replay the various conversations overheard, looking for clues to our future. But the future remained a blank slate. I wondered if the same conversations, the same sleeplessness, the same anxieties were taking place in thousands of Jewish homes across Egypt.

***

A little later, we all started to pack—everyone for their future life out of Egypt, and Papa and I to move to a nearby hotel.

Nona, Tante Rebecca spent long days sorting, discarding, and determining what to pack. The Egyptian regime only allowed twenty kilograms of belongings per person on their way to exile. Several faux-leather valises were delivered. Each was the size of a steamer trunk, all in hues of brown and red. As we filled them, Abdu piled them up in Nono's study. It was a violation of Nono's sanctuary, but nobody else seemed to care, not even Nona. The old rules didn't fit the new times.

When I was alone in the study, the big brown and red suitcases would conjure up images of a herd of cattle in the American West. I would fashion sharp cones made of cardboard to stand for the cattle's horns and pieces of string for their tails. A suitcase became my horse, a folded blanket a saddle, a broom a rifle and a rope a lasso. Perched on my stallion, driving my cattle through a Far West of the mind, I could daydream of roaming the vast expanses of a free land. After a while, the game felt too childish. It was like opening a comic book after reading a "real" novel—silly but fun.

A few days before they were to leave, Tante Rebecca went through old boxes of mementoes, picked her most precious photographs, and ordered Mayasoon to burn the rest. Later, when I climbed up to the roof, I saw Mayasoon throw the pictures into a metal barrel and put a match to them. No sooner had the flames gone up than a trio of *shawishes* in uniform appeared on the rooftop.

"What are you doing with these pictures?" asked the leader of the policemen.

"Don't you have eyes to see?" Mayasoon answered. "I'm getting rid of these pictures, that's what I'm doing!"

"Why are you burning them? What's in these pictures?" he asked, retrieving a few partially burned family pictures from the fire and blowing the flames out.

"Ya salaam! Like it's any of your business what's in the pictures! They're family pictures!"

"These are not your pictures! They're pictures of Jews!"

"Of course, they're not my pictures! They belong to my mistress's daughter, Madame Rebecca."

"Your *Jewish* boss asked you to burn these pictures?" The policeman turned to his colleagues with a knowing look.

"So?" said Mayasoon. "She's Jewish all right, but she's a better Egyptian than all of you!"

"Don't be insolent, woman! Why did your Jewish boss lady want you to burn them?"

"Because your government is kicking them out of the country! And she can't even take her pictures with her! Otherwise, I wouldn't be burning these pictures—and burning my heart with every one of them!"

"What are you talking about, woman?"

"Ya salaam, are you a stupid a'aragoz in police garb?" she yelled, referring to the dumb puppet of Egyptian folk stories. Taken aback by her fury, the shawish asked her why she was so mad. "Don't you idiots understand anything? When they go, our jobs go. We've worked here for twenty-seven years! This is our only home! Where will we go when they leave? Who will feed my children? You, bunch of clowns?"

"So that's why you're conspiring with your mistress to send smoke signals to the Zionists and their airplanes!"

"Einta mag'noon? Are you crazy?" She looked up to the sky. "What Zionists? What airplanes?"

The trio ordered Mayasoon to take them to her mistress's apartment and pushed her down the service staircase, which didn't stop her from yelling curses upon their houses. I followed them as they erupted into the kitchen where Tante Rebecca was working with Abdu.

"Ya sett, you're under arrest!" said the lead shawish in a solemn voice.

"What on earth for?" asked Tante Rebecca calmly.

"Espionage!" he said, pointing to the semi-burned pictures he'd salvaged and wrapped in a newspaper.

Tante Rebecca laughed at first then, realizing he was not joking, she protested, argued and threatened, to no avail. The shawish smirked, savoring his newfound power over his Jewish prey. Finally, Tante Rebecca hugged her daughters and told Myra, "If I don't come back, get on that ship and take care of your sisters."

"Don't worry, Mama, they won't hurt you," said Myra, trying to act strong and grownup. "They'll understand it's a mistake."

Suddenly, Abdu stepped toward Mayasoon and slapped her hard. "Mara!" he yelled, using a condescending word for woman. "Who gave you permission to burn these pictures?"

Mayasoon looked stunned at first, then she caught on. "Nobody!" she mumbled. "It's all my fault! I just thought—"

Abdu turned to the policeman and pointing to Mayasoon, he said, "It's my stupid wife who took it upon herself to burn these family pictures! This lady had nothing to do with it!"

Looking angry and bitter, the leader of the policemen grabbed Mayasoon by the arm and yelled, "We're taking you to the station! You won't get away with it!"

Abdu and Papa exchanged a glance, and my father handed him a wad of banknotes. Abdu rushed down the stairs after the policemen. I was angry. If only I'd had a sword to defend Tante Rebecca! Abdu was back with Mayasoon in no time.

"How did he do it?" Nona asked Papa.

"No revolution will ever trump the sacrosanct baksheesh!" he smirked.

***

After seeing *The Maltese Falcon*, I couldn't contain an urge to smoke. Everyone smoked all the time in Hollywood movies. I stole two cigarettes from my father's case and invited Viva to join me. We locked ourselves in the bathroom, opened the windows and lit up. I used a folded newspaper to fan the smoke away. The first few puffs made us cough a lot, but we got used to it. Holding the cigarette made me feel grown up, wise and tough—a miniature Humphrey Bogart. The next day, I stole another cigarette and smoked it alone on the rooftop in the servants' quarters. I enjoyed it even more than the first one. After lunch, I wanted another cigarette. Papa's case was almost empty, so I stole a few piasters from his pockets and went to the Palestinian tobacconist around the corner.

"A Belmont cigarette, please. For my father!" I said, putting a few coins on the counter.

"A single Belmont?" he asked. I nodded. He looked puzzled as he handed me a single cigarette. He took the exact change and handed me the rest of the coins. "Too much money," he mumbled, looking away. His unusual reserve told me I'd made a royal blunder. Only the very poor bought single cigarettes! I prayed he wouldn't tell my father!

Viva refused to share that last cigarette. She was going to the hospital with her mother for a check-up, and she feared that the X-ray machine would detect the smoke in her lungs.

"That's ridiculous, Viva! There's no way the X-ray machine could show smoke after a few hours!"

"You're wrong! I heard that the X-ray machine can see *everything*! Absolutely, totally everything! I hope it doesn't show the smoke from the last time!"

In the evening, Papa and Tante Rebecca came into my room and confronted me.

"How long have you been smoking?" Papa asked in an icy tone.

"Once, just to see what it's like," I conceded.

"Viva said you stole two cigarettes from your father's case and wanted to share another one with her," said Tante Rebecca. "What's the truth?"

I remained silent.

Papa said, "So, you stole two cigarettes *and* ran to the tobacconist to buy another one, saying it was for me. Did you think he was stupid?" I didn't answer. "He knows I buy several packs at a time, you idiot!" Further angered by my silence, he yelled. "*And* it's not bad enough that you smoke, you had to make your cousin smoke with you?"

"I didn't make her do anything! She wanted to smoke the first one, and I offered to share my second cigarette!"

"Would she have smoked if you hadn't?" Tante Rebecca asked me.

"I don't know." They were both staring at me. "Maybe not!"

"She's younger, so you're responsible!" said Papa.

"So punish me!" I yelled. "I've had enough with this! It wasn't a crime!"

"You wait here! I'm not done with you!" he yelled as he walked out of the room.

Tante Rebecca stayed behind and looked at me in silence. It wasn't a look of disapproval but rather of sorrow and concern. She put her hand on my shoulder and said, "I pray that you don't drive your father crazy when we're all gone. He'll need your help once it's only the two of you." She held my chin and looked into my eyes with apprehensive tenderness. "Do you understand?" she asked.

Fighting tears, I nodded my understanding.

***

Papa and I remained in the cavernous apartment for a week or two after the family was gone. Mayasoon and Abdu floated from room to room like lost souls, dusting, washing, swabbing, scouring, waxing, and polishing the silverware and the furniture as though they were preening the house for the high holidays.

On the given day an auctioneer came and opened the sale. Immediately Nona's apartment was invaded by a horde of men and women. They walked through the rooms, opened closets and drawers, examined furniture, silverware, porcelains and linen, lifted objects to gauge their weight. Items wanted by more than one person were auctioned, and for the non-contested items they bargained, extolled, denigrated, and ultimately bought the items, leaving the large items to be collected later.

After the sale, all that remained was my grandfather's library. The offers had been too low, and Papa said he'd rather give them away to an institution that would value them.

An elderly gentleman in uniform showed up as the auctioneer was ready to leave. He spoke French fluently and made a generous offer for the entire lot—books, shelves, framed drawings, and paintings, even Nono's brass bookstand which had been set on the floor after his desk was sold.

"Mabrouk, cher monsieur," said Papa. "Congratulations. Our family's library is now yours!"

I thought I was prepared to let my grandfather's books go, but the finality of the sale was more than I could take. Papa's words to the gentleman felt as though a sharp knife was slicing my heart, and I could feel my own thick blood dripping on the wooden floor of the study. I ran to the elderly gentleman and hit him with both fists, yelling, "You can't take my grandfather's books! These books are mine!"

Papa apologized profusely to the elderly officer who kept repeating, "Je comprends, cher monsieur! I understand!"

"There's nothing to understand! I don't care if you're the pharaoh of Egypt or Nasser himself, these are *my* books! You can't steal them!"

Abdu whisked me away while Papa continued to apologize and the kind officer continued to say, "Je comprends sa douleur, cher monsieur!"

After the gentleman left, Abu and Mayasoon went upstairs to their quarters. Papa and I walked through Nona's apartment for the last time. Almost everything was gone, except for the heavy furniture marked with red tags. I didn't care about any of it, but I had knots in my stomach when I entered Nono's study.

The bookshelves still stood, with their rows of books untouched for one last night. I sat on the floor in the study. The Turkish carpet that ran the length of the room had been removed, and the bare wood floor was hard and cold. I looked at the gold-stamped, leather-bound books that had comforted, charmed and enlightened my childhood, and I wept. Tomorrow the officer's men would come and cart them away. Tomorrow the temple would be reduced to rubble.

Papa came into the study and sat on the floor next to me. "I feel the same way, hijico mio. I grew up with these books too. I saw my papa's library grow and grow." His voice broke down to a whisper. "But even when they're gone, these books will stay with you." He extended his arm in a sweeping gesture toward the shelves and added, "Nobody can take this away from you. Everything in this room will continue to live—here." He gave me a tap on the forehead. "And here!" he added with a gentle poke on my heart.

CHAPTER 7

Winter of 1957

The Anglo-Swiss Hotel was neither Anglo nor Swiss. It belonged to a Greek family and catered to middle-class international tourists. Since the war the flow of tourists had thinned out, but the hotel had become a haven for Jewish families awaiting transit documents on their way out of Egypt.

Oddly, the Anglo-Swiss occupied the top floors of an otherwise residential building at 14 rue Champollion, a stone's throw from the Nile and the Egyptian Museum in Tahrir Square. A rickety elevator opened onto the sixth floor which housed the reception desk, the dining hall, the sitting room, and many guest bedrooms. A large stairway meandered up to the rooms and suites of the two higher floors. Papa and I had two rooms that offered splendid views of the Cairo skyline. They were spacious and airy, but once we moved in, our huge red-brown suitcases, piled up in the corners of the rooms like beached whales, dwarfed the space. I hated these ever-present reminders of the transience of our new lives.

"Unpack only what you need," said Papa. "We'll just be here until we get our exit visas in a few weeks at the most."

In the streets of Cairo, the ceasefire had brought legions of soldiers wearing blue helmets. They drove through the city in white jeeps and trucks bearing a smoke-blue emblem. Papa told me they were the soldiers of UNEF, the United Nations

Emergency Forces, sent to monitor the ceasefire between Egypt and Israel. He pointed to a UN flag mounted on the hood of a vehicle. I said it looked like a shooting target, but Papa told me to watch more intently.

"See the two olive branches surrounding the shapes of the five continents? It's the symbol of peace embracing the entire world. These boys' job is to keep the peace between enemies."

The *boys* came in a variety of colors and complexions. Most of the white soldiers were Nordic, and the troops counted contingents of golden-colored Asians, olive-skinned South Americans, and Africans of every hue. Papa said they were on leave from their observation posts on the Gaza strip or at Sharm el-Sheikh on the edge of the Sinai desert. "These boys remind me of the British soldiers in Cairo during the world war. They also came in every color and race from the entire British Commonwealth." Papa looked nostalgic. "Even the Palestinian Jewish brigades were among them—bunches of proud Jewish Tommies on their way to fight the Gerries in Libya."

"Tommies?" I asked. Papa went on with a litany of nicknames for the various troops fighting during the war—Gerries for the German enemy and on the good guys' side Tommies for the British, Yanks for the Americans, and Frogs for the French. He noticed my puzzled look. "It's short for Frog Leg Eaters," he added.

"Yuck! And the soldiers with the blue helmets, what are they called?"

"Blue Helmets!" he said with a grin. "Or Casques bleus! Or Cascos azules! Or—"

***

"It is cold in Europe," Maman said for the umpteenth time. We were in one of her favorite department stores where she took me almost every Saturday before going to our other familiar places. She knew I had more clothing than I'd ever need, but that didn't stop her from buying me new attires, blankets and even bedsheets. "I don't want you to catch your death on arrival in Paris."

She would pick up a garment, check its weight, feel the fabric between her fingers. "C'est de la vraie camelote! This is real junk!" she would say with a disdainful pout as she threw the item back in its bin. "Our department stores are not the same. Before the troubles they were as good, if not better, than Les Galeries Lafayette or Le Printemps in Paris. Even better than Harrods of London!"

When she found a suitable item, she would have me try on a size or two bigger than my fit. "You're still a growing boy. You'll outgrow your clothes in no time. And these things are very expensive in Europe."

What I saw in the mirror was a dwarf decked out in a giant's attire, but Maman was unswerving in her response, "We have to think ahead."

"We're not going to the North Pole, you know!" I would attempt to resist. "*Plus*, we're only allowed to take two suitcases and twenty kilos abroad. You've bought enough to fill twelve valises!"

"Don't worry about it," she would counter. "Some things never change. Monarchy or republic, a little baksheesh goes a long way. And what you can't take with you, Tante Magda and Oncle Hussein will send you by the diplomatic pouch. He's now a minister, just like Abel Hakim Amer and Anwar el-Sadat."

I wanted to say that Papa thought Amer was a Nazi, Sadat a buffoon, and Hussein el-Shafei a Muslim Brother fanatic, but I bit my tongue. "I'm sure Hussein el-Shafei has better things to do than help Jews take a ton of shirts and blankets out of Egypt."

"Don't you talk like your father! Tante Aïda is like a sister to me, and Oncle Hussein is not antisemitic!"

"First, he's not my uncle. Second, he *does* make speeches about throwing the Jews into the sea. I hear him on the radio, and I'm ashamed—"

"That's just politics! Propaganda for the masses. You know he doesn't mean it!"

"Still, I doubt my father would ever accept any help from him!"

"Your father is more stubborn than a mule! The war is over. Life is almost back to normal. Your grandmother and your father's siblings were too quick to leave. Everybody knew the bad times wouldn't last!" she said angrily. "Leaving Egypt makes no sense at this time."

I bit my lips and tried to change the subject, but she wouldn't have it. "You're just as mulish as your father. Why are you so eager to leave me?" she'd say, wiping an invisible tear from the corner of her eye. "Don't you love me anymore?"

I hoped she wasn't expecting an answer.

If I went home with so many bags and boxes, I'd have to endure my father's scoffs and taunts. Promising a good backsheesh, I got the *bawab*, the hotel doorman, to store the bags in the back rooms until I could smuggle them upstairs one by one.

Often, when Maman drove me home, she would hand the doorman a backsheesh. "Take care of my boy, please." The bawab would beam and bow several times while moving his hand from his chest to his forehead. "A'ala eini wa rassi, ya setti!" he'd say, "Upon my eyes and my head, my lady!"

***

After many months of closure, my school reopened with a new name. It was now the Lycée *Al Horreya*—the Arabic word for freedom.

This new incarnation was different from the school I knew before the Suez war. The Nasser regime had expelled the French faculty and administration, and the school had replaced them with French-speaking Egyptian, Lebanese and Syrian educators. As a result of the regime's decree of "Arabization" of the nation, the student body had lost most of its Jewish and Christian students and gained a majority of Egyptian Arabs. Although French remained the school's primary language, the studies of Arabic and Egyptian literature and history classes were now a large share of the curriculum.

I understood that these changes were a necessary evolution to reflect the new Egypt, but they put me at a disadvantage. Until then, we'd studied Arabic as a third language, after French and English, and few of us were fluent enough in Arabic to hold our own in the new curriculum. I didn't have a prayer of catching up. I would have despaired were it not for the certainty that I would soon be pursuing my education in France.

The silver lining in that new school season was the joy of reuniting with my mates, JP, Ike, Gil, Coco and Momo. We'd barely seen one another during the war and its aftermath. Not only was the lycée closed, but the streets weren't safe for European-looking people. At school, too many beloved teachers and too many of our classmates were absent. At home, we all missed too many loved ones who had either been expelled or forced to leave their country. I fiercely missed Nona, Oncle Léon and my aunts and my cousins. I even missed our bickering as we walked between home and school.

My mates and I returned to our rituals, listening to rock 'n' roll at JP's house or going to the movies. Since the war, French and British movies had vanished from the screens, and the theaters now played American and Italian films, along with the usual the Egyptian movie fare. Now and then a theater would play a film from the Soviet bloc, but they reeked of propaganda, blatant or subtle. Many Italian films dwelled on the hardship among the ruins of post-World War II cities, and it seemed that most of them starred Sophia Loren or Gina Lollobrigida or a sexy lookalike. American movies were often westerns or big Hollywood spectacles. Some were enjoyable, others not, but the extravaganzas set in ancient Egypt, like *Valley of the Kings* or *The Egyptian*, were so ridiculous they became the laughingstock of every Egyptian who saw them. Now and then, smaller films opened windows into different aspects of America, like *Blackboard Jungle*, *Rebel Without a Cause*, and *The Wild One*, reaching beyond the happy-happy Doris Day fantasies and depicting a real country with real people and real problems.

Emulating the characters with whom we identified, we got our parents to buy us blue jeans, sneakers and red windbreakers, and on weekends we paraded in the streets of Cairo like dark Levantine James Deans and Marlon Brandos. On Mondays, we would don our regular garb and return to our daily conformist lives.

A newcomer joined the lycée around Christmas and quickly gravitated to our little group. Quentin Barthes was the son of a Swiss diplomat who had been posted to Egypt. He had lived and grown up in various countries of Africa, in the wake of his father's postings, and he had an endless stream of stories about his adventures and mischiefs. I suspected that most of Quentin's African stories were tales inspired by adventure movies and halfpenny novels, but he cleverly injected the imaginary into the plausible, making it impossible to distinguish one from the other. He had a devilish sense of humor, and he talked about girls and sex with more knowledge than the bunch of us put together. He boasted of conquests and stolen kisses and canoodling with girls in the darkness of movie theaters. Nobody challenged Quentin's veracity, but we all suspected there was more fantasy than truth in his accounts. We let him get away with it because he was so entertaining.

I loved our playful times at JP's. His parents' life seemed to be a permanent celebration, although sometimes I sensed a dissonance, touches of sadness. On the surface, not much had changed since the revolution. The Lombrosos still traveled around the world, bought their clothes in Paris, their shoes in London and their electronic gadgets in Munich or New York. When we lingered at their house into the early evenings, it was not uncommon to see JP's parents in gown and tuxedo serving cocktails to their international guests before going out on the town. Yet, underneath the permanent feast that was their life, I felt a sense of loss and despair. It was the same undertone of forlorn hope I recognized in the frenzy of my mother's social activities, and in my father's escape into the night spots of Cairo. They all seemed to be sucking the marrow of life, knowing that it would soon run dry, perhaps snatching a few last moments of happiness from the jaws of looming destruction.

***

Almost a year after our entire family left the country, we were still in Egypt. The exit visa repeatedly requested was a long time coming. We relegated the big suitcases to a storage space in the bowels of the hotel to rub out the transient ambience in our rooms, but I began to feel like a hostage. It was as though the powers that be had pushed the "pause" button on a tape recorder and left me at a standstill.

Optimistic as always, Papa believed that the right amount of backsheesh in the hands of the right civil servant would produce the exit visas, but so far the bureaucrats he'd bribed had not delivered. Papa remained sanguine, but as the months went by, I was losing hope at a fast rate.

Maman had been right about one thing: I quickly outgrew the clothes she'd bought me, and they were now used by the children of Abdu and Mayasoon. Papa kept their family on a monthly stipend until they found a new family to serve.

At the Anglo-Swiss Hotel many of the dining room conversations revolved around Nasser's Jewish policies. The word 'sequestration' entered my vocabulary. Papa told me that large Jewish-owned businesses were placed under the administration of Egyptian nationals—preferably Muslims rather than either Copts or Christians for fear they would be too sympathetic to their fellow Infidels. Most owners of sequestered businesses were forced to sell their property for a pittance and leave the country. Smaller businesses suffered the opposite fate. They were assessed exorbitant taxes, and their owners could not leave Egypt until all levies were paid.

Papa was surprised at the tax bill he received for Dorville, his haberdashery. After the Suez war, the store's revenue had considerably shrunk. Most of his patrons, the British, the French, the Jews, and even the Egyptian aristocrats had either lost their fortunes or had left Egypt. His new customers, the rising elite of the new regime, were too few to make up for the lost revenue. Yet, as long as Dorville broke even, Papa wouldn't shutter it; he didn't want his longtime staff to lose their livelihood. The new taxes meant more palms to grease to avoid a shutdown.

On my mother's side, I heard no talk about leaving Egypt. She and her friends continued to believe that the current political situation was just a temporary crisis, and that life would eventually return to what it had been before *les événements*—the euphemism they used for both the revolution and the Suez war. Did they think that calling a military coup an *event*, and using the word *crisis* to designate a war, made reality less devastating?

So far, my mother and her husband were doing well. Albert's business had been under sequester, but Khadr Bey, Tante Aïda's husband, had used his political connections to be appointed as the administrator of my stepfather's enterprises. Being a close friend, Albert could pretend to report to Khadr Bey while running his business as he always had.

As Maman was telling me about Albert's business, I suspected she was implying that, given his powerful political friends, her industrialist husband was a far more important man than my shopkeeper father. It fell on deaf ears. I was happy for Albert, but his success didn't diminish my father in my eyes. My mother's news only pointed to the evidence that her life and my own were on diverging paths. Along with her husband, their children, her brothers and their wives, my mother would remain in Egypt while my father and I couldn't wait to escape from the lions' den.

***

On the weekends, if my father was busy, I would take long walks around the city. I wanted to explore the areas of Cairo I'd never seen before because, once we left for Europe, I might never return to Egypt.

One afternoon my steps took me to Fuad 1 Avenue, walking toward Nona's old apartment building. Not much had changed on my street, save its name—it was now 26 of July Avenue, the day of King Farouk's abdication. Walking along the familiar street brought back memories of Nona, my cousins, Abdu and Mayasoon, and my grandfather's study, and I fell into a wave of nostalgia and sadness.

The call of the muezzin reminded me I was late. I had homework to do before dinner. I ran toward the rue Champollion, and I was crossing a side street when a loud whistle stopped me in my tracks. A traffic policeman stood on the other side of the street, one hand holding the whistle while he gesticulated with the other hand like a disjointed puppet. Stuck in the middle of the street, dodging oncoming cars, I navigated my way across the street toward the shawish and jumped to safety on the sidewalk.

Before I could get my bearings, the policeman slapped me with all his might, projecting me against a lamppost, and slapped me again with the back of his hand. "Ebn el sharmoota yahoodeya! Son of a Jewish whore! When I say stop, you stop! When I say go, you go! You, sons of rabid dogs, are not the masters here anymore!"

He whacked me again, harder this time while unleashing torrents of invectives. I stood in front of him, speechless and incredulous, unsure about what hurt more—the humiliating blows, the painful slaps, the inability to fight back, or the hatred in the policeman's eyes. He was about to strike me again when a man shouted, "Stop, ya rakeeb!"

Surprised by the imperious order, the policeman darted an angry look at the newcomer, an older gentleman in a sharkskin suit holding an ornate cane. The shawish was about to yell back, but the words froze on his lips. He stood sharply at attention until the older man made a gesture of dismissal.

"Sergeant," said the gentleman. "The boy was wrong, but I'm sure he's learned his lesson!" When I stepped toward my savior, I noticed a small shiny military insignia pinned to the lapel of his suit.

We walked in silence for a street block, then the gentleman stopped and extended his hand. "Ma'al salama, ya ebni. Go in peace, my son." He added in perfect French, "I hope you won't hate us for what we're becoming!" He walked briskly across the street, his cane tapping the pavement like a soft military drum.

Back at the hotel, I went to my room and ordered a bucket of ice. I didn't want anyone to see my swollen cheek. An hour of ice on my jowl alleviated both the swelling and the physical pain, but there was no remedy for the psychic pain I felt—no remedy to heal the shame of being humiliated by the policeman's wallops; no remedy to mollify the rage at my powerlessness; no remedy against the sheer hatred I'd seen in the shawish's eyes. Had the old gentleman not stopped him, he would've reduced me to a pulp. I'd never seen an Arab beat up a *khawaga* before. Although I'd been brought up with the belief that we were all equal, I'd lived in a world in which Arabs were subservient to Europeans, and the policeman's violence had been unexpected. But then the man who'd saved me was also an Arab. It was a nightmare of confusion.

Papa came in as I was playing *Tutti Frutti* for the umpteenth time. He turned the player off and gave me nasty look.

"Could you please tell me what this 'Bada-boom bam boom' means?" he asked in an angry voice.

"You wouldn't understand," I said.

"Probably not! But I do understand your lousy grades in Arabic!" Papa said angrily. "Explain that to me, and why you've been cutting class these last few weeks!"

"I did it because I don't give a damn about Arabic! I won't need that bloody language to go to school in France."

"That's stupid on all counts. One, you're not in France yet. Two, it's never a waste to learn a language, and, three, if you don't pass your exams you won't attend school *anywhere*!"

"I don't care! I'm not learning the stupid language of the stupid people who hate us!" I said.

"Wait a minute! Now, you blame the Arabic *language* for some Jew-hating thugs?" Papa barked, increasingly irritated.

I wasn't mollified. "I don't care! I want nothing to do with these filthy Arabs!"

"I won't tolerate that kind of language, you hear?" Papa yelled in a rare outburst of fury. "We're not racists in this family!"

"*They* are the racists!" I yelled back. "I said I want nothing to do with this *shitty* country with its *shitty* dictator, and his *shitty* people!"

Papa slapped me. He'd never hit me before. I was in shock.

"I'm ashamed of you!" he hollered, shaking with anger. "I never thought I'd hear my own son speak that way!"

I stepped forward. "Go ahead! Hit me again!" I shouted. "Just like the shitty shawish bastard who beat me on the street!"

His anger dropped instantly. "What shawish?" he asked in an alarmed tone. "When?"

"Just now, on the way home! That rabid dog hit me because I crossed the red light!"

"Why didn't you tell me?" he asked.

"You didn't give me time to say a word!" I said. "Not that I would tell you anyway!"

"You *must* tell me these things!" he said. "I'm your father!" He turned the bedside light on and noticed the redness on my cheek I wasn't able to mask.

"I didn't want to upset you," I cried.

"Habibi, it's not for you to protect me!" Papa said. "It's the other way around! Don't ever keep anything like that from me!"

"What could you have done about it?" I asked, my anger turning to sorrow.

Papa didn't answer. We both knew there was no answer. Again, the feelings of impotence choked me, and tears gushed out of my eyes. I wanted to stop whining but I couldn't. "I'm sorry I said these things, but I can't stand it anymore! I'm fed up with the daily calls to slaughter the Jews on the radio! It makes me sick!"

"I know, hijico mio," he said. "It makes me sick too. But you must never let the poison of hatred come into your heart—"

"But they're the ones who are full of hatred! Why can't I hate those who hate me?"

"Because hatred hurts the hater more than the hated!" he said. "And it's not in your nature!"

"How do you know?" I asked, defiantly. "Maybe all this right and wrong stuff is just un tas de merde!"

"I know my boy," said Papa. "I recall a little boy who once bravely defended Mahmoud against a British officer who said something racist at the store. You don't remember?"

I shook my head.

"Mahmoud was fitting that British captain for a new uniform, and he pricked his leg by mistake. The Englishman kicked him and called him a dirty *wog*. And what did my little boy do? He stood up to the Englishman and said, 'He's not a dirty wog, he's Mahmoud and he's my friend!'"

Flashes of recognition teased my brain, too vague to form a memory. "What did the Britisher say?" I asked through my tears.

"He turned to Mahmoud and said, 'Sorry, old chap! Be more careful next time!' There wasn't a prouder father in the world that day!"

After my father left the room, I sat on the floor, trying to remember the incident with the British officer, but it was too vague a memory. It made me realize how much I missed Mahmoud. He had been a cherished presence throughout my childhood, my benevolent Arab uncle. Where was he now?

A little earlier, Papa had shut down his store. It was no longer viable. On the last day, Papa divided the store's equipment among his beloved staff, with the lion's share to Mahmoud, in the hope that they would start a business of their own. The memory brought tears to my eyes. I cried for all the losses I'd experienced in a year; I cried for my family now out of Egypt; I cried for Mahmoud and his staff; and I cried for the brotherhood we had all shared for so long.

CHAPTER 8

Spring of 1957

In the year-end tests, I failed by a hair's breadth in Arabic and math. The new principal ordered grade retention to help overcome my deficiencies in these disciplines. I did all I could to convince my father that repeating the grade would be a huge waste because my Arabic scores wouldn't matter at all once I went to school in France, and I would work hard to overcome my difficulties in mathematics. Miraculously he agreed and we went in search of a new school, but we encountered the same obstacles we'd had in previous years—the dearth of French-language schools.

Besides the lycée, the remaining francophone institutions were the Christian Brothers' schools and other religious establishments which were under the authority of the Vatican, not France. I was willing to go to a Christian school, but my father feared they would proselytize and convert me. Instead, he turned to my old boarding school and went to see Mme Victoria. She balked at taking me back, but Papa's feats of diplomacy won the day, and I was allowed to return to her school without repeating my grade.

On a gray autumn day, I returned to Maadi. I'd harbored a faint hope that the school would have changed, and it had, but not for the better. As in my former lycée, a staff of francophone Levantines had replaced the French teachers, and the number of Jews among the students had dwindled. Mme Victoria's rules were stricter than I remembered, and the state of my friendship with Renzo, her son, was uncertain.

Maadi had also changed. More cars were spewing their fumes onto the streets and a few new tall buildings had sprung up on the edge of town. At the Maadi Sporting Club, the British and French diplomats had been replaced by Americans and Eastern Europeans from the various Soviet republics.

Across the street, the atmosphere in the Gabr family was more subdued than it had been in the past. A deep sense of lassitude now tempered Tante Aïda's proverbial joie de vivre, and Khadr Bey rarely ventured out of his study during my visits. Even Hussein el-Shafei seemed to have lost some of his revolutionary fervor; he looked so preoccupied that I wondered if it portended another war.

But perhaps the biggest change was the growing distance that was setting in between my father and me. Our times together were not as enjoyable as they once were. I resented his choice not to leave Egypt with the rest of the family, and I felt numb and detached much of the time. Papa also seemed tired and defeated. Gone were the unbearable separation pangs and the tantrums of my early days, and gone the magical complicity and the closeness that had been my shield against the darkness; overnight, it seemed, I'd grown too old for our familiar games and we hadn't invented new ones.

Sometimes during my Sundays with him in the city, he would invite one lady friend or another to join us for lunch. He would introduce them as friends, but I could see they were more than that. Papa's female companions were intelligent and elegant, and they gave me a lot of tender attention. I suspected it was their way of winning my father's affections, but I didn't mind. I enjoyed the sense of power and control it gave me. Papa made sure that I didn't feel left out, and I tried not to show my likes or dislikes. As long as he didn't remarry. So far, there was no reason to worry. My father loved women the way a butterfly loves nectar, and he showed no inclination to settle down. With his flurry of conquests, I missed having my father's exclusive attention, but it seemed to be a fair price to pay for growing up.

***

If the French novelists of earlier centuries had awakened me to romantic love, Alice was the woman who gave me a first glimpse of sexual love. She was the shapely Coptic nurse who ruled over my dormitory of twelve boys ranging in age from ten to thirteen. She scrubbed our backs when we bathed, clipped our toenails and cleaned our ears, and she made sure our pajamas were immaculate and our teeth brushed morning and night.

Alice spoke French with a strong rolling Egyptian accent, stuffed with Arabic words and unwitting amusing mispronunciations. She apparently disliked the French or Italian forms of my first name and called me by its Arabic version, Elias. I loved her cheeriness, her exuberance, her playful sense of humor, and the seductive way she bounced when she walked. I hungered for her attention, and my ingenuity knew no bounds when it came to seeking it.

One of the many ways was to linger so I would be the last boy to get a bath. In the tub I would purposely let my soap bar fly out of my hands into the soapy water and make a show of not finding it. Alice would fetch it and hand it to me with a mocking smile that made it clear she saw through my stratagem. Sometimes she would punish me by scrubbing my back and legs so hard my skin would turn red, mumbling in her Franco-Arabic patois, "You dirty walad! Encore plus sale que les shahhâtin de la rue! Dirtier boy than the beggars on the street!" Other times, she would play along and rub me softly until I felt my body was dissolving in the tub water.

I suspected that Alice was good to me because she had a crush on my father. She would nonchalantly inquire, in her delicious syntax, about the ladies who came to the school with Papa on Sundays. "The lady she came with your Baba last Sunday, is she very nice motherly with you?" she would ask, or "Is he want to marry with her?"

"I don't think so," I would answer, adding sometimes, "She's not that smart. Certainly not as smart as you are!"

"You little boy already a liar like big men!" she would laugh and rub my chest in long, sensuous strokes that made me flutter with delight. It was hard not to stare at the undulating movement of her breasts as she moved. "Off to bed, clean boy!" she would say with a hearty tap on the back.

At night in the dormitory that housed a dozen boys, I'd lay awake, fighting sleep, pipe-dreaming about cuddling with Alice in bed and kissing her with passionate abandon the way people did in the movies.

A boy named Moussa noticed my interest and liked to imitate Alice's bouncy walk while pulling the front of his pajamas top to form an imaginary pair of breasts flapping in the air. "Hezz ya wezz!" he'd say, using a vulgar colloquial Arabic expression describing a goose shaking her behind. It infuriated me, and we began an escalation of insults until I used the mother of all insults in Arabic, *Koss omak ah'mar!*—a vulgar reference to the red color of his mother's overused private parts. Foaming at the mouth, Moussa came to my bed and punched me on the chest. I punched him back. We struggled on the bed. As I straddled Moussa and held onto his wrists to deflect his punches, the lights suddenly came on. Alice had stormed into the dormitory like a fury from hell.

"Stop!" Alice yelled. "Both of you! Right now! Stop doing dirty things in bed!"

I let go. She grabbed Moussa by the ear and propelled him to his own bed.

"What dirty things?" I asked, looking at Alice with utter disbelief.

"Don't give me innocent look! You know about what I talk!"

I continued to stare at her, still stunned by her behavior.

"I thought you good clean boy!" Alice shouted with utter contempt. "You very disappointing me!"

"We weren't doing anything!" I said.

"So, what you do on top of him?" she yelled.

"I was fighting with him!" I yelled back.

"Why you fighting with him?"

I looked down. I was too embarrassed to tell her the reason for the fight, but she was relentless.

"I asked you question—why you fighting him?"

"It doesn't matter anymore," I said, turning away.

"I will report both of you to Mme Victoria. You will both be severe punishment," she said, then pointing at me, "Especially you, dirty lying dog!"

She turned off the lights and stomped out. The boys in the dorm were roaring and howling.

The sheer injustice of Alice's accusation had cut me to the quick. I tossed and turned in bed, unable to decipher what had just happened. What "dirty things" did Alice think Moussa and I had been doing? Then I remembered the man who'd touched me with his penis at the old Koubbeh house, and it wondered if she thought that's what Moussa and I were doing. I wanted to tell her that it was nothing of the sort, but I knew she wouldn't believe me. I spent the night in an ethereal state between wakefulness and sleep.

Alice didn't report us to Mme Victoria and no punishment was meted out. But she exacted the worst of penalties by shunning me altogether. Our games ended, and she never mentioned Papa or his female companions. Alice had convicted and sentenced me for an imaginary crime.

***

My friendship with Renzo, Mme Victoria's son, had always fluctuated between friendship and rivalry, but there was now a new cause of friction. The Suez war had altered our relationships in school as it had in our world at large. Before the war, we didn't give a thought to a classmate's religion or political beliefs; after it, our identities became a divisive factor in our friendships and alliances.

For reasons I couldn't fathom, Renzo and I found ourselves on opposite sides of the spectrum. He now professed to hate anything British, French or Israeli and to admire Nasser, Stalin, Mussolini and Hitler while I'd been taught to worship Churchill, de Gaulle, and Eisenhower, the men who had vanquished Germany and Japan, and to hate all forms of authoritarianism. Our disagreements soon escalated into a mano-a-mano that mobilized all the intellectual power we could muster.

Bright, well-read, articulate and endowed with powerful oratory skills, Renzo was a formidable opponent. At recess, he held forth in the courtyard, pontificating about the Suez conflict, speaking loud enough to be heard whenever I was within earshot. I wondered if Renzo believed half the things he said or just wanted to be provocative—and I often couldn't resist his challenges.

"Egypt decimated Israel, England, and France in just a few weeks!" he'd bark.

"Idiotic nonsense!" I'd bark back, breaking all my resolutions. "The BBC says the opposite of Egypt's radio propaganda. Israel occupied the Sinai, the French and British the

Canal Zone, and Eisenhower forced them to retreat, not Nasser!"

"No! The BBC is nothing but British propaganda!" Renzo would state with a superior look. "Your Eisenhower only intervened to stop Egypt from throwing the Jews into the sea. Otherwise, Egypt's mighty Soviet MIGs would've destroyed Israel's nothing-army, and the Egyptian forces would now occupy Tel Aviv!"

I reminded Renzo that the Jewish nothing-army had defeated a coalition of Arab forces in 1948. One of Renzo's sycophants claimed that, with the help of Nazi officers advising Nasser, the Jews didn't have a chance. "Of course, Nasser needs Nazis to do the job! He is far too incompetent to win even a pissing contest!" I shot back.

Even though Renzo exasperated me, I couldn't help enjoying my jousts with him. Our verbal duels offered a good challenge in a sea of brainless conformity. We never resorted to personal attacks, and we sometimes reached moments of truth and unspoken friendship. But inevitably one of us would say something that would set off the other and ignite a new skirmish.

If there was a silver lining to these battles, it was that they had a healing effect on my sorry moods. Our wars of words distracted my mind from my feelings of alienation and from the pain of Alice's betrayal.

***

The mention of former Nazi officers helping the Egyptian military had entered my mind in a haunting way. I thought that the Allies' victory had eradicated the Nazis from Germany and from the rest of the world. Could it be true? I couldn't wait for my father's visit to discuss it with him.

"Why do you ask?" said Papa.

"Nothing. Just curious," I said nonchalantly.

My father wasn't duped. "Are you discussing these things in school?"

I shrugged my shoulders. He looked concerned, but he didn't probe further.

"Yes, there are Nazis in Egypt," he answered after a long pause. "Not in the government per se, but on its fringes. Some of Hitler's high-ranking men are now advisors to Nasser's secret police, the Mabahess, and to the military."

"So, Nasser is a Nazi?"

"No!" he said. "He was a Nazi sympathizer in his youth, but not a Nazi."

"What's the difference?" I asked.

"Nasser and his friends were members of the Green Shirts, a military Islamic youth group modeled after Hitler's Brown Shirts, but that didn't make them Nazis. In the 1930s, most Egyptian nationalists were pro-Nazi because they hoped that Hitler's forces would deliver them from British dominance. The Jews were the least of their concerns."

"All of the Free Officers too?"

"I don't know about 'all' but many were pro-German," said Papa. "One of them even went to jail for spying for the Germans during the war—twice, not once."

"Hussein el-Shafei?" I asked, suddenly concerned.

"No, it was that stupid puppet, Anwar Al-Sadat."

"OK, but if they weren't concerned with the Jews, why do they hate us now?"

"We're paying the price for their humiliation in '48 when a tiny Jewish army defeated a coalition of seven Arab countries. And again in '56 against a Soviet-equipped Egyptian Army in the Sinai. Arabs are proud people. They want revenge."

I wanted to know more about the Nazis in Egypt. Did they live openly or under disguise? "Both," said Papa. "Some

Nazis learned Arabic, some married Egyptian women and had families, a few converted to Islam, and others masqueraded as Eastern European businessmen or visiting professors."

"Disgusting!" I bellowed.

"Egypt is not the only country to employ former Nazis. Many other countries did, including the United States and the Soviet Union. They both recruited Nazi scientists for their nuclear projects, and other countries followed suit for a variety of scientific projects. But Egypt is unique in recruiting Nazis not for their scientific genius, but for their expertise in killing Jews."

Could the Nazis build nuclear bombs in Egypt and destroy Israel?

Papa thought it was unlikely. Egypt could not afford to feed its people, let alone build nuclear armament. Nor could Israel, a country still under construction. "But there's no shortage of brilliant Jewish scientists from Europe who've emigrated to Israel. So, if it came to nuclear war, guess who's more likely to win!"

As he drove me back to Maadi, Papa said, "You're a fool if you engage in discussion about Israel, Nasser and Nazis. You can't win this one!"

"Why not?" I asked even though the answer was obvious. "What's true is true!"

"Truth, like beauty, is in the eye of the beholder. And your friend Renzo is not the fascist you say he is. You two would be bosom friends if you stopped poking each other in the eye!"

"So that's your wise paternal advice—to keep my mouth shut when I hear nonsense?"

"Yes!" he said forcefully. "Just remember the Arab proverb, 'The dogs bark and the caravan moves on.'"

"What does that mean?" I ask.

"The caravan is a symbol of might and purpose. The dogs bark very loud to frighten the caravan and stop it. Guess who wins?"

***

At the noon recess, Renzo was standing in his favorite spot in the courtyard, lording over his cronies and ranting about a future war with Israel. "With the new MiGs, Egypt will wipe out Israel in a few minutes!" He mimicked a dogfight with each hand forming a fighter plane—his extended middle finger depicting the nose of the aircraft, his index and ring fingers bent as its front wheels and his thumb and pinkie extended in the shape of its wings.

"This plane here is an Egyptian Soviet-made MiG-15, the greatest fighter plane in the world," Renzo said with the voice of a newscaster. His left hand moved up in the air, simulating a jet fighter taking off. He looked at his right hand. "This one here is the French-made Israeli Mystère IV, not too bad but far inferior to the MiG." The right hand became airborne with loud sounds of jet fighters buzzing in the sky.

I had to admire, with some reluctance, Renzo's remarkable ability to tell a story with hand gestures, spitting sounds and a scarcity of words. Pitting his right hand against his left one, Renzo simulated a dogfight in which his planes rolled, cornered, tailed, looped, tipped their wings and flew upside down. He accompanied each maneuver with loud sounds of engines flying near and far, machine guns firing their fast rounds and buildings exploding. He ended the show with a high-pitched explosion as the Egyptian MiG downed the Israeli fighter into the sea.

I let out a loud belly laugh to signify my contempt for the performance. A boy named Fawzi walked up to me and spit in my face. I punched him. Another boy hit me with a blow that left me gasping for air. Before I could recover, he punched me again. I whacked him on the jaw, and we slugged it out until a school monitor separated us. He admonished both of us, but I was the one he dragged to Mme Victoria's office.

She glared at me with loathing and contempt. After an interminable silence, she said in an icy voice, "I'll call your father immediately and tell him to come and take you home. I've had enough of you! You don't belong here!"

I was too numb to react. My lack of reaction made Mme Victoria angrier. She lost her icy composure and shouted, "Maledetto! You're a bad element! You bring nothing but trouble to this school!"

I tried to tell her what had happened, but she was not in a listening mood. "Not only do you talk too much, but you talk nonsense! Dangerous nonsense!"

I turned away, but she yelled, "Look at me when I talk to you! I've done all I could to protect you, but no more! Last Sunday, the father of one of your classmates, a high-ranking officer, complained about you and your Zionist speeches! He warned me that, if it happens again, my school will suffer dire consequences!"

"There was no propaganda, Mme Victoria, but I had to—"

"No *buts*, no ifs—not a word!"

"All I did was defend myself!"

"Defend?" shouted Mme Victoria. "Don't you understand that we live in dangerous times? Don't you understand they can shut us down and put us in jail for any reason or no reason at all?"

"So, I should keep quiet when they say that all Jews should be thrown into the sea?"

Mme Victoria shook her head in denial. "Nobody in my school says things like that!"

I growled and didn't insist. We were beyond words. Abruptly, she stopped shouting and whispered, "Go to your dormitory, pack and stay there until your father comes to fetch you!"

***

When I walked into the dorm, Alice was packing my suitcase. "What's the crazy in your head?" she yelled. "You stupid boy! You get everybody in big sea of trouble!"

Her syntax made me smile once again. "Don't worry, Miss Alice. I'll be fine," I said.

"Why you always not keep your mouth shut down?" she asked.

"Not you too, Alice! Please!"

"You stupid boy! You not understand that Christian and Jews cannot speak free in Muslim country?"

"Alice, this was not about Muslims and Jews. It's about idiots saying idiotic things—"

"Children speak stupid things. You no have to answer all stupid things they speak! And you don't have to speak dangerous things! This is Egypt, not free country like Europe and America. It's Egypt! Under King Farouk, under Nasser, under Abu Ali, it's all the same zeft!"

I smiled. Abu Ali was the name of a mischievous character in Arab folk tales, and *zeft* meant worthless garbage.

"It's not funny!" she barked. She finished packing my suitcase. "Your books don't fit in suitcase. Too many books." She went out and returned with a large paper bag. She seemed to grow more annoyed with me. "Do you understand what I say? Here, Muslims is majority, Copts like me is minority, Jews like you even more small minority," she yelled. "So, if they say jump, you jump! S'ils te disent va manger la merde, tu manges toute la merde et tu ne te plains pas un mot! If they say go eat shit, you eat all the shit and you not complain one word!"

I'd never heard a woman use such coarse language, but I was less put off by the crudeness of the words than by their content. Every fiber in my body rejected the notion that being a minority meant accepting degradation and indignity. "It's not right, Alice! You shouldn't have to accept that! Nobody should!"

"Right, wrong, who cares? It's the same in all the worlds!"

"No, Alice, the strongest isn't always—"

A servant came in, motioned to Alice and went away. Alice lifted my suitcase and said, "You take books bag. Your baba is waiting."

Papa's Austin was idling by the front porch. Alice hurled my suitcase onto the back seat, grabbed the bag from my hands and threw it next to the suitcase and started to walk away.

"Goodbye, Alice," I said.

"Goodbye, Elias," she whispered. "Someday when you grow up—insh'allah that you live so long to become a man with wife and babies—maybe you understand that Alice is right, and you not forget me."

As the car took off, I watched Alice bounce her way back to the house, more beautiful and fetching than ever. When she was out of my sight, I closed my eyes. Words floated in my mind, slowly forming sentences. A letter to Alice—a letter I'll never put to paper but perhaps, by some magic trick, the breeze will carry my words to her ears . . .

Dear Alice, how could I ever forget you? You've awakened me to a world of desire and sensuality. I could never forget the new feelings and sensations, the painful and delicious longings, and the pleasure and despair you elicited, Alice. The memory of you will never fade.

***

What school next? The only remaining path for a French education was one of the francophone Christian schools. Papa chose the Collège des Frères, run by the order of St Jean-Baptiste de la Salle. Gathering information for my application, Papa looked through a pile of my fortnightly report cards, and sighed, "With these grades, a Dio Santo, it's a miracle if they accept you!"

"Sorry," I said sheepishly.

The next day, we drove to the meet the principal.

Brother Pierre-Sebastien had such a striking resemblance to my late uncle Maurice that I felt as though I were talking to a ghost. The principal looked at my report cards for a long time in ominous silence, then he put the papers on his desk, removed his eyeglasses, and said that his duty as a Christian educator was to give me a chance to redeem myself.

My first reaction was to tell him to shove his goddamn redemption, but I resisted that impulse. I knew Papa was on tenterhooks, and I was determined to spare him further aggravation. The priest asked many more questions, and I answered them as well as I could. His final question was how I felt about studying among students of another faith.

"I'm fine with that, uhm—" I stopped because I didn't know whether how to address him. "—sir!"

"Brother Principal will do," he said with a smile.

After a long and awkward silence, the Brother Principal pronounced his verdict. He would admit me to La Salle College next fall, but only if I met two conditions. The first condition was predictable. As the school year wasn't over, I had to spend the rest of remaining trimester studying Arabic, math and algebra with tutors. The second condition took me by surprise. The Brother Principal said that I needed to be acclimated to a Christian environment, and he thought that going to Christian summer camp would be beneficial. The camp's director, Father També, was well-known for handling wayward boys and bringing them back to the fold.

Papa let out a sigh of relief. I was neither relieved nor pleased. I didn't like being called *a wayward boy* and I didn't want to be *handled* by a tamer of children of any religion. Without asking me or even looking at me, Papa agreed on the spot.

As we were leaving, the Brother Principal said to me, "According to your transcripts, God has given you great flaws and great gifts, and nothing in between. Will you let us help you grow your considerable gifts to use them for the greater good?"

Again, I was tempted to ask, "Whose greater good? Yours or mine?" but I just answered, "Yes."

***

Besides going to a Christian school, I had another reason to be anxious. My thirteenth birthday was looming, and with it the prospect of my Bar Mitzvah. The ceremony called for reading from the Torah in Hebrew with the proper cantillation, and the tradition required a grasp of Jewish history, traditions, ethics, and elementary Talmudic law. I had gone briefly to Hebrew school before the Suez war, but those studies had fallen by the wayside in the chaos of its aftermath. The Bar Mitzvah wasn't important to me, but Papa was adamant. The ceremony elevated a male Jew from boyhood to manhood, and no member of our family had ever forsaken that essential rite of passage. We needed to find a Hebrew tutor urgently.

The rabbi at our synagogue was appalled by my lack of preparation for the ceremony. Papa suggested that I memorize the passages of the Torah I would be called upon to read, but that enraged the rabbi. There would be no Bar Mitzvah without proper Jewish education. Papa argued that memorizing a few lines would be a lesser sin than to forgo this important rite of passage, but the rabbi insisted that I study hard for the occasion, and he suggested that Papa hire a rabbinical student named Moshe to prepare me for the ceremony.

And the season of the tutors began.

***

Meeting the first of the Brother Principal's conditions, working with tutors in mathematics and Arabic, was promising a long season in hell. I felt like I was entering an endless period of atonement for my sins—atonement for the misdeeds and roguery that had gotten me expelled from so many schools and caused great pain to my father.

Math was difficult because I had difficulties that none of my classmates had. I often inverted numbers and symbols, and that handicap resulted in deeply embarrassing miscalculations in mathematics, algebra, and other scientific matters. I tried to convince myself that it didn't matter because I had no intention of becoming a scientist, a surgeon or an accountant. I wanted to be a writer like Alexandre Dumas and Victor Hugo. But the failures made me feel like an inferior being.

When the tutors were gone for the day, I read avidly on all kinds of topics. I knew I needed knowledge and experience to become a writer, and I was eager to begin. I dreamt of discovering the world as soon as I was old enough to travel on my own. I dreamt of learning all there was to learn in literature and art and history, and in many languages. I wanted to be able to read Virgil in Latin and Homer in Greek, Dante in Italian, Cervantes in Spanish, and Shakespeare, Dickens, and Mark Twain in English. But I was profoundly ambivalent about all things Arabic. Since my early childhood, I had loved the tales of Aladdin and Haroun al-Rashid and the wonderful tales and legends of Arabia. I loved the stories of the Golden Age of Islamic Spain which my father had described as the height of tolerance and enlightenment in the Middle Ages. But the current age was the opposite of tolerance and enlightenment. As Nasser and his cohorts had started the systematic destruction of the Jewish community, the Arabic language had come to symbolize tyranny, oppression and breach of faith in my mind. I knew it was more complex than that, but I didn't know how to overcome my growing aversion to the Arabic language and all that it represented.

***

Twice a week, sometimes three, I trudged to a private class in the monumental synagogue we called the Grand Temple or the Ismailia Temple because it stood in the heart of the European quarter built by Ismail the Magnificent. Its official name was Sha'ar Hashamayim, or Les Portes du Paradis, which meant The Gates of Heaven, and its glory was proclaimed in golden Hebrew and Latin letters on the front entrance of the edifice.

In earlier days, the Grand Temple was the sanctuary where our family's male members congregated on Shabbat and all Jewish holidays, often joined by the women who sat in a separate section in the mezzanine. After the family's diaspora, Papa and I stopped going to synagogue except during the High Holidays. Nona's absence made me realize that she'd been the anchor that kept us all moored to the Jewish faith and traditions. Without her and the rest of the clan, the Jewish celebrations had lost their joyful spirit. The Jewish faith and its traditions were at the core of my grandmother's being, and my primary reason for going through the ordeal of the Bar Mitzvah was to spare her another reason for mourning.

Since the rabbi had made attending the temple's Shabbat services compulsory, I kept my mind busy by observing, or rather discovering, the various architectural symbols peppered throughout the edifice. The mishmash of styles and epochs was disconcerting, but it didn't lack splendor and majesty. Over the weeks, Papa explained the characteristics of the various styles and periods comprised in the building. Sha'ar Hashamayim was a mix of neo-pharaonic, Art Nouveau, and neo-baroque architectures, and Papa told me his interpretation of the architects' vision. I'd never paid attention to the details of the synagogue's two façades, their massive porticoes and the turrets which Papa said evoked the pillars that bordered the Temple of Solomon. Nor had I noticed the wealth of pharaonic art in the two obelisks that stood at the entrance of the synagogue, the date palms on the walls or the bas-reliefs representing the Sunbird holding two sun-discs under his outspread wings. Detail after detail, the architects' intentions emerged—making every stone of the Gates of Heaven a celebration of the deep roots of the Jews in the land they'd inhabited since the early pharaohs' time.

I was awestruck by my father's knowledge about architecture. He said that he'd always dreamt of becoming an architect, but he came of age during the Great Depression, a time the family coffers were too depleted to afford him a university education. When I asked him if he regretted the missed opportunities, he responded without a trace of bitterness or self-pity, "Ç'est la vie. Maktoub!"

It was a surprising response. The word *maktoub*—"It is written!"—reflected the age-old Egyptian fatalistic belief that God had traced in advance the road map for every life from birth to death. It was the complete reverse of Papa's own teachings; he had always believed that we can shape our destiny through the power of our mind. Which was it? Man's hand or God's handwriting?

"The best khakamim are still debating that question." Papa said using the Hebrew-Ladino word for Sages, "It comes up in every passage of the Bible when Jews disobey the word of God. I think God offers a road map—it is written—and man chooses whether to follow it or not."

I didn't share with Papa my own feeling about God—that, if Yahweh was the master of my destiny, he manifested himself by his absence rather than by his presence.

CHAPTER 9

Summer of 1957

The Spring of Tutors came to an end, and on a bright summer morning, my father and I climbed into his trusty Austin and headed north toward the lions' den—Father També's summer camp in Ras-el-Bar. We left three days early. Rather than take the train, my father chose to drive to Ras-el-Bar to show me parts of Egypt I didn't know before we left the country for good.

Driving along the eastern branch of the Nile, the desert gave way to lush cotton fields and crossed irrigation canals that radiated upstream toward the Delta Barrage.

"In biblical times, this was the land of Goshen," Papa said. "This is the Egypt I hope you will remember—one of the cradles of civilization."

I was stunned by the sheer beauty of the Nile delta. In the open fields of the *ezbahs*, the vast plantations that extended beyond the horizon, legions of fellahin tended their fields. On the sides of the road, young boys led donkeys carrying huge piles of cut sugarcane and their elders walked on the hot earth or rode on bicycles or motorcycles with their bundles of cane precariously perched on their heads. It was a world of majestic eternity. I imagined that even in the days of the pharaohs the fellahin were using the same gestures, manning the same tools, and driving the same animals as their ancestors had for centuries.

Had the revolution improved their lot? I wondered.

We stopped to buy a stalk of sugarcane from one of the boys. He asked for too much money, and he seemed disappointed when Papa paid his price without bargaining. Emboldened, he asked for two extra piasters to cut the stalk for us, and Papa gave it to him. The boy opened a large cutlass, cut a stalk into several equal parts, carefully snipped a slit in the bark of each one, lifting it up so we could peel it easily. As he went through these steps, I became aware that this boy was my age, maybe younger, and that he was already earning his keep like a man. I felt guilty about my privileges. On an impulse, I slipped him a few piasters while Papa was walking back toward the car. The boy looked puzzled, but he took the coins and went to pick up his bundle of sugarcanes. I wondered if I'd hurt his feelings. He was a hardworking boy, not a beggar like the legions of boys in Cairo. I wanted to say that to him, but I didn't utter a word for fear he'd think I were the village idiot.

Papa and I sat in the shade of the car, munching on our sugar canes. A few yards away, a water buffalo was pushing a *noria*, the large waterwheel that pumped water from an irrigation canal into a reservoir through rattling pots attached to its rim. The huge *gamoussa* was blindfolded and a young boy kept spraying her with water from his *gargoulette*, a jug made of a porous clay that had kept the water cool. Papa explained that the blindfold served to spare the animal the dizziness and loss of balance caused by her endless spinning.

"Beautiful, n'est-ce pas?" said my father.

I nodded. "And sad."

"Because?"

"We don't belong here anymore."

"That, hijico, is the bittersweet story of the wandering Jews—the bitterness of loss followed by the sweetness of freedom—repeated every few generations," he sighed.

He started the car. "I know you like the history of Ancient Egypt, so I thought of something. There's an archaeological site along the way. I don't know if they're still open—they usually stop excavating in the summer because it's too hot—but they might still be open."

"What are they digging for?"

"They're exploring the site of the ancient city of Tell Attrib, an important city in the Old Kingdom period, around fifteen hundred years before Christ."

"Before Christ? Like 3500 years ago!?"

"Yup! We live on a very old planet, don't you know!" he guffawed.

***

We stopped in the city of Benha, near Zagazig, to get directions to the site of the ruins of Tell Attrib. Two European men sat at a table, sipping coffee, smoking cigarettes, and having an animated conversation in a language I didn't recognize. Papa went to their table, coughed softly to get their attention, and asked them in English if they knew the exact location of the archeologic site. They smiled and said they worked at the site, but the dig was not open to the public. As we walked away, I muttered, "Merde!" under my breath. They burst out in laughter. My face turned bright red. I didn't think they would speak French! My embarrassed look seemed to amuse them further, and they invited us to join them.

They were Polish, but they spoke an excellent French with an erudite Central-European flair. They talked about the excavations they'd been conducting since early 1957, shortly after the Suez war. The older man was tall and wiry and the younger one short and rotund and, since I'd quickly forgotten their unpronounceable Polish names, I dubbed them the professor and the apprentice. The professor said he'd worked on excavations in Egypt since the early thirties, except during the world war when he returned to Poland to fight the Germans. It was the apprentice's second foray in the trenches, except for a few periods of internship during his studies.

When their driver arrived in a Rover, the professor took us by surprise by inviting us to visit their digging site. "Since you and your boy are so interested in archaeology, I'll make an exception and give you a short visit to our site."

Papa went to our car, assuming that we would follow them to their destination, but the Egyptian driver laughed, kicked the Austin's tire, and cackled, "No good! You need Jeeba there!"

The professor said, "You can ride with us. We'll drive you back to your car."

We climbed into their Rover and drove a few kilometers through a narrow bumpy road before the driver veered onto a side trail marked only by the deep furrows dug into the hard earth by heavy vehicles. At the end of the track stood an encampment of makeshift huts and fly tents.

Our hosts gave us a quick tour. In the vast expanse of land that surrounded the camp, several men were digging with gentle and careful moves, under the supervision of European and Egyptian foremen. Others were examining fragments of pottery, bas-reliefs and pebble-like objects set on long tables under the tarpaulin fly tents. The apprentice kept enjoining us to step carefully and not touch anything. The professor likened their work to putting together the pieces of a jigsaw puzzle without the benefit of the picture on the box.

After the tour we had refreshments under a tent, and our hosts answered our volleys of questions about their work. The multitude of places and names made the conversation too confusing to follow. It took me a while to understand that Athribis, Tell Attrib, and Hut-heryib were the Greek, Arabic, and ancient Egyptian names for the same place, the capital of the Old Kingdom. I felt an incongruous urge to sing the "Istanbul, not Constantinople" song.

The professor graciously answered our questions, even though I had the distinct feeling that he'd fielded similar questions many times before and he'd memorized his responses. I was drawn to the passion with which he shared his knowledge. He must've known or guessed that we were Jewish because he spoke at great length of the large Jewish encampment that had existed in Tell Attrib during the Ptolemaic period. A century earlier, stones were found in the hills of Benha, one of them with the inscription: "In honor of King Ptolemy and Queen Cleopatra, the chief of guards, Ptolemy son of Epicydus, and the Jews of Athribis consecrate this place of prayer to God the Most High." He added, "The expression 'the Most High' is not indigenous. It was a translation of the Hebrew 'El Elyon' which meant temple or synagogue."

"The identity of this Cleopatra was still unknown because three pharaohs of the Ptolemy dynasty—V, VI, and VIII—had a wife named Cleopatra, but we will find out when new clues emerge."

I listened to the professor in utter wonderment even though I couldn't understand some of his complex information. As we got up to leave, the professor said we were lucky because they were about to close the site for the summer. They would return to Cairo to catalogue and analyze the riches amassed during the winter, and several guards would protect the site against grave robbers.

Papa thanked the professor and his assistant for their hospitality and wished them good luck.

"It's not luck we need!" the apprentice interjected. "It's peace! Wars are bad for archeology."

"A little luck never hurts!" said the professor, with a wink. After shaking Papa's hand, he turned to me, "I hope we didn't bore you, young lad!"

"No, sir. If I were older, I would ask to work on your team!"

He bowed in a courtly manner and smiled wide. "Most honored!"

***

We arrived in Damietta early enough to take a long walk along the fortifications that dominated the harbor. The morning barge to Ras-el-Bar was full, and we had to wait for the afternoon boat. We walked around Damietta's fortifications built as a defense against the Crusaders. It was easy to imagine the French galleons disgorging tall knights in full regalia, their shields adorned with coats-of-arms and their surcoats with large red crosses, holding lances whose pennants and oriflammes waved in the wind.

It was late afternoon when we boarded the rickety boat whose wood floor squeaked and whose mast hissed when the boatman maneuvered the sail. We landed in Ras-el-Bar in the early evening. A bright red *taf-taf*—an open trolley with two tram-shaped wagons pulled by a miniature tractor—awaited us on the wharf and took us to the Aslan Hotel at the other end of the peninsula. I noticed that the ubiquitous taf-tafs were the only motorized vehicles in Ras-el-Bar.

At first, I looked at my surroundings as if I'd never set foot on this peninsula. My mind had erased most of my memories of Ras-el-Bar and of Mme Victoria's camp. As the taf-taf moved along the unpaved streets, the sense of discovery took on shades of déjà vu. I recognized the *e'eshas*, the summer huts made of bamboo, straw, papyrus and reed, erected every spring and taken down every fall before the joined waters of the Nile and the Mediterranean flooded the village. Only a few resorts had solid walls and roofs. At the Aslan Hotel, a permanent structure sheltered the lobby, the dining rooms and the vast ballroom, but the guest rooms were lodged in ephemeral bamboo huts and bungalows.

A porter carried our luggage to one of the guest huts. There were two large beds with mosquito nets, and the closet contained huge white towels and robes. A strong smell of Flit pesticide floated in the air. The room opened onto the beach and the darkening sapphire-blue immensity of the Mediterranean as the sun was brushing the horizon.

As the evening wore on, the thought of being in a boarding institution once again filled me with anxiety. I asked Papa to let me stay with him another day before checking me in at the camp. "I'm not ready for the lions' den," I said. "I need a little more time."

"Time for what?" asked Papa.

I had no answer. He'd tease me to death if I told him how bizarre our situation was to me—my *real* father was about to let an *ersatz* Father, a priest I'd never even met, rule my life for a summer.

In the morning, Papa and I took a long walk in the village and along the beach on the way to the camp. I'd forgotten the supreme beauty of the Mediterranean whose colors changed imperceptibly from turquoise blue to sapphire-blue in a few hours; I'd forgotten the sheer joy of walking barefoot in the wet sand and feeling the shiny crests of its dying waves as they repaired to the shore, retreated regretfully, and rushed back toward the sand with renewed strength. All along the sand, servants dressed in bright white robes and red waistbands were opening beach umbrellas and readying chaise-lounges for the hordes of beachgoers that were already scrambling for a spot of hot sand. Before the beachgoers had settled, they were surrounded by an army of street vendors swaggering on the sand with big wicker baskets precariously balanced on their heads. They peddled their wares—mangoes, guavas, prickly pears, figs, candy, sugarcane juice, and Greek syrupy fritters called *locomadès*—in loud melodic singsongs while others cooked fava beans and ta'ameyas, eggs and fried cheese, or fresh fish and shrimp. I reveled in the comforting din of the beach as I braced myself for my imminent plunge into the unknown.

***

Father També's camp was made of three large *e'eshas*. We were greeted at the main hut by an ageless woman in a plain, habit-like gray dress with a white collar. She spoke in a soft voice as she introduced herself as Mademoiselle Bernadette. "Father També will see you in a few moments."

A tall, athletic man emerged from a door over which hung a huge wooden crucifix. He wore navy blue shorts, a blue sweatshirt with a white neckline vaguely reminiscent of a clerical collar. With his goatee, his long sideburns, and the battered blue-black beret he wore on the side with great panache, he looked like a swashbuckling buccaneer, not a priest. I was intimidated by his energy and magnetism. He shook my hand, uttered warm words of welcome and took us on a tour of the camp before what he called "our little talk."

The first hut held the recreation hall, the refectory and its attending kitchens, the prayer hall, the study hall and Father També's office. The other two huts housed the staff and the boys' dormitories. Crucifixes, large or small, were hung in every room. In the dorms, they hung over each of the white beds that lined the rooms, with a few exceptions. I hoped mine would be one of them. I didn't want a cross hovering over my dreams.

After the tour, we followed Father També to his study which was lined with books. While he spoke to my father, I walked toward the bookshelves that contained titles in French, English, Italian, Latin and Arabic, both religious and secular.

On the shelves of French books, along with the familiar volumes of Dumas, Hugo and Zola, I spotted names I'd never seen before. The English section had a plethora of books by Walter Scott, Charles Dickens, Rudyard Kipling, and Arthur Conan Doyle.

The tall priest was walking toward me with a bouncing step, like a large feline. "Like to read, my boy?" Father També asked.

"Yes, Father," said Papa. "That's all he likes to do."

Father També towered over me. "Cat got your tongue?"

"Yes, I like to read. Will I be allowed to read some of the books on these shelves?"

"Certainly! We read books every night as a group around the campfire, but you can borrow any book you want—if you can find the time between all our activities. Which books would you like to read?"

"All the ones I haven't read yet!" I answered, pointing to the shelves. "I've never read Maurice Leblanc, Gaston Leroux, Michel Zevaco." Pointing to a shelf of Arthur Conan Doyle's volumes, I added, "I don't know if my English is good enough to read his books."

"Good choices!" Father També said with a smile. "All the names you picked are superb prose writers. Michel Zevaco wrote cloak-and-dagger novels that rival anything Alexandre Dumas wrote." He saw the disbelief in my eyes and laughed, "Some people dismiss cloak-and-dagger novels as low-brow literature, but what is Dumas's *The Three Musketeers* if not an excellent cloak-and-dagger book?" I hadn't expected that much lightheartedness from a priest.

"Yes, uh, sir," I said, wondering how I should address the priest. Father També sat at his desk and cleared his throat. "You know, here, in the Jesuit world, we call priests like me by the name of Father. Do you think you could call me Father like the rest of boys in the camp?"

My answer came out before I could dwell on the question. "It's a bit strange since I already have a father!"

I braced myself for a reprimand, but the priest had a wide smile on his face and didn't seem to be angry at all. "Of course I'm not your father, and I can assure you in his presence that I have no desire to usurp his authority. Think of me as a father's assistant. Some of us are called Brother. We assist your fathers in your education. Calling us Father or Brother is nothing more, and nothing less, than an affirmation of respect. Can you understand that?"

"Yes, uh, F—" I swallowed hard. "Father!"

While he spoke to Papa, I look around the office. A large portrait of Jesus Christ dominated the room, and many rosaries hung around religious statuettes. Father També noticed my stare and smiled again.

"You have nothing to fear from Jesus Christ. We don't proselytize here. You'll see Jews, Muslims and Copts among the Catholic boys here." His voice slowed down as he enunciated slowly and clearly, "Only the Catholics are expected to follow our rituals. The other boys are free to practice their own rituals if they wish to do so. Our only expectation is that you have faith, whether you call your Almighty by the name of Jesus, Yahweh, or Allah. If you're an atheist, keep it to yourself," he said with a wink.

Something about Father També touched me deeply. He conveyed an aura of authenticity and strength made of kindness, understanding, power and self-assurance, which felt safe and solid—the opposite of what I had expected.

"I read your school reports. They show that you're quite a handful!"

I blushed.

"It happens, but it's not terminal!" he added with a mischievous smile. "At your age, I was a handful too! Difficult, rebellious, stubborn. Neither my parents nor my teachers thought my life would amount to much." He chuckled, "For my luck, the Lord put me back on the right path."

He turned to Papa and asked, "Where's the boy's luggage?"

"Well, Father, I thought I'd let him spend a day with me at the Aslan Hotel before he starts," said Papa.

"It's not a good idea," said Father També. "The boys who came on the train from Cairo arrived two days ago. The others who came from Alexandria and elsewhere arrived yesterday. They're already forming new friendships and groups among themselves. I don't want your son to be an outsider. I suggest you spend the rest of the day together, pack the boy's luggage and bring him back in time for supper."

I gave Papa an insistent glare, but he quickly acquiesced. Father També tapped me on the shoulder. "After supper every night, we sit around the campfire and read a book. We started last night but I'll catch you up with the story before we begin." He looked at his wristwatch. "Excuse me, gentlemen, but duty calls. Volleyball starts in five minutes."

Outside, kids of all ages were playing a variety of ball games. Older boys were playing soccer in a sandy field. Father També ran toward a volleyball court made of compacted sand, pulled a whistle from his pocket, wrapped it around his neck and blew it forcefully to get the boys to get in position.

As much as I liked the priest, I wondered how on earth I would fit in his world of crucifixes and sports.

***

Papa and I went to an outdoor restaurant near the point where the Nile and the Mediterranean come together and merge their waters. Young street urchins moved around the tables, wrapping jasmine necklaces over the women's shoulders and complimenting the men for the beauty of their companions.

"Ya Gamila, Wallahi al Azim! How beautiful, by Allah the Magnificent!" Some of the boys would kiss their own fingers and extend them like budding flowers in the traditional Egyptian expression that signified beauty. Amused and flattered, the men would buy the flowers and tip the boys according to their performance.

On the Nile side, boatmen stood by their feluccas and offered rides for a few piasters. We picked a felucca and climbed aboard after the obligatory bargaining exchange. We sat and waited for other passengers to join us. The boatman, who introduced himself as Amir, was a tall and sinewy man with a head of yellowish hair and striking green eyes. Papa noticed my gaze. "It's quite common for people in these parts to have blond hair and light-colored eyes. They are said to be descendants of Napoleon Bonaparte's soldiers," Papa whispered, even though there was little chance that Amir could understand French. "The French landed at Aboukir Bay, between Damietta and Alexandria. After Admiral Nelson destroyed Bonaparte's fleet, the French soldiers were stranded and had nothing better to do than, uh, to make babies with the young Egyptian peasant girls."

"They didn't take their wives and babies back to France?"

"They probably, didn't."

"That wasn't nice!" I said.

"No, it wasn't!" said Papa, unwilling to go further.

Five new passengers joined us in the felucca before Amir set sail toward El Lessan—which meant "the Tongue"—a narrow and long promontory that jutted out of the northern coast of the peninsula. It was the point where the Nile and the Mediterranean merged in a fierce embrace. It was both frightening and exhilarating to watch the everlasting duel between the river and the sea—the Nile pouring its water into the Mediterranean only to be pushed back by the sea's thundering waves, and coming back with a vengeance until the salty and the soft waters became one. In the furious mêlée the aptly named land strip appeared to move like the tongue of a mammoth whale. Amir skillfully kept our felucca at a safe distance from the whirlpool.

Papa stood at the bow of the boat, humming "Les feuilles mortes," his favorite love song. An American woman aboard the felucca intoned the English version of the same song, "Autumn Leaves." The merging of the two voices was so intimate and beautiful that I felt like a peeping intruder.

I was struck by the difference between the two versions of the song. In English, the lyrics were an affirmation of love and longing while in French they sang the end of love and lamented its inevitability. One of the French verses gave me the chills. It spoke of life separating a man and a woman, quietly and gently, and erasing the footprints left on the sand by the disunited lovers.

It made me wonder about the marriage of my parents and its end. Had they ever loved each other? I knew nothing of their first encounter or their life together before my birth. Nobody ever talked about that time, and if pictures of them together were ever taken, they had been burned or thrown out. Their love, if it ever existed, had left no trace other than my presence on this earth—and maybe the obsessional hatred that consumed them. Why didn't they move on? Was hatred another form of love? Did true love only live in the imagination of the writers of novels, movies and songs?

When we returned to the pier, Papa looked at his watch and said, "Supper time at Jesuit camp is upon us. We have just enough time to pick up your bags and knock on Father També's door."

"But it's still daylight," I protested. "We have plenty of time."

"You don't want to get on the wrong side of Father També on your first day, do you?"

"Never! I swear by God in Heaven and His Son on the cross!" I exclaimed with mock brio as I tried to ignore the wave of panic that was engulfing me. "Lest the Lord Jesus sends me right to hell!"

"Where you belong, Smart Ass!"

We went back to the hotel by way of the shore, our feet in the water. Papa was still humming the song from the boat. I was looking at the water merging with sand, imagining the footsteps of the song's lovers converging and diverging as the lightest waves covered them.

"If your lovers are so sad about being disunited, why don't they stay united?" I blurted out.

Papa smiled and tousled my hair, "If I knew the answer to that, I'd be God."

"All your love songs are stupid, especially this one!"

"If this one is so stupid, why were you tearing up on the boat?" Papa asked with a smirk on his face.

"Because I was *extremely* embarrassed by your singing with that woman. It was stupid and gooey."

"Well, boy, you say gooey, I say sentimental. There's nothing wrong with being sentimental and even a little gooey with a pretty woman."

"She was far from pretty! And her husband was even uglier!"

"That was her brother. And I'm not asking you to find her pretty just because I do."

I felt a pang of anger, and I said, "My mother is a lot prettier! And much more elegant!"

"I can't say we're in a free country anymore because we're not," Papa chortled, "but you were raised in a free household where poor taste is tolerated!"

"Ha-ha! Very funny! I would laugh forever if I weren't on my way to the lions' den!"

"Remember how the story ends?" Papa chuckled. "God turned the lions into pussycats, Daniel got out of the den safe and sound, and lived happily forever!"

"Barf!" I eructed.

***

Mademoiselle Bernadette took my bag and showed me to my cot in the empty dormitory. I sighed with relief when I saw that there was no cross above my bed. She unpacked my things, grousing that I had overpacked and wouldn't use half the clothes I'd brought. She sensed my disarray and added, "Don't feel bad. All newcomers, or rather their parents, make the same mistake the first summer."

I cringed at the word "parents." It conveyed images of togetherness that didn't apply to my life. I had no parents—just a father and a mother flying in opposite directions in separate crafts.

"Next time you'll know exactly what to bring!" added Mademoiselle Bernadette. Next summer I hope to be on a different continent, I wanted to say, but I didn't want to be unfriendly.

In the yard just outside the dorms, Mademoiselle Bernadette introduced me to some of my roommates before rushing to the main hut. Through the open door, I could see a squadron of cooks working over smoking pans and pots. The boys and I remained in the yard, sniffing one another out like puppies in a kennel, until the call to supper rang.

Father També was enthroned at the center of several tables assembled to form a large rectangle where everyone could see everyone else. For my first evening at the camp, I was seated next to Father També. Mademoiselle Bernadette served Father També a large glass of wine in a silver goblet, and three women wearing summer habits passed around pitchers of lemonade for the boys. Before saying grace, Father També introduced them to me as Sisters Theresa, Agnes, and Aisha, and introduced me as the newcomer. I counted thirty-seven mates whose ages ranged from ten to fifteen years.

Father També's prayer sounded like a vigorous conversation with an old friend to whom he was thankful, not like the usual drone of prayers. His words were repeated by the assembly, save a few boys who remained silent. The last "Amen" was the signal for the three Sisters and two young Arab helpers sporting large crosses around their necks to dole out the meal while Mademoiselle Bernadette served Father També and the few of us in his immediate vicinity.

It was one of the best meals I'd eaten since Nona had left Cairo. Through it all, Father També regaled the boys with stories of his years of studying for the priesthood in Rome and his ministries in Cameroon and the Ivory Coast. There was a sense of normalcy and a joviality about him that made me forget that I was a stranger among them. After dinner, Mademoiselle Bernadette opened a cabinet and handed us blankets and flashlights. It was campfire time.

Even though it wasn't quite dark, Father També lit a flambeau and led us to a tiny inlet at a distance from the camp. He gave me the torch to hold while he pulled logs and kindling from the huge canvas bag he was carrying. He let the older boys place them before giving me the signal to light the fire. I'd never done it before, but I didn't think it would be complicated. I was wrong. The flame didn't take to the logs and after several frustrating tries I threw the torch over the logs, but it bounced back a foot away. The boys howled, increasing my shame tenfold, but Father També flashed a wide smile, picked up the burning torch and gently lit up the kindling.

"You just missed a step—the kindling—that's all," he said. "Bête comme chou!"

I thought he was mocking me and answered, "Easy as pie for you, Father. We don't have campfires on the streets of Cairo, so how would I know?"

Father També ignored the sarcasm and flashed a wide benevolent smile. I felt like a fool because I realized that he hadn't been mocking me at all.

When everyone settled down, Father També handed me a well-worn book entitled *Le Chien des Baskerville* as he addressed the group, "Where did we stop yesterday?"

Several boys raised their hand. Father També chose the youngest one. "Dr. Mortimer told Sherlock Holmes that he saw footprints around Sir Charles's dead body."

"Excellent, Ibrahim," said Father També. "Before we resume, let me summarize the beginning for our new friend," he said, looking at me. "It starts in the offices of Mr. Sherlock Holmes, the well-known London detective. He is visited by a Dr. James Mortimer, who has come all the way from the moors of Devonshire to ask Holmes to investigate the mysterious death of Sir Charles Baskerville. Who is Sir Charles?" asked Father També pointing to a boy. "Thomas?"

"Sir Charles is the lord of the Manor of Baskerville."

"Good!" said Father També and went on with the story of the Sir Charles's ancestor, Hugo Baskerville, who offered his soul to the Powers of Evil in exchange for catching a wench who had escaped. He turned to me and said, "I'll fill you in later." Then he pointed to a boy in the group and asked, "Then what happened, Omar?"

Omar was tongue-tied for a moment, then whispered, "The hound came—"

"Not quite, Omar!" said Father També. "Boys, a fine novel is like a fine Swiss clock. Every single wheel in the clock makes the watch move forward at the right speed. In a fine book, the slightest detail may be a clue to something that will be revealed later, so pay more attention!"

The group fell silent. Throughout the evening, Father També unraveled the adventures of Sherlock Holmes, Dr. Watson and Dr. Mortimer, using different tones of voice for each protagonist. His Sherlock Holmes had a dry, sharp, impatient voice while Dr. Watson's tone was assertive when he was the narrator and slightly meek when he was Holmes's acolyte. For the various female characters, Father També's voice rose to different falsetto registers—an oddly realistic sound despite being spewed out by a barrel-chested man sporting a goatee. He told the story without looking at the well-worn edition that lay on his lap, recounting events like the troubadours of old. I could easily imagine him as a traveling minstrel in medieval times rather than a priest.

As the embers died in the campfire, and the story reached a high point, Father També said, "To be continued tomorrow."

"More! More!" the boys shouted. I surprised myself by joining them.

"Tomorrow!" said Father També. He got up and gave us the signal to extinguish the fire. We wrapped our blankets around our shoulders and headed back to camp. On the way back, walking behind Father També on the sand, I asked him so many questions about Arthur Conan Doyle that he shook his finger to silence me, "Too many questions. I'll lend you a biography of Mr. Doyle."

The next day, after lunch, he summoned me to his office and handed me a heavy tome. It was an abbreviated literary encyclopedia. "Take your time to read the full entry on Mr. Doyle. And, remember the rule, no flashlight reading at night under the blankets!"

Since there was little time to read during the day, I broke the interdiction the first night. I borrowed a flashlight from Mademoiselle Bernadette's cabinet and read the entire entry in a few hours. I closed my exhausted eyes, but sleep was slow to come. One sentence kept repeating itself, like the words of a song stuck between the grooves of a record player. It was in a paragraph in which Doyle speaks of his mother's bedtime storytelling. "In my early childhood, as far as I can remember anything at all, the vivid stories she would tell me stand out so clearly they obscure the real facts of my life."

He could have written that sentence for me. I too lived in the stories my father had told me—the magical stories that took me to lands of gods and goddesses and mythological animals and high seas. In the worst of times, these tales were my lifebuoy, but I recognized that sometimes they blurred the lines between "real" life and the colorful life I imagined.

***

After the first week, I let down my guard and began to enjoy summer camp. At the top of the pyramid, Father També ran all the athletic, artistic, and literary activities, which included the campfire reading group and the lending library, and Mademoiselle Bernadette ran the staff and everything else. Her devotion to Father També knew no bounds. She saw everything with his eyes and punctuated her observations with comments like, "Father També will be proud of you!" or conversely, "Father També will not be happy at all!" If Mademoiselle Bernadette had opinions of her own, she kept them to herself.

Father També was a sports fanatic who expected us to excel at all games. I'd had no athletic training, and I didn't know the rules of soccer, football, volleyball, or any game ending with "ball." I would often freeze in the field or miss a ball thrown in my direction. Father També would blow the whistle, run toward me and explain what I'd done wrong and what I should have done. He masked his impatience, but I could hear it in his voice. I felt like Dr. Jekyll and Mr. Hyde.

During the day, I hated being in a place where I felt incompetent and worthless, but in the evening my crippling feelings of inferiority would give way to a sense of mastery and sometimes of superiority. I was by far the best-read and most articulate of the boys in the camp, and I didn't mind showing it off. It was my revenge for the put-downs I had to stomach during the ball games.

During a game of soccer, I caught the ball with my hands. Father També blew his whistle, ran toward me and explained once again the rules of the game. His tone of exasperation made me cringe, and I yelled at the top of my lungs, "I hate this game! Why should I be running after a goddamn ball just to kick it? This stupid ball hasn't done me the slightest harm!"

A few of the boys gave me stern looks; others broke out in timid laughter. Father També wore a mask of pain and disappointment. "Blasphemy is not acceptable here, boy! You're excused!"

As I walked back to the dormitory hut, I was on the verge of tears. I had spoken my mind—I did think that ball games were imbecilic—but I hadn't expected that Father També's disapproval would affect me in such a painful way. I couldn't understand why the opinions of this goddamn priest mattered at all. I'd never cared about the opinion of teachers or other strangers before. Would I be once again thrown out for misbehavior? I felt sorry for my father. By the time I arrived at the dormitory, I was nauseous.

When Mademoiselle Bernadette saw me, she exclaimed, "Jesus, Mary and Joseph! You look like you've seen a ghost. What on earth happened to you?"

"I'm just a little woozy," I whispered.

She led me to the infirmary and took my temperature, listened to my lungs and my back with a stethoscope, and rendered her diagnosis. "This is the start of a nasty bronchitis. You're going straight to bed, young man."

"But Father També said he wanted to see me when he came back."

"Did you get in trouble?" she asked. I nodded.

"Whatever it is, it'll have to wait until you get better," said Mademoiselle Bernadette.

I crashed on my cot. A few moments later, Mademoiselle Bernadette came in with a cup of hot lemon tea and a handful of pills. "Take these," she said. "Then put your pajamas on and get some rest. Nurse's orders!"

***

In the morning, Mademoiselle Bernadette determined that I had bronchitis. She prepared a hot bath with Epsom salt and baking soda, then she had me gargle with a very salty water, and insisted that I eat half a dozen oranges throughout the morning "for the vitamins," and finally she served me a huge bowl of tea oozing with honey. I wondered if that regimen would heal me or kill me.

Moments later, Father També walked into the room. "Mademoiselle Bernadette gave me a mouthful because she believes you caught bronchitis last night on the beach," he said. "Wear something warmer next time, or we'll both be in the doghouse!"

In anticipation of a confrontation with Father També, I had expected the furies to spew hell and brimstone from Mount Olympus, not the kind words the priest was uttering. He wasn't even mentioning my bad behavior of the day before, and that made me nervous. As he went on, I blurted out, "Are you going to expel me?"

He was taken aback. "Why would I do such a thing?" he asked.

"I was rude yesterday."

"That, you were, my boy! I wasn't pleased at all, but I learned something from your outburst. Besides, I must confess that I like a spirited boy—in small doses, of course, because otherwise it would be total anarchy around here."

The priest smiled mischievously and sat on the cot next to mine. "We'll have a chat about all that when you're back on your feet. For now, I'm here bearing a gift." He pulled a book from his bag and handed it to me. It was his worn-out copy of *The Hound of the Baskervilles*.

"Since you missed the campfire last night and will again for a day or two, this will keep you up with your mates."

"Thank you, Father." It was easier now to call him Father. "You won't need it for tonight's reading?"

"No. I carry it just in case I have a memory lapse, but I'd rather speak it than read it to you boys. It's all in here," he said, poking his forehead. "You know, there was a time when people were telling stories without the benefit of the written word. Long before the hieroglyphs, the papyrus, the soot ink and the reed, people traveled from cave to cave and village to village to tell stories. Even today in parts of Africa and perhaps in Amazonian forests, the elders of the village gather their people to share stories."

"Like you do in the evenings on the beach?"

"Yes, just like we do here on the beach," he chuckled.

After Father També left, I read the installments of the previous night, then that of the night before. The latter left me flummoxed. Father També had replicated the story verbatim. No reading, just from memory. Many lengthy descriptions had been omitted or condensed, but he had reproduced the protagonists' dialogues to the syllable. How could he possibly remember them all? What was his secret?

***

Omar, one of the older boys, limped into the dormitory and rushed to his bed. His left knee and left hand were bandaged. Even though we shared a dorm, Omar and I had never had much to say to one another—he was one of the top soccer players, a total bore in my book, and I suspected he thought of me as a stick-in-the-mud.

"I took a fall and hurt my knee. Mademoiselle Bernadette fixed me up, but it still hurts—badly!" he said.

Omar was the oldest, tallest and most athletic boy in the camp, and his whining didn't fit his tough image.

"You made us laugh on the field when you told Father També, 'The ball hasn't hurt me! Why should I kick it?'" he said in a poor imitation of my voice, "That was pretty gutsy of you!"

"I just spoke my mind," I said with false modesty.

"I didn't figure you for a gutsy fellow," Omar continued. "I thought you were a sissy, the type who likes girls and books."

"I like girls and I like books," I said. Being called a sissy and a girlie boy because I preferred reading books to hitting balls was nothing new, and I braced for a fight while I devised ways to prevent any hostility. A guy this tall and muscular would make mincemeat of me in seconds.

He picked up on the rising tension. "Relax!" he said. "Didn't I just say you had guts? I don't care if you read books or not. I don't!"

"You don't read books?" I asked.

"Other than textbooks, no! This is what I like to do," he said as he fondled his crotch with his unharmed hand. "How many times can you come in a day?" he asked.

I didn't know what he meant, but his tone was clearly salacious. I looked away.

"W'Allahi al A'azim! God Almighty! You don't even know what I'm talking about!" he exclaimed. "I'll teach you!"

He unbuttoned his pants, exhibiting a large erect penis and began to knead it. "If you play with your zob long enough, some milk will come out," he said. I looked at him with visible disbelief. He let out a giggle. "It's the milk of manhood. It's pure mazag!" he said, using the Arabic word for pleasure and ecstasy. "Try it!" he said.

I was mortified to realize how little I knew about these things. Luckily, Mademoiselle Bernadette came into the dormitory to check on us. Omar turned over to hide his open trousers and his dangling genitals. "Father També will come and visit you shortly," she said to me. "And you, Omar, go join the other boys in the reading room! You're injured, not sick! You have no reason to be in bed!"

As soon as she was out, Omar fastened his pants buttons and decamped.

***

At lunch, Mademoiselle Bernadette served me a copious meal. "This is Father També's favorite. It'll give you energy." I ate every morsel of it and continued to read. When she returned to pick up the tray, I said, "That was the best chicken I ever had, Mademoiselle Bernadette."

"That wasn't chicken, dear boy," she said, appearing to be slightly peeved that I hadn't identified the delicacy. "C'était un civet de lapin, voyons!"

"Rabbit stew? I ate a rabbit?"

I must have looked so horrified that she exclaimed, "What's the matter? Is it contrary to the Jewish faith?"

"Not that I know, Mademoiselle, but I didn't know you could eat rabbits!"

"But you said it was delicious, no?"

"Yes, but now that I know I ate Bugs Bunny, I'm not sure I'll digest it."

"You have a good sense of humor," she laughed. "You will digest it fine. If the Lord didn't want us to eat rabbit, he would have made them inedible, like hippopotamuses!"

I laughed, but I remained ill at ease.

***

Alone in the dormitory, I remembered Omar's words about the milk of manhood and started to fondle my penis. It was very enjoyable, but no *milk of manhood* was forthcoming, and the intense mazag Omar had described didn't happen. I got bored and returned to Sherlock Holmes. In the afternoon, Omar returned to the dormitory, his shirt torn open on his bare chest. "Did you try?" he asked.

"Yes, but no milk of manhood for me!" I answered.

"That's because you're still a kid. You must be initiated first. After that, it'll come. Plenty."

"How do you get initiated?"

"I'll show you," he said. He unbuttoned his pants and gently massaged his penis. "Take off your pants," he commanded. I grew scared because his penis had become considerably larger, but I obeyed. "Turn around," he said with a panting voice. Suddenly, he was grabbing my shoulders with his strong hands, forcing me down on the bed, and straddling me. I tried to push him away, but he was too strong. There was a sharp pain when his penis entered me, but I couldn't breathe a word because he had covered my mouth with his hand.

"Do you like it?" he panted.

"Not at all!"

He moved faster, wheezing in my ear, "And now do you like it?"

"No! Enough!"

He got into a frenzy of jerks and muffled moans. A smelly and sticky liquid filled my ass. Puffing and wheezing, Omar pulled out, holding his half-erect penis and shoving a hand covered with a gooey liquid under my nose. "That's the milk of manhood!" he said, proudly. "Now you're a man!"

"It stinks like dead fish!" I said. "If that's being a man, you can keep it!"

He smirked. "Well, you are man now, whether you want it or not. The next time you rub your zob, the milk of your manhood will come out."

I felt sticky and dirty. I rushed to the bathroom and washed myself furiously. I was still somewhat wet when I returned to the dorm as Mademoiselle Bernadette walked in, holding a cup of tea.

"What are you doing? You have bronchitis! You'll catch your death!"

Using my pajamas in lieu of a towel, she rubbed me so hard that I feared she would flay me alive. I explained that I had showered because I'd been sweating so profusely that I was all sweaty. She stripped the bed, brought me a fresh pair of pajamas and made put fresh linen on my bed.

Omar was nowhere in sight, but the whiff of his sperm still hung in the air. Or perhaps it was just in my mind. I was engulfed in shame, not so much for the sexual act with Omar but for being so naïve and ignorant as to let him trick me into it. A long-buried memory resurfaced—back in Maadi, Alice erupting in the dorm as Moussa and I were wrestling and accusing us of "doing dirty things in bed." Now I understood what she'd meant, and I felt all the more humiliated. For now and for back then.

***

After Mademoiselle Bernadette released me from bed rest, Father També summoned me to his office.

"Let's have that talk now. Do you think I'm upset that you're not good at sports?"

"Yes."

"Well, I'm not. I didn't like that you were impertinent and took the name of the Lord in vain, but I'm not upset by your poor athletic performance. You can't be blamed for that, but it concerns me. You're bright and quick-witted, but you only have a life of the mind. Your body is clumsy and awkward, and it can't keep up with your mind. Here, we believe in Mens sana in corpore sano. You studied Latin, right?"

"A sound mind in a sound body."

"Are you interested in learning anything other than literature and history?"

"Yes, but I'm not interested in playing ball."

"You make that very clear," he chuckled, then added, "There is a reason for your physical difficulties. Our job is to find that reason and find a remedy. I'm not here to punish you, I'm here to help you."

"With what?"

"You tell me. Why do you dislike playing ball so much?"

"I don't know!"

"I'm sure you have some idea," he insisted.

I searched my mind for some joke to crack, but Father També's look stopped me cold. I hesitated for a while and finally said, "By the time I see the ball, it's too late to hit it. I hate it!"

"That's an honest answer," said Father També. "Your father told me about your bad eye."

"He did?" It surprised me because Papa and I hadn't talked about my bad eye for a very long time.

"There's nothing shameful about your impairment. Many great men have suffered from afflictions, but it was often those ills that propelled them to excellence." He saw the sudden sadness that had descended upon me. "Are you afraid to fail?" he asked.

"I'm afraid of nothing!" I exclaimed.

"Only fools are afraid of nothing. The bravest soldiers are petrified on the battlefield, but they conquer their fears. That's the definition of courage." Father També took a book from his desk and handed it to me. "Read the underlined words," he said.

The book was *Arthur Conan Doyle: A Life in Letters*, and the underline sentence was, "I went on board the whaler a big straggling youth and I came off a powerful young man."

"That's the author we're reading now. While he was a medical student, Conan Doyle got a job as a surgeon on a whaling ship and traveled to the Arctic Circle. He learned about the brutality of the hunt for whales and about the camaraderie of the men on board."

Taking the book from my hands, Father També said, "You're also a straggling youth, and I want to help you become a powerful young man. But I can't reach the goal without your help. Will you help me help you?"

I nodded my assent.

"If I understand correctly, your worst obstacle in ball games is that your eyes don't follow the ball, right?"

"Yes. Do you have a magic potion for that?" I asked.

He smiled. "Yes, I do have a magic remedy, and I'll ignore your sarcasm and tell you. There are two basic ways to overcome an obstacle—you jump over it, or you go around it. Since you can't play fast ball games, I can make up a program of exercises and sports that are easier on the eyes—softer and slower ballgames, gymnastics, running, swimming and riding a bicycle."

"I can't swim or ride!"

"If you learned how to read, you can learn to ride and swim. So, here's my proposition—"

This priest never ceased to surprise me. Teachers didn't propose, they commanded. They didn't ask for acquiescence, they demanded obedience.

"Here's the deal," he continued, "you'll be dispensed of the fast games you dislike, but you'll spend the same number of hours on soft sports and learning how to swim and ride. Agreed?"

I nodded. He crushed my hand with his powerful grip. "Any other problem?" he asked.

"Yes, I mean no! May I borrow the book of Conan Doyle?"

He roared with laughter as he fished the book out of his pocket and gently threw it at me. "Why do you think I brought it with me?"

***

Most Sundays and sometimes on weekdays, Father També would pile us up onto a large felucca and sail toward El Lessan to observe the merging of the Nile and the Mediterranean Sea. We would drop anchor a few feet from the shore, and the taller boys would jump into the waist-deep water from the starboard side of the felucca while a wobbly gangplank was deployed portside for the rest of us. I hated gliding down onto sludgy soft mud bank of the Nile that was full of nasty jellyfish.

I'd already had three or four swimming lessons without making much progress. As long as Father També or one of the older boys propped me up, I could stay afloat, but as soon as they withdrew their support, I would flail in panic, even though I knew the waters were too shallow for me to drown.

"Enough for today!" said Father També. "You can go back to the felucca."

Mortified, full of anger and self-pity, I stepped on the gangplank and went to hide my shame in the felucca. It wasn't fair. Everyone around me could swim like a dolphin while I sank in the water like a crippled hippopotamus. I was fighting a losing battle, and I had to do something about it. I went to the back of the felucca and looked down. The waters were deep enough, and I was tempted to jump, but I took a step back instead. I wondered, if I had jumped, whether I would have sunk or drowned—and, in a fit of rage, I jumped. As I hit the water, words crossed my mind—the gladiators' salute, "Ave Caesar, morituri te salutant!"

I hit the sea floor hard and rebounded back. The waters were deeper than I thought, and I was scared witless, but I was propelled by a force greater than my fear. With my arms flailing and my legs kicking, I was thrust forward—neither truly swimming nor drowning! I heard Father També shout, "Keep moving! Don't stop! Keep swimming!" He caught up with me and swam by my side, still shouting words of encouragement. After a while I lost my momentum but continued until the salty water filled my lungs. I coughed and gagged and threw up, but I reached the shallow water. I threw up again, but I didn't care. It was a barf of victory.

"Congratulations, boy!" Father També said. "You're well on your way to becoming a swimmer!"

My feet planted in the mud of the Nile, impervious to the jellyfish that was rubbing its slimy back against my right ankle, I savored the moment and sent a grateful silent thank-you to the gods and goddesses that had watched over me.

Not resting on our laurels, Father També tackled the next challenge—bicycling. Once or twice a week, he led his flock, divided by age groups, for a mile-long walk to a bicycle rental shop run by a one-legged man named Waleed. Mademoiselle Bernadette closed the procession.

Waleed's fleet of two-wheelers was primarily composed of black or dark green pre-World War Two Raleigh, Armstrong and Humber bicycles with straight handlebars. Teaching me to ride was a long and arduous undertaking for Father També and an ordeal for me. I had no balance at all, even with training wheels. I was inclined to use the brakes as much as the pedals, and I feared relinquishing control to a machine. Finally, I learned to ride with training wheels and, at Father També's urging, go faster and faster—until the day the ride felt different. I looked down and panicked. Father També had lifted my training wheels without my knowledge. Instinctively, I pedaled faster and faster. Riding at last! Then I did a false move and fell off the bicycle. My knees hurt like hell, but I was proud to have slain the dragon. I just prayed I could do it again.

In the following days, I suffered many a scrape in many a fall, but the good Jesuit, patient to a fault, would put me back onto the saddle and urge me to keep going until the last shred of fear was gone.

Most of the boys had a favorite bike and Waleed tried his best to pair each boy with his chosen wheels. One bicycle commanded my attention—a sapphire-blue Raleigh with the number 9 attached to the back of the saddle. It was of the same vintage as the others, but it had been refurbished and painted in a hew that stood out in the sea of black and green machines.

Father També shook his head and pointed to a smaller bicycle, but I insisted, "My mother says that nine is my lucky number and blue is my lucky color."

"Far from me to argue with a mother's beliefs!" he chuckled.

By mid-summer, I was holding my own on the saddle.

***

At night, around the campfire, Father També finished a novel and started a new one with a warning that it would be a scary one. Most of the boys yelped with joy and excitement. I'd never liked horror films, so I was prepared to hate the new book from the get-go, but the first lines of the story caught my attention:

> The Opera Ghost really existed. He was not, as was long believed, a creature of the imagination of the artists, the superstition of the managers, or a product of the absurd and impressionable brains of the young ladies of the ballet, their mothers, the box-keepers, the cloak-room attendants or the concierge. Yes, he existed in flesh and blood, although he assumed the complete appearance of a real phantom; that is to say, of a spectral shade.

How could I resist such prose? By the end of the second chapter of *The Phantom of the Opera*, I gave Gaston Leroux a seat in my literary Pantheon. Unlike my campmates, I didn't experience his novel as a scary story, although it had its chilling moments, but rather as a heartbreaking tale of tragic unrequited love. Many of its passages gave me goosebumps.

Papa came to Ras-el-Bar every other weekend and was pleased that Father També had no complaints. As usual, I was not invited to stay with him at the Aslan Hotel—Father També didn't want me to miss the evening readings—but we had two entire days to catch up. We would walk on the beach or sail on a felucca and talk about the books Father També had read to the group and the ones I'd read by myself.

Toward the end of summer, a shadow colored our reunions. Papa seemed preoccupied and impatient. He would start a sentence in a tone that presaged a serious announcement and switch abruptly to small talk. He would throw furtive glances at his watch long before I was due back at camp. I asked jokingly if he were impatient to get rid of me. His immediate response was, "Fashar! God forbid!" but it failed to convince me. Something was off. True to my new detective models, Doyle's Sherlock Holmes and Leblanc's Arsène Lupin, I decided to conduct an investigation.

That night I told Papa that I wanted to go back to camp by myself, and he agreed—too readily for my taste. He walked me to the *taf-taf* stop, gave me more than my usual allowance money and walked away with brisk steps. I jumped from the trolley and followed him at a distance. As a precaution, I had left my sweater in Papa's room, so I'd have an excuse for my return if I were caught.

Papa walked into the lobby and joined a blonde woman at the bar. She was strikingly beautiful. They ordered drinks and listened to the music. When the piano man played a romantic melody, Papa and the woman got up and stepped onto the dance floor. He held her close and she put her head on his shoulder. They danced well and they looked happy together. I wondered who was the mysterious blonde? Did they come together from Cairo or had they met here at the Aslan Hotel? Why didn't he tell me about her? Did he tell her about me? At first, I felt a pinch of rejection, jealousy and possessiveness, then a sense of joy and relief entered my bittersweet dance of emotions. I hadn't seen my father this happy in a long time. I'd always been aware that, unlike my mother who had a brand-new family to share her life, my father had fleeting relationships and no family near him aside from me—a source of more trouble than comfort for him—and I was thankful for this mysterious woman.

When I climbed aboard the taf-taf, I was oscillating between joy and forlornness, hopes for my father's happiness and fear of the shackles of new entanglements.

***

I had a lump in my throat when Father També announced that the book he was about to begin would be the last book of the season. "It's a book that some of you may have read in picture-book form or seen in a film adaptation, but nothing replaces the original work of art. This book is one of finest literary creations by one of the greatest writers in the world. When you've all progressed in the English language, I hope you will read it in the original language. For now I'll read the Prologue and see how many of you will recognize the book: "If sailor tales to sailor tunes, / Storm and adventure, heat and cold, / If schooners, islands, and maroons, / And buccaneers, and buried gold, / And all the old romance, retold . . ."

I knew the answer, but I didn't want to show off. I'd been called Father També's pet behind my back, probably because he spent more time helping me exercise than he did others, not understanding that it spoke of my need for help rather than favoritism, and I needed to deflect that perception by toning down my literary fluency.

"Come on, boys!" thundered Father També. "The author already told you it's a story about sailors, adventure, buccaneers, buried gold and—" Father També pulled a black patch from his cassock and put it on his left eye. We all laughed.

"What are you, a bunch of ignorant boys?" The silence was getting uncomfortable, so I raised my hand with some reluctance. "*Treasure Island*, maybe?" I answered.

"Excellent!" said Father També. "And who is the author of *Treasure Island*?"

Another long silence before I answered with deliberate imprecision, "Something Something Stevenson?"

"The first *something* is Robert and the second is Louis," he chuckled. "Robert Louis Stevenson was a contemporary of Sir Arthur Conan Doyle and Sir James Barrie, the author of *Peter Pan*. They all went to the University of Edinburgh at the same time. Stevenson's best-known novels are *Treasure Island*, *The Master of Ballantrae* and *The Strange Case of Dr. Jekyll and Mr. Hyde*. He also wrote poems, one of which sums up his life and was inscribed on his gravestone."

Father També removed his eye patch, put it in his pocket, and read the poem first in a French translation, then in its original English. His Levantine accent in both languages gave the words a resonance and a magnitude that moved me.

> "This be the verse you grave for me:
> Here he lies where he longed to be.
> Home is the sailor, home from sea,
> And the hunter home from the hill."

In our discussions after each reading, Father També liked to describe the lives of his favorite writers, always emphasizing the connection between their personal experiences and their work. It was new territory for me. Until then, I'd never given much thought to the worldly lives of the likes of Dumas, Hugo, and Balzac. In my mind they were demigods who had sent their divine compositions down from Mount Olympus for all to enjoy. Father També opened my eyes to the fact that the dead writers in my literary Pantheon-in-the-Sky had been people of blood and flesh who'd been shaped, like all mortals, by the places, the people and the events of their lives. Only these mere mortals had been armed with ink and paper, and the talent to use them—and their creations had made them immortal.

I pondered the power of great stories. By some miracle, here we were, a bunch of boys of various origins and religions, sitting on a beach in an ancient country at the confluence of Africa and Western Asia, listening to the words of a Scotsman, translated into French, and read by a Levantine Jesuit priest who loved literature as passionately perhaps as he loved the Lord.

On the way back to camp, Father També noticed that I was pensive and asked me if something was wrong. I said no, but the man had the uncanny ability to make me disclose my most private thoughts. I spoke of my musings about the mortality of artists and the immortality of their art. He listened attentively and said, "You had an epiphany. Do you know what that is?"

I shook my head.

"I'll spare the various meanings of 'epiphany' in Christianity because I'm using the word here in its secular sense. An epiphany is a moment of deep insight into life, a moment of deep understanding of something essential," he said. "In your epiphany, you grasped the meaning of the legacy of great artists. Long after their bodies have turned to ashes, long after their material life is forgotten, the power of their art lives on to enlighten generations to come. It's their gift to the world. Let that epiphany guide you throughout your life."

"Me? I'm not a great artist!"

"It applies to all of us. We all get a chance, at birth, to leave our mark in the world. You'll get yours when the time comes. God gives some chosen people a mission and the talent to carry it out. If you're one of them, you cannot, must not, let any obstacle, situation or people derail you from your path. You must follow your north star wherever it will lead you."

Back at camp, Mademoiselle Bernadette had prepared chocolate cakes and urns of lemonade. Father També congratulated each one of us for our singular accomplishments and blessed the lot of us with his usual panache.

The next morning, we boarded the barge to Damietta where a train would take us back to Cairo. Throughout Ras-el-Bar, men were dismantling the *e'eshas* of the vacationers who'd already gone home. There was a soupçon of autumn in the air. As the barge floated away, I watched with a twinge of sorrow Father També standing on the platform, waving us goodbye, and I thanked him silently for all the riches he'd brought to my life.

CHAPTER 10

Fall of 1958

In the days following my return to Cairo, I felt like a different person. I'd gained self-confidence and maturity; I was less moody or sad, and I was filled with newfound energy. It was like my mind was outgrowing my skull, just like my body was outgrowing my clothes, and I switched from elation to despair for no perceptible reason. Sometimes I felt like a giant lizard undergoing a metamorphosis, shedding my old skin without having grown a new one, and feeling naked, exposed, and terribly vulnerable.

Talking with my father offered no solace; his response was always that I was going through the "normal" troubles of adolescence, and it would pass in "due time." In my mind, "due time" was a euphemism for eternity.

September was approaching. Going back to school was imminent, but this time it was to the La Salle College, an unfamiliar environment. Although Father També's summer camp had allayed some of my apprehensions about going to a Christian school, it was yet another plunge into the unknown.

September also meant resuming my Hebrew studies and preparing for my Bar Mitzvah. It was a huge burden because it meant little to me. I loved my Jewish heritage, and I loved the Bible for its epic stories, not its religious teachings. Being a Jew would not have been a major factor in my life if the world in which I lived hadn't singled me out as an enemy and made me a pariah, and it was with a heavy heart that I returned to Moshe, the rabbinical student who'd taught me at the synagogue before summer break.

I'd never liked or disliked Moshe before. It was difficult to connect with a dour and insipid man who seemed to have no interest in life besides his studies. He had been boring but not mean, but now he was boring *and* mean. His disdainful attitude made it clear that he believed my "Jewishness" had regressed after my "Christian summer." His repertoire often included hostile comments. "A good Jewish boy, by the time he's ten-years-old, should be able to read from the Mishnah. At twelve, he should read the 613 commandments of the Torah!" or "At the rate we're going, you might become a Bar Mitzvah by the time of your funeral!"

I didn't complain to my father, not only because I thought I should fight my own battles but also because it seemed that my Bar Mitzvah was growing in importance in my father's eyes. The way he spoke about it, it became clear that it was about much more than just a coming-of-age ritual; it was a symbol of resistance against Nasser's oppression of the Jews. In my mind, such resistance was futile. Egyptian Judaism was already on the verge of extinction. We were already ghosts of glories past. But I faked enthusiasm for Papa's sake and did my best at Hebrew studies, ignoring the pettiness of my tutor.

A few days before my birthday, Tante Marcelle helped Papa organize a party for the occasion. Marcelle Haroun wasn't really my aunt; she was the sister of my aunt Marie, a distinction without a difference. After the entire family left Egypt, Tante Marcelle was our closest remaining relative. Whether it was by affection or by a sense of obligation, she was active in helping my father in the merciless task of raising me. I felt particularly close to her, in part because I knew I'd never see her after we moved to France.

Tante Marcelle and her husband, Shehata Haroun, were a rarity. They were Jewish anti-Zionists and staunch Egyptian nationalists. Shehata Haroun was born René Silvera, but he had changed his name to the Arabic Shehata Haroun to proclaim his devotion to Egypt. He defined himself foremost as an Egyptian nationalist, second as a communist, and third as a Jew. His political activities had caused him to be imprisoned by Nasser's regime along with fellow communists, Muslim Brothers, and petty criminals.

Long before Israel became a state, Shehata had proclaimed that the mere existence of a Jewish nation would disrupt the entire Middle East and bring about the end of all Jewish communities in the Arab world. At family dinners, Oncle Léon and Papa would usually interject and extol the virtue of Israel as a refuge for the persecuted Jews from both Arab countries and Europe, and Oncle Shehata would respond with long diatribes against Israel. When these conversations would run out of steam, they would give way to jest and banter, leaving no blood on the floor. Papa would tease Shehata and say, ""Every family needs a black sheep to challenge them!" and Shehata would retort that we were all dancing on deck while the Titanic sank.

***

A mere few days remained before school started, and I was apprehensive. I spent much of these days reading the classic novels of the previous century. One of my favorites was Stendhal's *The Red and the Black*. I was enthralled by the descriptions of the uprising of the people during the 1830 revolution, and I recognized elements of the burning of Cairo six years earlier. But the passages that struck the loudest chords were those portraying Julien's lover, Mme de Rênal, the beautiful older woman who dies of, and for, her love of Julien. It made me wonder if there would ever be a Mme de Rênal in my life. Would I ever know such absolute passion? And *when?*

Between chapters, I would open my hybrid history-and-literature textbook, a large volume with illustrations in vibrant colors, to better understand the 1830 revolution. On the first page devoted to that period of history, a large reproduction of Eugene Delacroix's painting, *Liberty Leading the People*, dominated the entry. It depicted the people of Paris taking to the streets, led by Marianne, the goddess of Liberty, an arresting and beautiful bare-breasted woman holding the tricolor flag of the republic. I stared at the painting. The naked breasts of the goddess were full, vibrant, alive, mesmerizing, and they looked like they were daring me to touch them.

Spellbound, I brushed a timid finger over Marianne's left breast, and it gave me a light electric jolt as if I were touching her real flesh. There was a rush in my groin, and I touched my hardening and expanding penis, stroking it gingerly at first, then with increasing frenzy, reaching a state of painful ecstasy that culminated in an eruption of white sticky fluid gushing all over me. It brought back the memory of Omar holding to my nose his fingers wet with the same smelly fluid and promising that someday my *zob* too would disgorge "the milk of manhood." For once, that bastard Omar hadn't lied. It was what he called *mazag*! I went back to reading, keeping one eye on the breasts of the goddess Marianne and the other on the novel. After a few passages of passion between Mme de Rênal and Julien Sorel, I wanted to feel that pleasure again. The second time it lasted longer and was even more pleasurable—so much that I did it again, growing bolder in exploring various touches and rhythms to prolong my pleasure before reaching the ultimate *mazag*.

The more I masturbated, the more daring my fantasies grew. In many of them the breasts of Alice, of boarding school memory, and those of Marianne floated in a dance of twirling veils. In others I would be in a warm pool of soapy water and Alice would join me, shedding her sheer toga as we danced to a sensual melody—then by magic our bodies would dissolve in jolts of ecstasy, and we would become one.

***

On my thirteenth birthday, Tante Marcelle came early to co-host the party with my father. She directed the servants to arrange an appetizing buffet and a side table with a mammoth chocolate cake. My buddies from the lycée also came early enough to allow us time together before the other guests arrived. Quentin, who'd returned from Switzerland, snuck in a few bottles of beer, which I poured into coffee cups to escape detection. JP brought a slew of recent records from France and America, and we had a pre-party celebration. The beer, Quentin said, was made by Belgian Trappist monks in remote cloisters, and the lightheadedness it left in its wake quickly tamed my anxieties.

A visitor I'd never met before came into the room, and Papa welcomed him with a bear hug. Short and very thin, he wore a gold-colored sharkskin sports coat over a starched jet-black shirt and impeccable pressed black trousers. A red silk kerchief spilled out from his breast jacket and a golden ankh, the pharaonic symbol of life, shone over the black of his shirt. Papa motioned me to join them.

"This is my cousin, Nisso. You wouldn't remember him!"

I shook my head. There was something vaguely familiar about the newcomer, but I didn't remember ever meeting him.

"Come on, cousin, of course not!" said Nisso. "He was barely six or seven when I last visited Tante Hélène!"

Tante Hélène, who? It took a moment to realize that his Tante Hélène was my grandmother! Few people ever called her by anything other than Mama or Nona. The newfound cousin turned to me and extended his hand. "But I remember you well, young man. My name is Nessim el-Khouri, Nisso for you."

I took an instant liking to him, and I wanted to talk to him, but Tante Marcelle called me to join her.

Throughout the afternoon, most of the children living at the Anglo-Swiss Hotel came, some with their parents in tow. The owner of the Anglo-Swiss, Dimitrios Giannopoulos, came with his son Ari and several of his Greek relatives who were visiting Cairo, among them a gorgeous blond woman whom Dimitrios introduced as his cousin, Calista Christina Christakos. Papa, as mesmerized by her as I was, told her it was my birthday party. She extended her hand and congratulated me in perfect French, then she excused herself and departed. I had the impression that the lights in the room had dimmed by a notch.

"Gorgeous woman!" Nisso muttered. "She looks like a pagan Greek goddess!"

"Not pagan—she's a super-Christian goddess!" said Papa. "Did you notice there's not one but two 'Christ' in Christina Christakos?"

After the excellent food and many sets of Frank Sinatra songs, an epidemic of sleepiness was spreading among the guests. "Your party is wilting, little cousin," said Nisso. "Do you want me to jazz it up a little?"

"Yes, please, Uncle Nisso."

"Just Nisso, my boy. The *uncle* part makes me feel like a decrepit old man."

"All right, uh, Nisso. How do you jazz up a party?"

He smiled. "Moving people is my thing, lad. I'm a dancer, a choreographer, and a dance instructor."

A dancer! Curiouser and curiouser! In my family, men were lawyers, teachers, doctors, and some were business owners. I'd heard a story about a great-great aunt who'd been a ballerina in Vienna and had perished in Hitler's camps, but no other performer until now. A man dancer in the family was a promise of fun.

Nisso stopped the music and said, "Hello, boys and girls—well, the boys far outnumber the girls, so a special hello to the three brave young girls among us. Anybody want to learn a few steps?"

Silence. Everyone looked intimidated and unwilling to move. He played tango music and said, "Come on, kids. Dancing is fun! I want to hear a loud 'Yes!' from all of you!" Nisso said. The youngsters shied away, but three grown women raised their hands. Nisso chuckled and picked the oldest among them. "Three yeses is a good start."

Nessim's gracefulness and elegance on the floor dazzled everyone. "He was always the King of the Tango, the Fred Astaire of the family," Papa whispered, an edge of nostalgia in his tone. I was surprised that Papa had never mentioned Nisso, but I remembered that Nona had eight siblings, and an army of nephews now dispersed over the five continents.

When Nisso tried to coax the young ones into learning the tango, there was little enthusiasm, so I whispered in Nisso's ear, "How about a little rock 'n' roll?"

"I like rock 'n' roll music, but it's more gymnastics than dancing—but why not? There's nothing wrong with gymnastics, right?" he said with a wink.

Nisso alternated rock 'n' roll and ballroom dance music, dancing or showing my friends and their parents a few twists and turns, keeping the party alive until the end.

When almost everyone had left, Nisso took his leave, saying to me, "The music of your generation is fun and innovative, but I hope someday you'll learn our traditional dances. Especially the tango. It's the mother of all dances!"

Tante Marcelle was the last to leave the party. Her little girls were fast asleep, and two servants helped her take them downstairs to a waiting taxi. As the cab moved away, Papa remarked said wistfully that both Tante Marcelle and Nisso would never leave Egypt, we would lose them forever.

I shared Papa's sorrow, but it irked me that Papa never had a word for my mother and the maternal family I would leave behind. How could he be so oblivious to this part of my life?

***

At breakfast with Papa the next morning, I fired a barrage of questions about the cousin who had emerged from the blue.

"It's not complicated," said Papa. "Nessim is one of Nona's countless nephews. As children of the same age, we played together a lot."

It surprised me. Nisso looked much younger than my father. Papa saw the look in my eyes and tapped his belly. "Dancing keeps you looking so young! No such luck with me!"

"If he's Nona's nephew, shouldn't Nisso's last name should be Cohen? Where does el-Khouri come from?"

"He changed it when he converted to Islam," Papa said with a mischievous smile. "And, actually, he didn't change his name; he just translated it."

"Huh?"

Papa chuckled. "Simple! The Hebrew word 'Kohen' means priest. The Kohanim were the priests of the Temple of Jerusalem, and Nisso is their descendant through his father, Nona's brother. You know the Arabic word for priest?

"Imam? Sheik? I've never heard of a Khouri!"

"Both Imam and Sheik mean leader, not priests—imam for a religious leader, and sheik for a secular leader in a village as well as in an empire. A Khouri first designated a Levantine Christian leader, but today it means a priest in all religions."

"So, are we Kohen too through Nona?"

No, son. The status of Kohen is only transmitted to male children. Nona's brothers are Kohen, but not Nona. Which means you are not a priest!"

"Okay with me! So why did Nisso convert to Islam?"

"He had his reasons. The most important one is that he found peace in Islam."

"I don't understand!"

"You don't need to understand. Only Nessim el-Khouri needs to understand Nessim el-Khouri!"

The newfound cousin perplexed and fascinated me. I sensed Papa was holding back other things about Nisso's life, and it made me want to puncture the mystery.

"Why have you kept him hidden all these years?" I asked.

"Last question and last answer, all right?" Papa waited until I nodded my assent.

"I didn't keep Nisso hidden. We were in close contact until the madness of '56. After the war, his brothers and sisters moved to Europe, and I assumed he'd gone with them. Nisso made the same assumption that we had left Egypt at the same as Nona and the rest of the family. Just a few days ago I ran into a friend and learned that my cousin was still in Cairo, ergo, we reunited. Here goes your deep mystery!"

"I'm still curious about why Nisso converted." I said.

"Maybe he'll tell you someday."

***

Maman held another birthday party in her apartment. Her brothers and their wives, their children and assorted nannies were present, along with some people I didn't know or remember.

It was great to see Tante Aïda, Khadr Bey and their boys, and I was relieved that Magda and Hussein el-Shafei hadn't come. Hussein had risen to be Nasser's minister of labor after a stint as minister of war, and his importance in the ruling regime only exacerbated the schizoid feelings I had around him, depending on whether he wore civilian clothing or a uniform covered with medals.

I couldn't wait to reunite with Tante Toto. I'd never been close to my maternal aunts and uncles, but I had a soft spot for Tante Toto. It had been a long time since she'd joined us on my Saturday outings with Maman. She'd missed my last birthday because she had had what Maman called her "problèmes de femmes," whatever that was. The first thing I noticed when I walked into my mother's apartment was the grim expression on the face of Oncle Moni, Tante Toto's husband. My heart sunk.

I joined my mother in the kitchen and asked her where Tante Toto was. She looked distraught and said in a hushed tone, "Didn't I tell you? Oh, God, I was sure I'd told you!"

"Told me what?" I asked. "Did something happen to Tante Toto?"

Maman pulled me further aside and whispered, "Tante Toto left for Europe a while ago with her parents. They're either chez nous already or on the way there."

"What?" I yelled. "Tante Toto's gone to Israel? Why?"

"Hush!" she whispered. "We never mention that country. Or Tante Toto in the presence of Oncle Moni. She left him, and he's lost without her."

"Why'd she leave him? Was he mean to her?"

She shook her head.

"Why then?" I asked repeatedly until she relented.

"All right, all right. Toto wanted children and Moni couldn't give her that."

"Why not?"

"Mon chéri, what happens in a couple is their business. Besides, you're too young for these things."

"Why did she leave without saying goodbye?" I asked in a voice strangled by grief. "Did she forget me!?"

"Fashar! God Forbid! Tante Toto adores you, and she'll never forget you. She just thought it best if I told you myself."

"But you didn't tell me!"

"I was waiting for the right moment," said Maman, an embarrassed look in her eyes. "I didn't know how to tell you."

"So which is it?" I yelled. "It can't be both 'I told you' and 'I didn't know how to tell you'—so?"

"Hush now! We don't want to make Oncle Moni more upset than he already is!"

"What about *her*? *She* wouldn't leave like that if she wasn't hurt and upset!"

"She'll be fine. Don't worry about her," Maman whispered in my ear. "There are no children, so Tante Toto pourra refaire sa vie, she'll be able to make a new life for herself."

I went into a bedroom to be alone. I hated the French expression Maman had used—*refaire sa vie*, which meant *remake* one's life. It was often applied to my father by family and friends. "Il n'a pas encore refait sa vie." Why on earth did people think that marriage and divorce could *make, unmake,* or *remake* a life? In spite of an uncertain future, my father seemed to enjoy his *unmade* life, full of lovely lady friends, books, poetry and history, while mother's fully *remade* life— new husband, two new stepchildren, and a newborn baby— was still consumed by old and bitter grievances.

A few tears dripped down my cheeks as a gush of memories flooded my mind, quick images flashing like fireflies— Tante Toto lifting me up in her arms when I was a baby and dancing and singing softly along with the radio; the sense of closeness and safety that I felt in her arms; her quiet love, so much more comforting than my mother's intense bursts of passionate love. I remembered Tante Toto coming to my boarding school during my mother's pregnancy, and taking over the Saturday visits. Her kind reaction when she came to announce the birth of my baby brother; her understanding that I felt betrayed, and her loving soothing words, along with scoops of ice cream, that eased my sorrow. I would miss her for the rest of my life.

I allowed myself a good cry, then washed my face and rejoined my birthday guests.

***

A few days after my birthday, Moshe reported to the rabbi that I was not ready to read from the Mishnah and therefore the ceremony should be postponed or cancelled. Papa was devastated, of course, and I felt bad for him and mostly for Nona. I knew they would be ashamed of me. No member of our family had failed to become a Bar Mitzvah.

Papa requested an audience with the rabbi. Before he could plead for some kind of dispensation, the rabbi said, "I will hear you, but first we'll have a better discussion if I explain the full meaning of the Bar Mitzvah. According to Jewish law, the Bar Mitzvah is a given. Any Jewish boy becomes a Bar Mitzvah automatically when he reaches the age of thirteen. It's separate from the Bar Mitzvah initiation ceremony!"

Both Papa and I were baffled, perplexed, and speechless. We stared at him with wide open eyes of disbelief.

"The ceremony is just a confirmation that the boy has become a man—a public celebration, if you will—but it is not a condition for a Jewish boy to be a Bar Mitzvah." He turned to me, "Like I just said, according to Jewish law, you are a Bar Mitzvah, and now that you're a man, you must behave like one!"

"No male in our family has ever skipped that sacred ritual," Papa moaned.

"Then you must study hard and return when you're ready, young man!" said the rabbi as he looked at me. "There's no set limit about when to go through the ritual. I've seen men in their sixties and seventies go through it. I repeat, you're a man in the eyes of God, and as such you can participate in a minyan. Do you know what that is?"

"Yes. It's the minimal number of Jewish men required to perform a prayer."

"How many men are required for that quorum?"

"Ten."

"Good. You can also fast on Yom Kippur, wear the tzitzit, you know, the prayer shawl with fringes, and you should observe the 613 commandments of the Torah. You know what they are?"

"No. Sorry."

The rabbi laughed. "I don't either. I read them though, and so will you. Of these 613 commandments, you'll see that there are 365 negative commandments, which means you must abstain from performing them, and 248 positive commandments, which means you must obey them. Understand?"

I nodded.

"You should also know that you're now allowed to marry—"

Papa and I both laughed.

"You don't have to," said the rabbi with a wink. "But under Jewish law you can, just so you know! Good luck, young man!"

***

On Sunday, Papa and I had planned a day of riding at the Pyramids, lunch at the Mena House, and a movie in the evening, but I felt that something was off during breakfast. Papa didn't tease me or ask me about the progress of my Bar Mitzvah preparations, and he looked anxious. As we were leaving, he announced that a friend would join us.

"Do we have to, Papa?" I blurted out. "I have things I want to talk to you about."

"We can talk later. On the way home or when we're back this evening."

It was odd. Was it another girlfriend? Usually when Papa had a new paramour, he would arrange for a short meeting over tea to check the waters before including her in further outings. An entire day with a new girlfriend before taking the temperature was a troubling first.

My irritation grew when Papa double-parked in front of a posh building and told me to sit in the back.

"Why should *I* sit in the back? Let *her* sit in the back."

"You're the gentleman, she's the lady," said Papa, slamming the car door.

A long while later, he emerged from the building, holding a blond-haired woman by the arm—the mysterious woman with whom I'd spied him romancing at the Aslan Hotel in Ras-el-Bar.

She opened the car door, leaned over and kissed me on the cheek. "Sorry we kept you waiting, darling, I was just emerging from my beauty sleep," she said in a soft voice. "I'm Rachel Wertheim."

The woman's easy familiarity with me took me aback.

"Get in the back seat, my boy!" said Papa.

I didn't move. Papa grabbed my arm and motioned to the back seat.

"Let him sit in front. I don't mind, Alfie," the woman said.

I burst out laughing and remained motionless in my passenger seat. *Alfie?* Papa had nicknames in various languages—Al, Fred, Freddo, Fareed, Fritz, and others—but Alfie was not among them. *Alfie?*

"It's all right, Alfie," Mrs. Wertheim repeated.

"No, Rachel! I want him to sit in the back seat."

"All right, *Alfie*, you win!" I said and got out of the car, a wide fake smile spread from ear to ear.

Papa was not pleased. If he was wondering why I was being so rude, he wasn't alone. I couldn't fathom why I so disliked that woman!

At the Mena House, one of our favorite tables was available. I loved it because it was close to a large bay window that offered a breathtaking view of the Great Pyramid. All three pyramids had the magical effect of making me feel safe and protected as they stood tall above the sand in perfect stillness. They pointed to eternity, impervious to the chaos beneath their stones. This time, though, the trifling chatter between my father and his new conquest was casting a shadow over my emotional bond with the monuments I'd adored from the first time I'd laid eyes upon them.

It must have been the tenth time I had heard Papa tell a new potential conquest the story of the Mena House from its humble beginning as Khedive Ismail's hunting lodge to the height of its glory when it hosted Empress Eugénie of France. It had always amused me, but not this time.

"Really?" said Rachel Wertheim. "The Empress came to the Mena House?"

"Yes. She came in 1869 for the opening of the Suez Canal, representing her husband, Napoleon the Third. Of course, the Khedive enlarged the hunting lodge and turned it into a palace for her sake. He even built that large Avenue of the pyramids to spare her the sight of some of the ugliest slums of Cairo."

"How gallant!" she purred.

I rolled my eyes toward the ceiling. Papa gave me a nasty look and moved on to the story of the Britishers who bought the lodge from the khedive and transformed it into a luxury hotel named after King Menes of Memphis. During the war, around 1943, there was a conference with Franklin Roosevelt, Winston Churchill, Chiang Kai-shek, and their staff, here on these grounds. They turned the Mena House into a fortress for the occasion. There was even a Royal Air Force observation post up there," he said, pointing toward the Great Pyramid.

"Alfie," I asked. "Don't forget the story of Agatha Christie."

"What story is that?" he asked, surprised.

"You know, the story about *Death on the Nile*."

He shook his head. "I don't remember that story, so why don't you tell it, son?"

"Agatha Christie wrote *Death on the Nile* right in the lounge of this hotel," I said. "There's a rumor that she shot a servant in the head and watched him die, just to make the murder scene realistic. That's what makes her such a great writer!"

"Pay him no mind!" Papa interjected, a falsely amused smile on his lips. "This boy has a vivid imagination and a nasty sense of humor. Agatha Christie did write her book here, but no one was killed."

"That's reassuring!" Mrs. Wertheim simpered.

God, she is beautiful, I thought, but so vapid! How could my father be enamored of a woman so dull-witted and so uninspiring? I broke the silence by looking at my watch. "Time to ride the camels, no?"

La Wertheim, as I now called her silently, looked uneasy and looked at my father.

"Are you up for it, Rachel?" he asked.

"Yes, Alfie," she said, looking terribly apprehensive.

***

We stepped onto the hot sand. Beneath the Great Pyramid, a group of camel and horse drivers, their animals, and multilingual dragomen were awaiting tourists. One of the dragomans came toward us, speaking French. Papa's response in fluent Arabic told him we weren't tourists, and he retreated.

A superb white dromedary drew my attention. Before I could declare my choice, the camel driver said, "Good choice! Her name is Leila," he said. "Not the cheapest, but the best!"

"We'll go elsewhere," said Papa, again flaunting his perfect baladi Arabic to let him know that we were not tourists. Most vendors had different rates for non-Egyptians, shamelessly charging white tourists and sheikhs from the Gulf's oil-rich kingdoms exorbitant fees.

"For you, ya khawaga, ya balash!—it costs nothing, sir, it's free!" the camel driver would say, opening the bargaining ritual, even though both parties already knew their settling price. Once they agreed, Papa picked a tame sandy grey camel for La Wertheim and a dark near-black one for himself. I kept Leila.

The camel driver, whose name was Muneer, helped Mrs. Wertheim get on the saddle. Papa held her hand while the camel stood on its hind legs first. La Wertheim let out a scream. "Lean back, Rachel!" Papa instructed. She yelled again when the camel stood on its front legs. She was too high up to hold Papa's hand, and she held on to her saddle with all her strength while mumbling prayers to God and mother, "Ya rab! Ya mama!"

I bit my lips to contain my laughter. Atop the camel, the woman seemed terrified, yet she was making a valiant effort to please Papa. I had a fleeting pang of guilt as I climbed on my camel. Muneer moved to help me, but I gestured him away. I'd ridden camels for a long time, and it was second-nature to lean along with the camel's movements rather than against it—first back as the camel raised its butt, then forward when the camel rocked its front legs and settled in its upright position. It was the ritual of bonding with the animal before embarking on a journey.

We set out toward the Sphinx. My white dromedary, Leila, was quick and responsive. I stroked her neck with my right foot, and she answered with a gentle roar and a quicker pace. "Yalla, ya Leila," I whispered to her as I yanked the bridle to veer away from the group. The camel driver rode after me, but I waved him away and pointed to La Wertheim who still look terrified. Leila trotted faster toward the open desert, cutting through the scorching air, the light thump of her hooves on the soft sand gently punctuating the silence of the desert. It was a silence, a stillness and a weightlessness that reached deep into my soul.

On my frequent camel rides, I would often daydream of escaping from Egypt, retracing in reverse the footsteps of Abraham and Joseph when they both came into Egypt, the former to escape famine, and the latter as a slave in this land. With a map and a good compass, it would take forty days, I guessed, not the biblical forty years. I wouldn't have to cross the Red Sea, as my ancestors did. Instead, I would go further north and bypass both the sea and the Suez Canal. The only things I would miss would be pyramids—abandoning them would be like losing a limb.

A shout from Muneer wrenched me out of my reverie. He was galloping toward me, yelling, "Ya khawaga, your baba wants us to go back." He grabbed Leila's bridle and turned her around, making clicking sounds to egg her on. Startled, I slapped his hand with my stick until he let go of the bridle. We returned to camp at a doleful half-trot.

***

"Will you please explain your appalling behavior?" Papa asked after we'd dropped off Mrs. Wertheim at her home. His icy, controlled tone was louder than a shout. "What's going on?"

"What difference does it make? It's not like you give a damn!"

"You owe me an explanation!" Papa said.

"I just don't like this stupid woman acting like she's my mother, calling me 'darling' and 'sweetie' and kissing me and stuff. She's not my mother!"

"That, she's not!" said Papa. "She's much nicer. Besides, any man would be flattered when a pretty woman calls him 'darling' or 'sweetie' and kisses him!"

"I don't know about pretty," I retorted. "My mother is a million times prettier!"

"Beauty is in the eye of the beholder, as the saying goes," said Papa.

"What if the beholder is blind?" I yelled. "My mother is smarter and prettier than all your women put together!"

Most of the time, I chose to ignore Papa's sarcastic remarks about Maman but not this time. I was driven to push back hard.

"Okay, father, maybe she's not ugly, but she's not smart either." I heard the shrillness in my voice and tried to tone down my response without success. Using the Ladino feminine word for bovine or stupid, I said, "Don't you see she's a complete bova?"

I thought it would be funny since Papa often called me "bovo" as a tease. It wasn't funny and it backfired. "Very witty! Hilarious!" His tone was icy cold. "Now take the wax out of your ears and listen carefully, will you?"

I groaned something that sounded like a yes.

"You're my son. I'm happy when you and my friends like each other, but you're free to like or dislike anyone. What you're not free to do is behave like a bully with a misguided sense of superiority!" Poking my shoulder with his extended finger, he added, "You have no rights whatsoever to disrespect and humiliate anyone—man, woman, child or dog!"

Even though I knew I deserved it, the violence in Papa's voice shook me up.

"Sorry," I mumbled.

"You should be! Now I want you to answer a question."

"Okay," I mumbled.

"Who, in your opinion, is the moral giant of the day?" he added. "The mosquito who thinks he's an eagle? Or the butterfly who showed grace and tolerance in the face of that buzzing fool of a mosquito?"

"The butterfly," I answered reluctantly.

"And what will the foolish mosquito do tomorrow?"

"Apologize?"

"Right! You'll write a groveling letter of apology full of sincere and convincing contrition."

"Contrition, all right, but sincere?"

"It's not a good time to be a smartass!"

Our spats always ended up with a joke and a kiss. Not this time. It made me wonder if Rachel Wertheim would be a passing fancy, like so many others—and I feared this time would be different.

***

School started. Like my old lycée, the Collège Saint Jean Baptiste de La Salle, also known as Collège des Frères—the Brothers' College—was in the familiar Bab-el-Louk neighborhood, but it was an altogether different country, a country for which I had no guide, no maps, and no navigation tools.

At La Salle, the men in black cassocks were called *Brothers*, followed by their first name, although there was a *Father* in the lot. If one didn't know their first name, one was to call them Cher Frère—Dear Brother. There seemed to be strict rules of hierarchy among them, but their pecking order wasn't clear to me. Just as I'd struggled at first to use the word "father" to address Father També, I had to make a huge effort to call these black-clad men Brother."

As there were many Jews and Muslims among the newcomers, most of the Brothers made efforts to make us feel welcome in the vast sea of Christianity. We were dispensed with catechism and New Testament classes, but we all had to attend Old Testament class since all three monotheistic religions recognized the Hebrew prophets and kings. There were no classes to study Islam or Judaism as religions

The Brothers ran the school like military barracks, professing no tolerance for tardiness or slovenliness in appearance or speech. Most classes began with the Ave Maria, recited either in Latin or in French, at the whim of the teacher. At the summer camp, I'd never paid much attention to the meaning of the "Ave Maria" prayers, perhaps because I couldn't decipher Father També's Latin rendition. Listening to it in this new environment, recited at a slower pace, every word of the prayer jumped at me.

Sancta Maria mater Dei . . . Sainte Marie, Mère de Dieu . . . Holy Mary, Mother of God . . . For a boy steeped in the stories of the Hebrew Bible, as told by my father, it was a shock to hear that God had a mother named Mary. Even when I finally understood that the prayer did not refer to the God of the Bible but to Jesus, the son of a virgin, it seemed unreal, maybe even sacrilegious for a Jew. The very notion of a God other than Yahweh contradicted the teachings of the Old Testament. Everywhere in the Bible, the Creator unleashes his wrath upon the Jews for worshipping other gods.

I had confusing feelings about the Christian world I was entering. It was dominated by guilt and fear and presented a world in which we were all sinners and a great many of us were bound for Hell. It offered the sinners a simple covenant—it promised the healing of all wounds, the forgiveness of all sins, and even a laisser-passer to Heaven in exchange for total submission to Jesus and to the teachings of the Catholic Church. It was seductive and I was tempted to convert at times, but a chorus of ancestral voices would rise within me and would castigate me for contemplating, even for a second, the sacrilegious notion that there could be a God other than Yahweh.

To my surprise, I liked most of my teachers at La Salle, and particularly Brother Bertrand, who taught classes in history, literature, and Old Testament. He was a short, soft-spoken man whose demeanor was the opposite of Father També's flamboyance, but his classes were just as spellbinding. He taught history as more than a series of chronologies of kingdoms and dynasties; he made it come alive by encompassing politics, religion, literature and arts to form a complete recreation of the world in its time. Just as Father També had turned adventure books into exciting living experiences, Brother Bertrand made events like the fall of Babylon to the Persian Empire feel as though they were happening to us.

I was beginning to enjoy the way the Brothers taught us. I loved the study of rhetoric and oratory, the fine art of honing one's command of language to present ideas and theories persuasively, in writing and in verbal debate. Learning about the opposition between Plato's Academy and Aristotle's Lyceum opened a world of philosophy and politics that captivated my imagination.

The only thing I truly hated about the Brothers' methods was their practice of corporal punishment, in particular the so-called *règle de la règle* which meant the "rule of the ruler." It was a fearsome sentence that consisted of lashing the palms of the wrongdoer's hands, alternating the sharp and the flat edges of the ruler, until a confession or an act of attrition was obtained. Among the lesser forms of punishment, the most used was *le piquet* in which the accused was made to stand facing the wall in the corner of the classroom for long periods of time—an exhausting position made all the more painful because the offender wasn't allowed to touch or rest against the wall when he lost his balance. I couldn't reconcile these barbaric practices with the high-level intellectual pursuits of the Brothers' institution.

When I brought back a few good grades, Papa would exclaim, "Hallelujah!" Poking my cranium, he would add, "Three cheers for the good Brothers! I didn't think anyone could drum a little sense into this kavesa dura of yours!"

"Me? Pig-headed? You have the wrong boy!"

***

In this new school, as in my previous ones, I grappled with my ineptitude in mathematics, algebra and the sciences, but I compensated by getting excellent grades in literature, history, geography, and Bible studies. In my old secular school, there were no Bible classes, but the Old Testament classes at La Salle were a gift from heaven because I knew I would do well. I'd been steeped in Bible stories since my earlier childhood. My father venerated the Old Testament, both as the greatest history book and as the greatest epic novel ever written. Whenever I would point to its implausibilities, Papa would dismiss them as poetic license, just as he did with the farfetched tales of Homer's epic poems. That fluency afforded me excellent grades which minimized my lousy grades in science and enhanced my overall scores.

But things fell apart when Brother Bertrand fell ill and was sent to France for treatment. As he taught history, literature, and Old Testament, the Brothers appointed three teachers to replace him.

The new teacher for the Old Testament was the opposite of his predecessor. It was *mapalá* as Nona would say in Ladino, a word which meant misfortune, disaster and ruin.

While Brother Bertrand was eloquent, Brother Norbert, a tall and beefy man with bulldog jowls, was dull and uninspiring. There wasn't a scintilla of humor in his long windy speeches full of loud platitudes.

I was horrified by the way the good Brother spoke about Jews. He called them *Israelites* rather than plain Jews and described them as a prehistoric race whose only reason for being had been to herald the advent of the son of God. He took great pleasure in excoriating the foibles and trespasses of the Israelites—from the murder of Abel by Cain to the fall of Sodom and Gomorrah, from King David's killing of Bathsheba's husband, Uriah, to King Solomon's dalliances with foreign women. He was careful to avoid attacks on Judaism as a religion, but his animus was blatant enough to fill me with anxiety. Until that moment, I had only been exposed to political antisemitism, the Jew-hating speeches of the crowds on the street or the policeman who hit me on Fuad Avenue, but I'd never seen such hatred emanating from people like Brother Norbert—white Europeans without a known political agenda.

After hearing too many harangues disguised as historical details, I'd had enough. I raised my hand and asked, "Why did Jesus Christ convert to Christianity?" I asked.

Brother Norbert gave me a look of utter disbelief. "Come again?"

"I'm asking how the son of a Jewish carpenter became a Christian God."

"You think you're clever, don't you!?" yelled Brother Norbert. Eyes glaring, his face, already covered with rosacea, had turned into a darker shade of crimson. He yelled, "How dare you show such disrespect?"

"No disrespect, sir!" I protested. "I just want to know."

"The New Testament, and therefore Jesus Christ, is not within the purview of this class," he said, looking at me, "but I'll say this. It is not the Lord Jesus who abandoned the

Israelites. Rather it was the Israelites who turned on him and his preachings before crucifying him!"

I raised my hand again and blurted, "I thought the Romans crucified Jesus!"

"Silence!" he barked. Turning to the other pupils, Brother Norbert said, "Again, boys, this is beyond the scope of this class! The crucifixion and its ramifications belong in your New Testament class." He pointed at me, "To which you're not invited."

Turning to the rest of the class, he added, "If you can't wait to brighten your horizons on the matter, read the Gospel according to John!" He paused. "Of course it's not mandatory for the non-Christians among you."

My father didn't have a copy of the New Testament, so I stopped at Monsieur Michel's bookstore and bought one in a French annotated version. As Brother Norbert had suggested, I read John's Gospel first, then the rest of the Gospels. The apostle John was the harshest in the condemnation of the Jews, calling their leaders the "children of the devil" for rejecting Jesus as the Messiah.

To my surprise, I liked Jesus, the Christ. I'd never known much about him before joining Father També's summer camp, and even there the good Jesuit didn't talk much about him to non-Christians for fear of appearing to be proselytizing. Now, reading the Gospels, I saw him as an itinerant rabbi, practicing his ministry and gathering disciples along the way throughout Galilee and Judea. I didn't understand why the high priests of Israel had rejected him rather than accept him as a new prophet, maybe even as the Messiah. His preachings, as presented in the Gospels, were in keeping with the Jewish prophets who'd preceded him. They'd all advocated obedience to the Lord, righteousness, goodwill, kindness and all forms of love. What made the high priests think Jesus was subversive? Perhaps if they had accepted Jesus as the Messiah, the Temple might still be standing tall in Jerusalem, and the world would have been spared twenty centuries of persecution and destruction.

My love affair with Jesus took a bad turn at the Resurrection and the Ascension. Prophet, Messiah, why not, but son of God? A god himself? Every fiber of my body and soul rejected the notion that there could a God other than the great white-bearded Lord in the sky.

***

What came through in his classes was Brother Norbert's deep belief that the Jews were guilty of the martyrdom of Christ. He was all but subtle. He would read from a list of Old Testament predictions of Jesus and the coming of the Messiah, the books of Genesis, Isaiah, Mica, Hosea, and others, pointing out that these prophecies were spoken by Israelites, an implication that the entire Jewish population had rejected the vision of their own prophets. Whenever Brother Norbert spoke of the Jews, he would look in my direction, as if daring me to contradict him or protest. I did my best to appear indifferent to his taunts.

After goading me for several few weeks, Brother Norbert finally got to me. As I heard him quote another Old Testament prediction of the coming of the Messiah, I couldn't stop an instinctive shrug of the shoulders and a roll of the eyes. Brother Norbert crossed his arms. "New pearls of wisdom to share with us, young man?"

"There's a contradiction between the two quotes," I said. "In the Book of Samuel, it says that the Messiah will be the son of David, but the Book of Isaiah affirms the Messiah will be the son of God."

"Is there a question here?" asked Brother Norbert.

"Yes," I blurted out. "Is the Messiah the son of David or the son of God? Maybe they're one and the same—or were there two different Messiahs?"

A shroud of deadly silence fell over the classroom.

"This is not a question! This is blasphemy!" Brother Norbert roared. "I've had it with you!"

He came down from the podium, holding the long wooden ruler he often used as a pointer.

"It's time for the rule of the ruler! Extend your hand!" he barked.

He hit my knuckles with the ruler until I extended my left arm in the position he wanted, my palm facing upward. "You must learn never to offend the Lord again!" he yelled.

It was my first encounter with corporal punishment. I'd seen some Brothers inflicting it on unruly students, but I'd been spared so far. The first strike stunned me. Brother Norbert smiled and hit me harder, and again, counting the blows, "Two for blasphemy, one for insolence, one for effrontery!"

He stopped after a few strikes, but he ordered me to keep my arm extended. When it became so painful that I couldn't sustain the position, Brother Norbert would force my arms back to place with a few thumps from beneath, wait quietly, then strike again without a warning.

"Any more blasphemous questions, little miscreant?"

For a fleeting moment, my mind slipped out of my body. Like a fly on the ceiling, I could observe the scene in all its grotesque ugliness—a fat grown man using a school implement as a weapon on a defenseless youth. A part of me was tempted to confess anything to end the ordeal, but the instinct to resist was stronger. I understood that the purpose of the exercise extended beyond physical punishment. It was meant to break my spirit. I could not, would not, give in—I knew the damage to my soul would be greater than scars on my flesh.

As the strikes got harder and more sustained, tears of pain gathered in the corners of my eyes, and a few drops of blood peered out of my fingers, but the pain only fueled my resolve to resist.

"Just confess your misdeeds! Show contrition!" Brother Norbert whispered, almost begging. "I have no wish to hurt you."

"Jews don't practice confession, Mr. Norbert."

More blood oozed out of my hand. Brother Norbert relented and used only the flat side of the ruler, striking softer blows. I could read his thoughts as though they were mine. The good Brother feared he might have overstepped his mandate. If I were seriously injured, he might suffer consequences. Abruptly, he lowered his arm and gently pushed mine downward. I hardened my jaw to avoid showing relief or defiance. Looking away, Brother Norbert barked, "Go to the corner and face the wall! Now!"

An oppressive silence set in, broken only by the faint sound of a furious pen scratching paper. A few heavy footsteps, then Brother Norbert shoved a sealed envelope under my nose and yelled, "Take this to the Brother Principal's office! Post-haste!"

***

The Brother Principal read the note and asked to hear my side of the story. He listened quietly and thought for a long time before giving me his verdict—a seven-day suspension to begin immediately. I was so stunned I couldn't say a word.

"You may think it's too harsh," the Brother Principal said, "but a lesser punishment would be akin to rewarding rebelliousness and insolence. I don't doubt you started out with good intentions, but the best intentions can go awry without a dose of humility. You turned your question into a defiant debate with your teacher. That's arrogance to the extreme!"

Before I could protest, the Brother Principal made a commanding gesture to silence me. "Enough said. Before you go home, stop by the infirmary and have Sister Elise look at your hand."

I bypassed the infirmary and rushed home. Papa had left a note saying that he'd be out for the evening. It was a relief. I needed solitude. My swollen hand was hurting, but the injury to my spirit cut far deeper.

I wished I could talk to Father També. Throughout the summer, under his influence, I had gathered my old grievances and discontents, thrown them in a funeral pyre, and put them to the torch. I had returned to Cairo renewed, reconciled with the world, and fueled with hope and energy. Now, that foundation was crumbling. I felt as though the embers from the funeral pyre had not fully died down, and once again, anger and rebellion were stoking the fire. I didn't know whether I had the will or the power to extinguish this new blaze.

Papa took my suspension with equanimity. Was it by solidarity with me or because La Wertheim was in his life and my travails no longer mattered? Either way, I looked forward to seven days of reading and hanging out with my friends.

***

When I first stepped into Brother Norbert's classroom after my suspension, he flashed a triumphant smile and said, "I see the prodigal son has returned. Truly repentant, I hope!"

I didn't know who the prodigal son was, and I didn't care. I answered with a noncommittal groan and sat at my desk, determined to stay out of the evil Brother's gunsight for the rest of the school year.

A few days before spring break, another change of guard took place. Brother Zachary, our kindly Arabic teacher, announced that he was going home to his native Lebanon to tend to family matters. I was disappointed. Like Father També, Brother Zachary seemed to understand my learning difficulties, and he would help me rather than excoriate me for my mistakes. I hoped that his replacement would be just as kind and helpful.

In his last day at La Salle, Brother Zachary came into the classroom with a younger man and introduced him as Anwar Kamal, the teacher who would take over after the holidays.

The newcomer wore European-style clothes, and in his first address to the class he stated that he was Muslim and should not be called Brother Anwar, but Ostáz Kamal. I wondered why the Brothers had selected a secular Muslim rather than another Christian Arab as our new teacher.

Ostáz Kamal spoke to the class about the profound cultural changes that were sweeping the heartland since the revolution, stressing the need to expand our knowledge of Egyptian literature and history. His jet-black eyes were full of both fire and ice. He spoke with a fervor and an intensity that reminded me of Gamal Abdel Nasser's speeches on the radio. My body stuttered with anxiety. If Ostáz Kamal proved to be a nationalistic zealot like Brother Norbert was a religious zealot, I would be in harm's way in a short time.

Tahrir Square in the 1950s

Father, Mother, and Aunt Lily

Paternal Grandfather

Paternal Grandmother

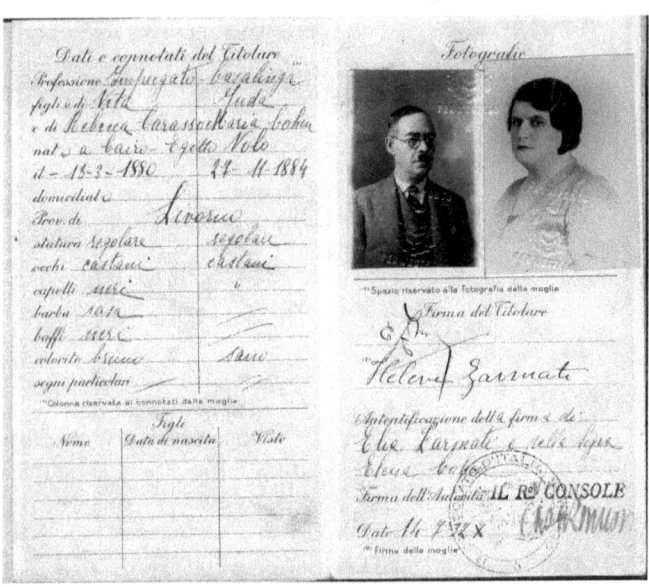

ID Card Paternal Grandparents

Uncle Leon & Grandmother

Maternal Family Picnic

Maternal Family & Father at Beach

Father as a Young Man

Mother as a Young Woman

Father & Son in Alexandria

Mother & Son on Felluca in Alexandria

EZ on Grandmother's Rooftop

EZ & Cousins

Father & Calista - son's favorite girlfriend

Aunt Aïda & husband Khadr Bey

LaSalle College commencement 1959 - EZ, 2nd row, 3rd from left

CHAPTER 11

Winter of 1958

Easter break was an opportunity to return to the carefree camaraderie of my band of brothers. Just before the break, JP's parents had gone to Paris and returned with piles of new records—singles, albums, and the new Extended Play 45 rpm discs which contained two songs per side. The new bands that kept popping up from America bore odd and whimsical names like the Marvelettes, the Contours, the Shirelles, the Four Preps, and the Tune Weavers. In France too, singers of a new generation were rising, and the Egyptian press took pride in noting that many of the new French musical stars were born in Egypt—Dalida, Richard Anthony, Claude François, and Georges Moustaki. The magazines failed to mention that they were Egyptian Christians and Jews who had fled their native country because they had no future there.

We didn't often speak of politics in my multicultural, multi-faith, multi-everything group of friends. We didn't have to. We knew that many of us were on the verge of exile, that we would be dispersed among the various countries that would give us shelter, and that we might never be together again. All that mattered was having fun before the deluge—and fun meant shrinking our conversation to the two most important topics, girls and rock 'n' roll.

As always, Quentin had juicy stories about his sexual adventures. He described with relish the night he had sex with two girls at the same time when his father was on a diplomatic visit to Denmark. He loved Scandinavian girls because they were less prudish than European lassies, and he hated that Egyptian girls didn't put out. He thought Egypt was a sexual desert. I objected that there was a lot of explicit sex in the Arabian Nights stories, but Quentin dismissed it as "sex on paper."

I asked him to elaborate on his experiences with "real sex, not paper sex" but he demurred. "A true gentleman never divulges a lady's secrets," he answered. I didn't want to embarrass him, so I didn't share the obvious—we were all long on fantasies and short on reality, and truth mattered not at all when it came to love and sex.

***

I saw little of my father during Easter break. When he invited me to outings with La Wertheim, I would plead the need to study or plans with my friends. It did not fool Papa, but he let it go. In time, Papa and I established a tacit pact—he wouldn't ask me to join them except for special occasions like the high holidays, and I would be on my best behavior.

The special occasion was the Passover Seder, which was hosted by Papa's friends, the Moreno family. Rachel Wertheim was included in the invitation. Papa's friends seem delighted that, after years of failed matchmaking, he was finally involved in a lasting relationship, and they treated the couple as though they were on the verge of marriage.

Throughout the seder, I observed Papa and Rachel with as much objectivity as I could muster. I had to admit that Rachel Wertheim had a soothing effect on my father. She was beautiful and affectionate, and her even-tempered demeanor seemed to lighten his spirit. I didn't know what to make of the relationship. My father didn't seem to be madly in love, but he was far more serene than he'd ever been. I wished I could like her, but it wasn't easy. Her perpetual smile of bovine contentment and the platitudes that came out of her mouth made me cringe. Why, I wondered, not for the first time, had God created such a beautiful woman and denied her a good measure of intelligence? It seemed like a cruel joke.

The next day, I took a long walk along the Nile. I was despondent. I feared that my father's relationship with Rachel Wertheim was becoming permanent, and that prospect was disturbing. I didn't want a stepmother. I couldn't even imagine living with my own mother. My one-day-a-week relationship with my mother—some love and a lot of freedom—was all I wanted.

Along the Corniche, I passed an elegant woman who left a whiff of familiar perfume in her wake. It had an aroma of orange flower that took me back to distant and opaque memories. Slivers of images flashed through my mind like fireflies in the night, forming the fuzzy silhouette of a young woman lulling a baby to sleep. Was I the baby? Was the woman my mother? My beloved Tante Toto? It was a powerful visceral bond, and I had a pang of longing for that unknown young mother. Moments later I felt an urgent need to see my own mother. I'd never felt that urgency before, and I kept walking because I didn't want to give in to that impulse. Then I lost control. Without thinking, I turned around and walked in the opposite direction. I crossed Tahrir Square and walked along the Corniche for a few yards, then stopped abruptly. When I emerged from my half-conscious state, I was standing across the way from my mother's building, wondering whether to go inside or run away.

A visit to my mother's abode was a rare occurrence. Since I had not been allowed to fraternize with Maman's husband or her children, I only saw her in restaurants, film theaters, and museums. I was content with this arrangement because outside activities reduced the time my mother would spend on long tirades against my father which turned our visits into an ordeal. It was easier to be with my father because, aside from some snide remarks about my mother, he barely acknowledged her existence. Caught between the maternal fury and the paternal silence, I had withdrawn into a no-man's-land in which I could ignore their permanent feud.

Now, standing in front of my mother's home, I was at a crossroads. If I went up and saw Maman and her husband, I would be meeting with my father's disapproval. If I walked away, I would be rejecting my mother once again, and I would be suppressing the impulse that had led to the very place where I stood. The old rules were unfair, and I could no longer accept them.

I crossed the street and walked into Maman's apartment building.

The new doorman didn't know me. When I told him where I was going, his look of utter surprise made it obvious he didn't know the lady on the top floor had another son. I was both amused and saddened by the evidence that I was as peripheral in my mother's daily life as she was in mine.

The *bawab* took me to the top floor and pointed to her door. I knocked. He remained in the elevator like a watchdog anticipating trouble. A maid opened the door. Before she said a word, my mother appeared right behind her. She wasn't surprised at all. She smiled as though she had been expecting me, and she held me in a tight embrace. All I could hear were my mother's muffled sobs over the receding creaks of the wooden elevator on its way down.

***

Throughout the rest of Easter break, I ignored Papa's interdiction and paid several visits to my mother. I'd only known her as the beautiful and fashionable woman who paraded me around town on our Saturday outings, and I slowly discovered a different woman. She was still elegant, but she wore less makeup, and she went without the shield of jewelry and other regalia—and, most of all, she was so busy with her toddler that she had less time for her usual obsessive chatter about my father's cruelty toward her. It was odd but pleasant to see her as the materfamilias, and occasionally I felt a pang of regret for the life I might have had if she'd been my full-time mother. But such thoughts were quickly reversed by the fear of being smothered by her love. Everything about my mother was excessive and often overwhelming.

At first, I was standoffish with Albert. I'd wondered for years what his part in my parents' divorce might have been, but my grudges vanished when I understood that, if my parents had remained together, their marriage would have been a greater nightmare than their divorce. Maman's second marriage seemed to be more harmonious.

In time, Albert's kindness and thoughtfulness won me over, and I opened up to his children. Simone, the eldest child, was a few years older than I was, and she introduced me to the French Impressionists' paintings that figured in her impressive art books. Her brother Sidney was too young to be my friend, but we were nice to each other, and I stopped cringing when Maman called Sami *my little brother*. It was still odd to be in the environment of her *other* life. Sometimes I felt like an imposter, an actor playing the role of the son—but I also felt that our estrangement was mending in slow increments.

***

A gift from my mother led to a confrontation with my father. It was a membership to the Gezira Sporting Club. Maman had simply added my name to the list of her children when she renewed her own membership. I thought it was a nice gesture, and I accepted it with gratitude.

I never expected Papa would order me to reject the gift. I asked for his reasons, and he said all I needed to know what that he had good reasons. I demanded more specifics. He said Maman's gift, like everything *she* did, was a Trojan horse, a way to increase her nefarious influence on me. I asked for examples of her bad influence. He said I was too young to understand. I yelled that I was old enough to recognize a dictatorial bully when I saw one. He got angrier and tore up my membership card, mumbling I would thank him someday. I said I would get the card replaced and use it with or without his permission.

The Gezira Sporting Club was a prestigious sporting facility located on the island of Zamalek, adjoining the west bank of the Nile between downtown and the Giza plateau. It was home to international championship tournaments in every imaginable sport, particularly tennis and horse racing. I knew it well because both Papa and Oncle Léon had been members at an earlier time. Papa had let our membership expire after the Suez war because he believed we were on the brink of departure—but that was two years earlier, and we were still on that same brink. I was happy to return to the Club because many of my friends had remained members.

In the following argument with Papa, he repeated that I was too young to understand. I let out a howl of frustration and yelled, "I am old enough to know that you're a dictator, a Jewish Nasser! I'm old enough to resist tyranny! So I'll be going to the club to be with my friends! And, about my mother, if you stop me from seeing her and her family, I will not see your sharmoota anymore!"

I hadn't intended to call La Wertheim a whore, but I couldn't control my rage, and I said it almost unwittingly. I should have apologized, but I couldn't because I'd be losing ground in my efforts to assert myself. Papa was just as enraged as I was.

"Go to your room!" Papa ordered.

"I'll go wherever I want and whenever I want!" I opened the door, then turned back and said what I'd wanted to say for most of my life, "I hate you and my mother *both* for poisoning my life from my first day on this crappy earth! Allez au diable, tous les deux! To Hell, both of you!"

Shaking, I ran to my room, picked up my piggy bank and a book, and stormed out of the hotel.

***

The sky was darkening, and I had nowhere to go. I pondered my next move while circling the massive granite pillar at the center of Midan el-Tahrir. I didn't want to go to my mother because getting her in the middle would make things worse. I couldn't remember JP's telephone number, and I feared that going to his house would cause his parents to call my father. I walked through the streets aimlessly, praying for a solution to my troubles.

As I walked, I tried to devise a way to leave Egypt by myself and go to France. For inspiration, I tried to remember the plot of all the adventure novels I'd read. Every scenario included finding my way to Alexandria and stowing away on a ship bound for Marseille. I would also need the layout of a typical cargo ship, so I'd know where to hide. I wondered if JP could help. His father owned a fleet of ships that ferried tourists to Luxor and Aswan. I hoped he also owned a cargo ship or two.

What would happen if I were caught? Would the captain allow me to work for my keep—or did that happen only in the movies? Would I be arrested on arrival? So many unknowns!

Was I delusional or was this plan viable? It was frightening and exhilarating all at once.

I headed toward JP's house in Garden City, hoping that his parents would be out for the night as they often went to theaters and concerts. The bawab told me that the *khawaga* was at home. I didn't know if he meant the father or the son, and I rang the bell with some apprehension. JP opened the door. His parents were out, and the servants had retired for the night. I let out a sigh of relief and told JP that I was starving.

"Easy fix!" he said. "Kitchen's all yours!"

We raided the refrigerator and feasted on breads, cheeses, cold cuts, cookies and chocolate ice-cream. His attention perked up when I said I'd run away from home and I was going to France. He gave me a you're-out-of-your-mind look, but I ignored it. "I need your help," I said.

"Me? Help? How?"

"I need you to get me a list of the next cargo ships bound for Marseille."

"Not too difficult. What else?"

"After I decide which ship is best, maybe you can find a floor plan or something to help me find hiding places."

"Unlikely, but you never know. I'll ask my father. I'll have to figure out a way to do it and avoid suspicion."

We talked about my plan in detail in an effort to anticipate pitfalls and perils. How to sneak onto the ship, where to hide, how to find food and go to the bathroom, what to do if I were caught, and finally where to live and support myself if I made it to Paris.

Playing devil's advocate, JP said, "You might be arrested and jailed for illegal entry, then what?"

"I would ask for political asylum. I think it would be justified because we are persecuted."

"What if they jail you for illegal entry!" JP asked.

"Que sera sera! I thought about that. They might let me go because I'm a crazy teenager—or I'll go to jail, do my time and move on. At least I'll be free! No parents at war with each other! No Egypt-Israel war either! And no persecutions! I'm ready! You'll come to visit in Paris. I'll live in Montparnasse like Modigliani in *Montparnasse 19!*"

"That's a movie, not real life. Dream on!" he chortled.

"Look, this is probably a harebrained plan, but what choice do I have? I'm dying here."

He nodded and said, "I'm skeptical, but I'll help if I can."

"All I need is the layout of a damn ship!"

"How will I get to you?"

"General delivery at the main post office in Alexandria."

"All right. Do you have enough money?

"I have twenty pounds and change."

"Let me see what I can do!" JP emptied his pockets, then he went through his house in search of cash. After opening drawers in most rooms, he found thirty-five Egyptian pounds and a small jar full of piasters. With his gift and my savings, I felt like a millionaire. I got up to leave.

"You can sleep here if you want," JP said. "My parents won't mind."

"Thanks, but no. I don't want to raise suspicions. I'll sleep at the train station."

As we shook hands, JP said, "Maybe we'll be in Paris at the same time someday."

"Next Year in Paris!" I said. It sounded like a prayer.

It was too early to go to the train station, and I wanted to fine-tune my insane plan. I walked in the balmy Cairo night. The Nile sparkled in the semi-darkness, and the opulent mansions and apartment buildings shone like crystals in the velvety night. Looking at the thousands of scintillating bulbs in hundreds of windows, I thought that if I had a *malleem* for every one of these lights, I could pay for a first-class passage to Marseille and feed all the beggars of Bab el-Hadid, the Cairo central rail Station.

***

Outside the Central Railway Station stood the colossal statue of Ramses II that dominated Cairo. It was another symbol of pharaonic Egypt, along with the pyramids of Giza. The towering statue had been moved from Memphis to Cairo after the revolution.

Bab el Hadid never slept. Day and night, it was a cauldron of frantic activity with honking taxicabs loading and unloading people and goods; porters pushing carts piled sky-high with luggage, shouting their way through the crowd, and rushing back to greet the arriving multitudes. Outside, innumerable street urchins begged for a coin and inside Nubian peddlers chanted their wares. Bab el Hadid was Paradise, Purgatory and Inferno rolled into one prodigious crucible of humanity.

I stared at the impassive face of Ramses the Great, towering over the swarming city, and wondered if he would be proud of what had become of his kingdom. Perhaps the granite colossus had ceased to care; he had left the Valley of Man centuries ago. "Goodbye, King of Kings," I whispered. "I will remember you with fondness."

The ticket counters were closed while a squad of men swept the vast floor. Since I couldn't buy my ticket to Alexandria, I sat on a bench and closed my eyes for a moment.

When I reopened them, a man in uniform was tapping on my shoulder, asking me if I were lost. I said no; I was just on my way to Alexandria. He asked to see my ticket. I said I hadn't bought it yet. He asked to see my fare money. I put my hand in my pocket to retrieve my stash, but my pockets were empty. I was incredulous—a thief had picked my pockets while I slept!

The Railway policeman laughed at my story, pulled me by the elbow and dragged me to an office while I vituperated against the thief.

"Give me your parents' telephone number!" he ordered.

"I don't have parents," I said. "I'm an orphan."

It felt like a repeat performance of my encounter with a policeman at the Maadi train station. Had that been a rehearsal for this situation?

"Who do you live with?" he insisted.

"I live alone," I answered. "But I'm on my way to be with my uncle in Alexandria."

"You don't have any money to go to Alexandria," he glowered.

"I know! Somebody stole my money! I'll go home and get some more!"

"Wanna malli eh!" he grunted. "What do I care? If you cannot prove who you are, you'll stay here!" He left, locking the door behind him. He came back several times throughout the day. With every return visit, I said I was hungry; each time, he poured a cup of water from a clay jar and handed it to me. "Show me your money, and I'll bring you the best food in Cairo!" he would say before he would leave, slamming the door with all his might.

In the evening, I surrendered. In less than an hour, Papa was at the door.

There was a deadly silence during the short drive home. Papa had looked worried when the policeman had unlocked the office, but once he ascertained that I'd suffered no harm, he stopped talking to me or even looking at me.

It's only when he parked the car that he asked in a low voice, "Would you rather live with your mother?"

I shook my head and said, "No! Absolutely not!"

Papa made a slight gesture to signify he wanted to hear more.

"All I want is to be left alone," I continued. "I want to go to the Gezira club with my friends and have a life without being torn between you and my mother every time." I couldn't hold in my tears. "You two don't have to be friends, but you can be nice enough for my sake. If Jews and Arabs could end a war, why can't you two?"

Without a word, Papa put his hand on my head, as though he were blessing me, and nodded. I didn't know whether it meant consent or just understanding, but at least it was neither rejection nor denial. When he nodded for the second time, I noticed a lone teardrop fighting gravity at the corner of his eye.

***

School resumed, and I attended my first class with Ostáz Kamal, my new Arabic teacher.

Things didn't go well from the start. When our previous teacher, Brother Zachary, taught us the high form of Arabic, he would not hesitate to speak in the colloquial language of the street or even in French if he thought it necessary. Ostáz Kamal only spoke the classical form of Arabic.

It was anathema to me. I could speak colloquial Arabic with ease, and I could read and write Arabic script, but I lacked the grammar and vocabulary to be fluent in classical Arabic. Ostáz Kamal didn't tolerate the lesser forms of Arabic.

At first, Ostáz Kamal was rather patient with me, but it didn't last long. He didn't seem to understand that I could not possibly achieve the proficiency he expected because I lacked the proper foundation in the Arabic language. I was a product of the pre-revolution system of education in French schools which treated Arabic as a third language. I didn't know if Ostáz Kamal was aware of that history, or if he simply didn't care, but the atmosphere in his classroom quickly became unbearable. When he scolded me or called me lazy, using many synonyms of sloth in his vast Arabic vocabulary, I responded with defiance and open resistance—which led to the inevitable corporal punishment.

Ostáz Kamal's variation on the rule of the ruler turned the penalty into a game of speed and surprise. He manned the straightedge with playful randomness which made it difficult to guess when he would strike the next blow. My reaction was to enrage him by feigning total indifference to the pain he caused.

The first three sessions of the rule of the ruler ended in a stalemate, but on the fourth round I lost control and grabbed the ruler with both hands and yanked it away from Ostáz Kamal.

A deadly silence descended on the classroom. Ostáz Kamal and I stared at one another like two gunfighters in a bad western movie. I felt quite silly holding his ruler, and the sheer absurdity of the moment caused me to giggle hysterically. A silence fell over the classroom as though Ostáz Kamal and my classmates had stopped breathing. Not knowing what to do, I handed the ruler back to Ostáz Kamal.

He wiped it off with his handkerchief and went back to the blackboard, resuming the lesson where he had left off.

I had expected a summons to the Brother Principal's office. It didn't come that day, or the next day, or anytime during the rest of the week. I couldn't fathom why Ostáz Kamal had let it go. For the rest of the term, he graded my homework without comments, harangues, or admonishments. Ostáz Kamal had washed his hands off me. I was relieved, but it was relief mixed with inexplicable sadness.

***

That escapade had a deep effect on the way Papa and I related to one another. I was now a teenager, I was coming into my own, and I was chafing under the rigid rules of yesterday. Papa seemed to understand that he no longer had the power to exercise control over me or over my relationship with my mother, but he still had the power to influence me. I loved him and trusted him, and I was eager to maintain the closeness we'd had since I was born. In turn, the more Papa was showing acceptance of my needs, the more I wanted to please him. I looked inward and examined my behavior and found it wanting. What I saw in that inner mirror was a selfish boy who was controlling and intolerant, just as I thought my father was with me. I had exercised control by rejecting the woman he had invited into his life. I had hurt them both, and I felt guilty.

The change in my life seemed to extend to my mother. My newfound openness to her affections made her realize that her constant grievances were hurting and alienating me, and she could win me over without being the eternal victim. She didn't give up her complaints altogether, but she toned them down sufficiently to allow me to breathe in her company.

I spent the rest of Easter break reading, masturbating, swimming in the pool at the club, and pondering my future. Would I ever reach France and fulfill my destiny? Was there a destiny to be had? At night I often I lay awake thinking that the sudden changes in my life were too good to be true. How long would this state of peace last? When would the house of cards come tumbling down?

***

On the morning of my finals, I woke up with a sharp pain in my abdomen. The pain was exhausting, but it was only intermittent and bearable, so I asked Papa to drive me to school.

"What's the matter?" he asked. "A case of severe exam jitters?"

"No," I answered. "I'm just tired, so I want to save my energy for the blasted exams."

As I passed Brother Norbert in the schoolyard, he gave me a sneer of disdain. Evil eye, I thought. I was sure the bastard was praying for my failure, but I was too dog-tired to care. There seemed to be a war between my body and my mind—my brain still sharp and ready for the challenge and my flesh aching and ready to go to sleep.

The first assignment was to write an essay on the influence of Greek and Roman mythology on the French theater during the reign of the Sun King. I tackled the task with gusto, silently thanking my father for his bedtime readings of endless passages of the plays of Racine, Corneille and Molière during my early childhood. I was happy with my work and anticipated to receive a high grade for it. I was almost done when the stabbing pain in my abdomen returned, along with alternating waves of chills and fever. I asked for permission to go to the bathroom, but my legs wouldn't carry me. As I got up, I stumbled, and the lights went out.

When I opened my eyes, I was in a room with glaring whitewashed walls. Both my father and my mother were watching over me. It was such an unexpected sight that I thought I was dead. What else would bring these two people together, standing on either side of my bed, breathing the same air, and looking at me with such sorrow and worry? Was I at the bottom of my open grave? Was it Hell or Purgatory? It was clearly not Heaven because the pain in my groin was unbearable. I struggled to keep my eyes open. I wanted this last moment of my life to last a little longer, but once again the lights went out.

A man dressed in white brought me back to life with gentle slaps on my cheek. My mother was no longer present, but a faint trail of her perfume still hung in the air, affirming that her presence in the room had not been a dream. After the man in white pricked my arm, the pain in my belly diminished and almost vanished, and my body began to float in the ether. Now and then, I would wake up and see a woman, also in white, lifting my bandage and cleaning the blood-stained incision that went from my navel halfway to my crotch.

When I regained consciousness, the surgeon came to examine me and told me I was out of harm's way. He explained I had suffered a ruptured appendix which had caused a nasty reaction called peritonitis. He'd removed the appendix, leaving only the huge red incision, but an infection remained, and I was not ready to go home yet.

Never again did I see my father and my mother in the same room at the same time. They alternated their visits to avoid that possibility. I wondered if the whole thing had just been a hallucination.

A nurse came to change my bandages several times. Between her ministrations and my parental visits, I slept, ate, and slept again. My slumber was visited by erotic dreams, wet and dry—mostly visions of Alice and her prominent breasts. I wanted to masturbate, but I feared it would exacerbate the pain in my abdomen and I resisted the urge. I quickly learned to keep one hand firmly on gut to ward off spasms and convulsions and use the other hand to pleasure myself.

In time I was sent home with instructions to both Papa and me on how to clean the wide ugly red scar that divided my belly into two parts of unequal size.

When I got home, Papa told me that Rachel Wertheim had received her exit visa and transit papers to the Commonwealth of Australia. A few days later, Papa brought Rachel to my room to say goodbye. She was gracious as usual, but she looked sad and defeated, probably heartbroken over the looming separation from Papa. He looked sad too. I was overcome with feelings of guilt and shame for having treated her badly for as long as I did. I hoped she would remember the last months during which I'd been on good behavior for my father's sake.

***

The Brother Principal summoned Papa to La Salle. Since I hadn't completed the finals, he had relied on my previous scores and on my unfinished exam room essay to determine my final results. As expected, my average grades in literature and history were high; in the other matters they were passable, and to my utter disbelief Ostáz Kamal had given me the grade of *Maqbool*, Acceptable, instead of my customary *Daeef* or *Daeef Gedan*, Weak or Very Weak. There was no such surprise with Brother Norbert. He had given me the grade of two out of twenty on Old Testament studies, perhaps because a grade of zero would have been too suspicious.

The Brother Principal told my father his conclusion. He thought that excellence in the humanities trumped mediocrity in sciences and Arabic, and he had given me a conditional pass—a summer of remedial classes in Arabic and Egyptian literature with the tutor of his choice. The Brother Principal dispensed me from Bible tutoring after Papa subtly alluded to my performance before and after the change of teachers. The tutors would set the frequency of the classes. If they gave me a passing mark, I would move up to the next grade. The Brother Principal also said that, fail or pass, I would be transferred to a different campus of the La Salle schools. He gave no explanation for that decision.

"I'm looking forward to a lovely summer of Hebrew and Arabic. Long afternoons with the most pedantic Bar Mitzvah tutor, Moshe, and Arabic with God knows Who—"

A big grin appeared on my father's lips.

"What—!?" I asked.

"*God knows who* is Ostáz Kamal. He's the tutor the Brother Principal has assigned for you during the summer."

"What? How perverse can he be? Why in the world would he pick Kamal of all people—!"

"I asked the Brother Principal that question—a bit more diplomatically of course. He said that Ostáz Kamal has 'shown much benevolence in the face of misconduct' and he thought it would be a good lesson for my wayward son!"

"Benevolence? Almost killing me with a ruler, that's benevolence?"

"Simmer down! We can debate the validity of corporal punishment, but not the facts! You thought Ostáz Kamal hated your Jewish hide, and he ended up saving it instead! You should kiss the ground he walks on!"

"Yuck!"

"Or, at the very least, stop fighting the wind and give your teacher a chance to help you!"

CHAPTER 12

Summer of 1959

Summer break began. I spent the week before the start of my tutoring with Ostáz Kamal alone in my room, reading, masturbating, and feeling sorry for myself. My good friends were in Alexandria or in Ras-el-Bar or at other summer resorts, getting suntans and cruising the beaches for girls while I remained stuck in the scorching heat of Cairo with my Arabic and Hebrew tutors for sole company.

A young American I'd befriended at the Anglo-Swiss went back home, bequeathing me a few books, among them novels by Ernest Hemingway, Ralph Ellison, and Scott Fitzgerald. It was an opportunity to improve my English language skills.

I started with Hemingway's *The Old Man and the Sea*, which I thought would be the most accessible of the lot, but it wasn't an easy read. I didn't identify with the old man and his obsession with the fish, and I didn't care much for boy's worship of Joe DiMaggio, an athlete I'd only heard of because he was or had been married to Marilyn Monroe. I didn't finish it.

I couldn't finish the following book, Ellison's *Invisible Man*. The first few lines of the book hit me like a jab in the gut: "I am an invisible man. I'm invisible, understand, simply because people refuse to see me." It was so powerful I could taste the blood oozing from the narrator's pen. I wasn't familiar with the slang of American Black people, and I couldn't find much in my slang dictionary, so I had to give up at the end of the prologue. I knew that it was an important book, and I vowed to read it in full when I became more fluent in American English.

The Great Gatsby was daunting. I had to consult my encyclopedia to understand the back cover blurb. There were references to times and places I'd never heard of before—the Jazz Age, the Roaring Twenties, the American Dream, speakeasies, bootleggers, and flappers. The lure of these words was irresistible. They promised to unveil an unbridled world of gin and sex, greed and power, and romance and tragedy. Fitzgerald's story of love lost, love regained, and love lost again was enthralling. The image of Gatsby spending his nights staring at the green light on the dock of Daisy's house had a hypnotic quality that stirred deep longings in me. Even with my limited English skills, I recognized the author's limpid prose as the mark of a master stylist.

After reading a few chapters, I ran to Monsieur Michel's bookstore, my favorite on Emad-el-Din Street which had many other booksellers. I loved Monsieur Michel's polyglot kingdom full of books of every known European language. I asked him if a French translation of *The Great Gatsby* existed. Without consulting a catalogue, he led me to a shelf and handed me a French edition entitled *Gatsby le Magnifique.*

I continued to read the book in English, comparing the difficult passages with the translation. It was an illuminating experience. The French version contained a scholarly preface that placed the novel in its context of 1920s America, and there were numerous footnotes clarifying references that I couldn't understand in English. I couldn't fully grasp the notions of American exceptionalism and the American Dream. Didn't all or most nations think of themselves as exceptional? How did this concept come about? The American Dream appeared to cover every aspect of life. The philosophies of freedom, democracy, equality, and fairness were equal in both the American and the

French Revolutions. I remembered my father explaining that they both stemmed from the Age of Enlightenment, and they had inspired one another. Why did the Americans see themselves as more exceptional? How was the American Dream different than the dreams of most nations on the planet?

I wished I had an American friend with whom I could discuss these things.

***

The moment I dreaded had arrived—my first tutoring session with Ostáz Kamal. When I came down to the lobby at the appointed time, Papa and Ostáz Kamal were sitting at a table in the dining room, drinking Turkish coffee and talking. They had completed their financial arrangements, and the teacher had set up a study table at the far end of the room. Papa instructed me to order anything Ostáz Kamal desired from the kitchen and left us.

"We have more work than we have time for," Ostáz Kamal said before outlining the intensive syllabus that awaited us. It encompassed Arabic language written and spoken, and Egyptian literature and history. I quivered at the sheer enormity of the task. Ostáz Kamal noticed it and said, "I looked at your report cards, and I know you can do well when you're motivated. So, are you motivated enough to study hard, or are we both going to waste our time?"

"I will study hard." I said.

"Good! Who are your favorite writers—in any language?" asked Ostáz Kamal.

"Alexandre Dumas who wrote—"

"Of course!" he said. "Who else?"

"Victor Hugo, Emile Zola, Chateaubriand, Stendhal, and in translation Sir Walter Scott, Conan Doyle, Dickens—"

"A fine selection, well balanced between romanticism, lyricism, and realism. No Egyptian writers?" I shook my head. "Did you read any Egyptian books?"

"Yes," I answered, racking my brains to find a title. "*Alf Layla Wa Layla.*"

"Which one?" he asked. "The classic *Thousand and One Nights* or the play *Shaharazad*, written by Tawfiq al-Hakim around 1930?"

I answered with some trepidation, "I read the classic *Thousand and One Nights.*"

"Which one of the three versions is the classic one?" he asked again in a matter-of-fact tone. "The ninth century Arabic translation from the Persian, the twelfth century Egyptian *One Thousand and One Nights*, or the nineteenth-century Syrian version?"

"I didn't know there were that many versions," I said, feeling my face turn red. "I only read it in a French translation."

"At least you're honest. Explain to me why a boy as well read as you are is not interested in the literature of his native country?"

All I could say was, "The lycée I went to didn't have as many classes in Arabic. We studied Arabic language, not Arabic literature or history."

"That was the way before the revolution. I hope you understand that things have changed. There are no more parallel societies with separate schools, separate languages and separate courts. To live in Egypt, you must learn its national language and its literature!"

I nodded my understanding.

"Is there *any* Egyptian writer you've heard about?" I could hear the contained disapproval underneath the words. It didn't bode well.

"Yes, Naguib Mahfouz!"

"What do you know about him?"

"I met him at Uncle Hussein's house!" I answered.

"*Your* uncle Hussein?"

Savoring his look of utter surprise, I added, "Yes, Uncle Hussein el-Shafei. Naguib Mahfouz comes to his parties."

"Hussein el-Shafei of the Free Officers is your uncle?" he asked, still incredulous. "And you met Naguib Mahfouz?"

I said that the writer was a good friend of my mother's and that we often saw him at Groppi's or at the Café Riche. If he noticed my mother, he would bow from his seat, and she would reciprocate, but he never came to our table. He was only sociable at parties. The extent of our connection was shaking hands with my mother at Tante Aïda's parties and exchanging pleasantries. At the two famous cafés we all frequented, I'd observed him for afar. At the Café Riche, the writer was often engaged in animated debates with the people who came to his table, but at Groppi's he was often alone, immersed in a book or a newspaper, oblivious to the world. I spoke in a way that suggested a connection with the famed writer that didn't exist, and Ostáz Kamal's envious look was sweet revenge.

I hadn't forgotten the corporal punishment in his classroom. I was determined not to hold a grudge and to try hard to work with him, but I was on guard. Ostáz Kamal acted as though nothing negative had happened between us, and he asked me if I knew the storied role that Groppi's and the Café Riche had played in both Egyptian revolutions, in 1919 and again in 1952.

I didn't. He said the two watering holes were like the Paris literary cafés before the French revolution. In Cairo, the literary crowd fancied Groppi's while the political intelligentsia preferred the Café Riche, but ultimately both places had seen Egypt revolutionize the Arab world with its advancement in politics, literature, music, science, archeology, and in all forms of art.

"Since you've met Naguib Mahfouz," Ostáz Kamal said, "we will work on his masterpiece, the trilogy *Thulathia al-Qahra*, which includes *Bayn al-Qasrayn*, *Qasr al-Shawq*, and *Al-Sukkariyya*."

I must have looked overwhelmed because Ostáz Kamal repeated the titles, articulating each syllable so I could understand their meanings—*The Cairo Trilogy* comprised of *Between Two Palaces*," *Palace of Desire*, and *Sugar Street*.

"Naguib Mahfouz is our Egyptian Balzac or Charles Dickens," he added. "Maybe it's time for you to read writers of your own heritage!"

I wanted to yell that this was an absurdity. The culture he called my heritage was the very culture that rejected me—and he was asking me to embrace it!? But I remained silent. In his changing country, I was a beggar and not a chooser. I had a fleeting memory of Alice saying that minorities had to eat shit if their rulers demanded it.

Exercising all the restraint I could muster, I just said, "I'm just not fluent enough in Arabic to read an entire novel!"

"Let me be the judge of that!"

"I cannot make up for what I've not learned!"

"Fair enough. If you want to learn, I'm here to help you. Your father told me you're awaiting a visa to join your family in Europe—but until then, without a proper education, you'll face a dismal future in any country. It would be a shame for a bright lad like you!"

Ostáz Kamal's tone of empathy stunned me; I hadn't expected him to show a smidgen of compassion for me. He noticed my surprise and looked me in the eye. In a flash, I saw myself through his eyes, and I didn't like what I was seeing—a precocious and arrogant European-educated kid with a disrespectful attitude toward Egyptian culture. If we traded places, perhaps I would have the urge to beat that obnoxious brat senseless. My defensiveness dropped a notch or two.

"And to look at the bright side," he added, "you might become an authority on Arab literature and teach it someday at the Sorbonne or wherever Allah intends for you to be!"

My guts were in knots. Not a chance, I thought. I was so fed up with life in Egypt that I wanted to forget its existence.

As though he'd read my thoughts, Ostáz Kamal went on, "If you can't accept the new order of things, I will pray that you leave Egypt soon because the jinn are out of the bottle, and nothing can put them back in!"

"I'll do my best!" I said, unsure that I had a best to give.

***

If the American dream truly existed, I was looking at it at the Gezira Sporting Club.

The girl was unmistakably American and thoroughly the stuff of dreams. In her tennis attire, with her soft and shiny golden hair bouncing over her shoulders, her luminescent skin, her eyes full of glee and her buoyant laughter, she was breathtaking.

Maman and I were having lunch at the Lido, the poolside restaurant at the club, and the American girl sat three tables away with a couple who were clearly her parents. The father talked fast, punctuating stretches of words with sips from a martini coupe while the mother inhaled smoke from a long cigarette holder and listened to her husband with an indulgent smile. Whatever the man was saying made his daughter roar with laughter—a distinctive laughter that sounded like the chime of glass marbles shaken in a crystal bowl. I tried to look away, but my eyes kept returning to her. She was everything I'd imagined Fitzgerald's Daisy Buchanan to be. Sadly, I was no Jay Gatsby, and I knew I wouldn't even dare to say hello.

By luck, a trio of my mother's friends came to our table, freeing me from the filial duty of listening to Maman's monologues. The girl caught my gaze and looked back at me, a half-smile on her lips. I turned away, berating myself both for being so obvious and for not sustaining her gaze. I excused myself, saying I was going for a walk, and left my mother in the good care of her friends.

When I returned from my stroll a half-hour later, another group occupied the Americans' table. I was both annoyed and relieved—and then I spotted her. She was standing at the soft-drink fountain by the buffet, with no parents in sight. My feet led me to the buffet of their own volition, and I stood in line behind her, inhaling the scent of suntan oil and chlorine that emanated from her delicate skin. She moved to the side to make room for me at the counter. I smiled and thanked her, but, inexplicably, the words came out in Arabic, "Shukran gazeelan!"

The girl turned toward me with a broad grin that revealed a row of sparkling teeth. "I don't speak Egyptian. Do-you-speak-Eng-glish?" she asked, enunciating each syllable, as though it would cause her words to self-translate.

"A little," I answered in English.

"Oh, good!" She extended her hand. "Hi, I'm Pat O'Keefe from Toledo, Ohio. Who are you?"

"Pato—?" I repeated, feeling mighty stupid.

"Pa-tri-cia-O—" she said, drawing an apostrophe in the air, "—Keefe. But my friends just call me Pat."

I shook her hand a tad too long and introduced myself. We picked up our drinks and stepped away.

"I'm glad you speak English!" she said. "I don't have any friends here. I've only been here two days!"

We sat on a bench, away from the dining area, sipping our lemonade. Up close, I gauged she was about my cousin Lena's age, sixteen, perhaps a little older, and that alone was intimidating because I wasn't quite fourteen. Patricia said her father was in Egypt to oversee the construction of a chain of luxury hotels and that she and her mother had joined him for the summer. She spoke so fast it was hard for me to follow.

"Please, speak a little slower, Mademoiselle Pat!" I said. "My English is not good."

"Oops, I'm sorry, I forget you're a foreigner!"

I couldn't suppress a giggle.

"What?" she asked in a tone of alarm. "What did I say?"

I cleared my throat while I summoned up the right words in English. "With respect, Mademoiselle, you're the foreigner here. I'm the native."

She laughed and turned beet red at the same time. "Oops and oops! Give me three seconds to take my foot out of my mouth, please!"

I'd never heard that expression, but it made me laugh. "I'm sorry if I embarrassed you, Mademoiselle—"

"Nah, don't worry about it, but—" She stopped for a moment and added, "please don't Madmazelle me! Where I come from, nobody says Madmazelle. I'm just Pat!"

I gulped. In my world, nobody ever went from first sight to first-name intimacy so quickly. I knew from the movies that Americans were less formal, and I liked that directness more than our excessively proper behavior, but it was still disconcerting. We continued to talk, or rather she talked and I listened. She spoke about her hometown of Toledo and her school, her friends and their activities. I thought it odd that Americans would name their cities after existing European cities, but Pat explained it was commonplace in her country. "We have New York, New Jersey, New Mexico, and so on. We even have several cities named Memphis in several states," she said.

"Do these people know their cities are named after the capital of the Old Kingdom of Egypt?"

"Some maybe, but the majority? Not sure. Why is it called the 'Old' kingdom?"

I thought I'd impress Pat with a quick history of the dynasties of pharaonic Egypt, but her interest waned very quickly, and we were back to Toledo, Ohio. I loved to hear her talk. Her America was as exotic to me as my Egypt was to her. I didn't understand everything she said, but I enjoyed the infinity of expressions that moved across her face when she spoke, the halting cadence of her voice, and the way her pitch rose a notch as her tales grew in momentum. I wished I were a painter and she were my model. I could easily imagine my brushstrokes capturing the gentle waves of her hair, her small upturned nose, her high cheekbones, her fleshy lips, and her eyes. It would take several shades of blue, grey, and green paint to recreate the ever-changing hues of her eyes.

Pat noticed my stare, smiled, and stopped in mid-sentence. "I'm sorry. I haven't stopped talking. Your turn! What's it like to live in your spectacular country?"

How to answer that? I could neither come up with the usual clichés about Egypt nor answer truthfully about life in my *spectacular* country. I changed the topic by asking her what she planned to do during her visit. The list of places Pat wanted to visit was long enough to keep a dragoman busy for a year. Without thinking, I offered to show her around Cairo. Her eyes sparkled, and she gave me a beaming smile. Her immediate acceptance threw me. An Egyptian girl's ritual would've been to refuse an invitation at least three times before accepting it, with the unspoken condition that she could obtain her parents' permission and secure the presence of a chaperon.

Pat looked at the tiny watch she wore as a pendant around her neck and frowned. "Oh my God! How did it get so late? Gotta go!" She bolted up, extended her hand, and said, "Nice to've met you!" Before leaving, she asked the very question

I feared would come up. "By the way, I'm sixteen as of three weeks ago. You?"

I'd been mulling over a viable answer to this inevitable question, but my overheated brain had drawn blank after blank. If I told Pat my true age, *finita la commedia*! And if I lied, and she found out, *finita la commedia* too! And, even worse, even if she did not find out right away, how long could I hold my own with a girl who was almost three years older than I was? How long could I be the Great Pretender?

As if by magic, the voices in my head fell silent, and I heard myself answering nonchalantly, "You're a little ahead of me! My birthday is next September," I said. "But I like older girls!" It worked—too vague to be a lie, and subtle enough to bypass the question about age.

She didn't respond, so I hastened to add, "You know, Egypt is a land of black magic and there's a djinn under every bed. My mother is a sorceress who could alter the big calendar in the stars and make me a year older than you!"

She giggled and punched me on the shoulder. "You're funny!" She punched the other shoulder. "In a weird kinda way!" She looked at her watch again. "Gotta go! See you 'round!"

Merde! Triple merde! Stupid me! Why didn't I ask to see her again?

Several yards away, Pat slowed down and made a balletic volte-face, facing me as she walked backwards. She cupped her hands and shouted, "I'll be at the pool after lunch next Monday! And Wednesday too!" Then she made the reverse pirouette and glided out of sight with the grace of a ballerina.

***

I didn't go to Sporting Club on Monday for fear of appearing too eager in Pat's eyes, but I rushed there on Wednesday after my morning session with Ostáz Kamal. I was a little early, and to my great annoyance I saw my mother and two of her friends having lunch on the terrace of the Lido. I didn't want Pat to meet anyone who might reveal my true age, and I moved to turn back, but Maman had seen me and was waving at me. I joined her at her table, and drank mango juice until Pat appeared, waltzing in toward the pool. I mumbled an excuse and ran toward her.

"Hello!" I said, haltingly. I'd been rehearsing a few brilliant lines for two days, but I'd forgotten every one of them.

"Are they your relatives?" she asked, pointing to Maman's table in a movement that made her hair twirl.

"The one in the middle, facing us—that's my mother."

"Oh, my God! She looks like an Egyptian queen or something!" she exclaimed. "She's so beautiful! So elegant! So mysterious too! Like an exotic Ava Gardner!" Pat said. Astonished by my lack of response, she added, "You know Ava Gardner, yes?"

I nodded and tried hard not to roll my eyes. Beautiful? Elegant? Yes, to everyone's eyes but my father's. Exotic? Perhaps in other continents, but not in this one. But mysterious? Maybe to some, but she was the most predictable person in my world. I did all I could to stifle my laughter. But, hell, if having an exotic Ava Gardner look-alike for a mother would help me attract this dream girl, I would wipe our slate clean of all past wounds and grievances!

Pat told me about her first days in Cairo. "My mom and I went shopping in that huge bazaar, Khan-something. It's a place out of *The Arabian Nights*. Your country is amazing! One moment you're in the desert under the pyramids; next, you're walking in sophisticated stores that might be in Paris, if they weren't so hot; and now, right here, we could be in an English countryside, but also boiling hot! Gosh! It's nothing like what I expected!"

"What did you expect?" I asked.

"Well, a more Arabian place, I guess, not so modern and civilized—"

"You mean, um, a country of men riding camels and women covered with veils?"

She blushed. "Not at all!" She looked away, then laughed. "Well, uh, maybe, kinda sorta, a little!" she said sheepishly. "You must think I'm the stupidest girl in the world!"

"Not at all! Many tourists expect Egypt to be, how you say, primitif country?"

"Same in English—primitive."

"Primitive, yes, and then they see we have electricity, cars, and golf courses, and they are gobsmacked—"

"Gobsmacked, eh? Is that Egyptian for flabbergasted?" she asked.

"I think it's an English word—I mean the real English, not the American English."

"You're mean," she said with a chuckle.

To make amends, I added, "Well, you weren't altogether wrong, you know?"

Her eyes opened wide. "You're kidding me, right? What do you mean?"

"No, I'm not. A kilometer or two from here, there are sections of Cairo with no electricity and no water. Women wear veils and black cloaks named abayas, and men wear galabeyas and ride donkeys, if they can afford it, and kids run around in the mud."

"They don't go to school?"

"Some do, but many just beg in the streets or pick pockets at tramway stops."

She looked at me with shock and disbelief. "Little kids?"

"Yes, over there—" I said, pointing to the east, "you'll see lots of children begging for a few malleems to take home for food."

"How much is that?" she asked.

"A malleem is one-thousandth of a pound." Misinterpreting the look of utter horror on her face, I added, "Don't worry. You won't see them here or at your hotel."

"It's not that!" she said. "An Egyptian pound is worth thirty cents, so they beg for one-thousandth of thirty miserable cents? Really?"

"That's what poverty is, Pat—and Egypt is a very poor country!"

"Darn! Isn't your government doing anything about it?" She looked distraught. "We don't have such poverty in America!" she said.

I refrained from saying it wasn't true. I'd seen a movie with Henry Fonda about farmers losing their land, and another one showing Negro cotton pickers in the Mississippi Delta. They didn't appear to have a better life than our fellahin of the Nile Delta. It was one more topic I wanted to discuss with an American, the huge contrasts I saw in American movies—but not with this particular American. With Pat, I only wanted light-hearted boy-girl banter, fun and humor, and some romance, if I were lucky. But I didn't know how to surmount the two impossible obstacles—the difficulty of courting her with my poor English skills, and my inability to make small talk in any language. In French, I had the ability to make people laugh but with Pat I felt naked and vulnerable.

Patricia asked me to show her around the Sporting Club. The grounds were so large that I was only familiar with a small part of the Club's venues. There were fields for soccer and rugby, croquet and cricket, tennis and squash, and innumerable venues for a multitude of other sports I couldn't identify. Pat was a devotee of many of these sports, most of all horseback riding, and the sight of riders practicing jumps atop their majestic Arabian horses elicited a symphony of squeals of joy. Pat was knowledgeable about every type of obstacle, and she enjoyed explaining them to me. I listened, not because I cared a hoot about the bullfinch or the coffin or the shark's teeth, but because I delighted in her delight.

"Do you ride?" she asked.

"Horses?" I confessed that my horsemanship didn't go beyond mild gallops on the sand beneath the pyramids, and I was better at riding camels.

"To each their own!" she said. She looked at her pendant watch. "Shoot! It's late! Gotta go!"

***

Over the next weeks, Pat and I saw each other almost every day at the Gezira Sporting Club, except for an occasional lull when she and her parents took quick trips to Upper Egypt or Alexandria. We managed to work around my study schedule, and I took to reading and doing my homework by the Lido swimming pool so Pat could join me. When she wasn't traveling, Pat played tennis with a group of young American and European boys or girls, all older than me.

Even without hearing their accents, the Americans distinguished themselves by their casual dress, their casual manners, sipping coca-colas straight from the bottle or chewing gum as they talked. The Europeans, and a few Australians and New Zealanders, were the opposite. They paraded their formal elegance and haughty manners in the ways of the dying colonial empires. Many of them were the offspring of diplomats or industrialists; they were groomed to be princes who would own the world someday, and they behaved as if they already did. They cut such glamorous figures that I wondered why Pat would even look at me. It thrilled and flattered me when she bid her friends goodbye and ambled toward my table.

Pat would look at the books and magazines piled up on a chair and laugh. "I guess I don't need to ask what you do while I'm away, do I?"

I couldn't tell whether she liked my bookishness or mocked it, but it didn't matter because she seemed to enjoy my company. She'd tell me about her travels and I'd answer her questions about Egypt and Egyptian customs. I didn't always understand her American speak, but she made me laugh. If guesswork failed when we spoke, I would draw a question mark in the air and she would slow down and use different words to convey what she meant, and when I couldn't find the right word in English, she would finish my sentences and ask if she got it right.

Patricia had the uncanny gift of creating immediate intimacy. I soon learned too much about the loves of her older sister, Jan, who attended college in a place called Ivy League. She also liked to talk about her parents, whom she called by their first names, Joe and Bea—an unthinkable offense in my world. Pat's life in Toledo, Ohio, was all about after-school sports events and parties with her legion of *best* girlfriends, each one paired with a boyfriend who drove his parents' car and won awards at athletic competitions.

Pat's stories weren't always thrilling, but they opened a window onto an America different from the various Americas I'd seen in the movies. Her America was not as heroic as the America of westerns and war films, not as sophisticated as the high society characters in Fred Astaire's musicals, not as corny as Doris Day's comedies, and not as violent as the America of the newsreels in which policemen sicced big dogs against defenseless Negro protestors. Pat's America was a prosperous and industrious society, a little savorless, a little self-centered, and somewhat insulated from the rest of the world except perhaps in international organizations. In a way Pat resembled her country—she could be self-absorbed and generous all at once.

"What are you grinning about?" Pat asked, interrupting one of her stories. "What's so funny?"

"I just noticed that your family and friends all have one-syllable names or diminutives."

"What on earth are you talking about?"

"Well, you have a president called Ike, a vice-president called Dick. Your parents are Joe and Bea, your sister is Jan, and all your friends have names like Sue, Fay, Gus, Jack, and Cal!"

She giggled, "Good golly, Miss Molly! I never noticed that! Only a foreigner would see these things!" She caught herself and exclaimed, "Oops, again! I mean a foreigner to America! You know what I mean, right?"

I gave her a reassuring smile, and she sang, "You say diminutive, I say nickname; you say gobsmacked, I say flabbergasted. Let's call the whole thing off!" Then she giggled, "So what's your nickname?"

I wasn't about to reveal my ridiculous diminutive, Loulou. I'd hated it ever since I'd seen a portrait of Napoleon's wife, Empress Josephine, parading her loulou de Poméranie, a disheveled tiny Pomeranian Spitz that looked like a peacock rather than a dog.

"If you want to be an honorary American," Pat said, "you must have a one-syllable nickname! How about El?"

"That's fine if you think I'm God!" She gave me a quizzical look. "El is Hebrew for God,"

"No, you don't qualify! How about just E, the letter E?"

I nodded my agreement. She came close and wrapped an imaginary ribbon around my neck. Her scent of suntan oil and lavender soap made me want to take her in my arms, but I didn't dare.

"Okay, E! I now declare you an honorary American!"

As I walked home, I lifted my eyes toward the pair of lions that guarded the Gezira entrance to the Qasr-el-Nil bridge and smiled at them—and at the end of the long bridge, at the

Tahrir Square entrance, I saluted their two other siblings. The quadruplet felines had been the benevolent witnesses to the ebbs and flows of my life. I could have sworn that they were winking as though they were amused by both the exuberance and the jitters of first love.

***

My life was becoming a maelstrom of activities. Between my Hebrew teacher, Moshe, and Ostáz Kamal, I was losing my mind. If studying the Modern Standard Arabic was painfully difficult, learning Hebrew was pure torture. Since Suez, there was nothing meaningfully Jewish in my life. My father and I rarely celebrated the high holidays, and even though my Hebrew tutoring demanded that I attend the synagogue on the Shabbat, I managed to skip many days. I was only studying Hebrew because I knew my grandmother would die of grief if I walked away from our religion.

Moshe was still mumbling about the negative influence my Catholic school had on my Jewish studies, and the combination of his droning voice and his colorless personality bored me to death. I made prodigious efforts to stay with the program, but these very efforts only caused further estrangements from my roots.

The work with Ostáz Kamal also felt like force-feeding, but it was more rewarding than I'd expected. The world of Naguib Mahfouz captivated me. Although there were no Jewish protagonists in the trilogy, I recognized more similarities than differences between the traditions of the al-Jawwad family and those of my great-grandparents. Life in a traditional Arab family of Islamic Cairo was indistinguishable from that of an Orthodox Jewish family in the neighboring Haret el-Yahood, the Alleys of the Jews. In both religions, an inner civil war existed between medieval traditions and modern aspirations. Even in our modern age, the traditions in both mosques and synagogues had major similarities. The men still prayed at the heart of the prayer hall while the women were relegated to the back of the house or to the upper floors.

Entering the world of Naguib Mahfouz was a journey of discovery. It was as though I were swimming in a cesspool of contradictory sensations and emotions. It reconnected me to a part of my life I'd forgotten, a part largely influenced by Arab traditions—the smells and textures of the Koubbeh house, the perfume of fresh linen, the women's henna rituals, the aroma of the array of spices in the kitchen, and all that had been a source of warmth and comfort in my early childhood. It was a feeling of déjà vu, accompanied by a touch of distance and alienation. Being the son of a European father and a mother with deep Jewish-Arab roots had been a source of great anxiety in my early childhood, but the persecution of the Jews by the new Egyptian regime had led me to embrace my European roots to the detriment of the Jewish Arab side of my being. In the last few years, I thought the matter was settled, but the study of Mahfouz's book revitalized the duel between East and West that had torn me to the core.

Ostáz Kamal seemed both surprised and pleased with my enthusiasm for Mahfouz's work, and something was opening in our communication. While he remained as exacting and fastidious as ever, he showed more compassion for my mistakes and more willingness to help. In return, I stopped seeing him as the Arab Avenging Angel. Was it just a lull in our yearlong antagonism or the beginning of a reconciliation?

We spent much time studying the passages of the book set in the period leading to the Egyptian revolution of 1919 and comparing it to the 1952 revolution. Both had shared the goal of dislodging the British from Egypt, but the first revolution only achieved partial success. Egypt became a sovereign state, but the British retained full control of Egypt's foreign affairs and of the Suez Canal. I thought it ironic that the second revolution had just abolished the monarchy that was created by the first one, but I kept quiet. Ostáz Kamal was proud of Gamal Abdel Nasser. He said he was the greatest Arab leader since Saladin, not only for his military prowess but also for the agrarian reforms that redressed the suffering of the people.

I resisted the temptation to point out that the victorious British-French-Israeli forces had been chased out of Egypt by the president of the United States, not by Colonel Nasser, but I concurred with Ostáz Kamal's assessment of the Raïs's social accomplishments. I, too, would have admired him were it not for his fierce Jew-hating speeches on the radio.

"May I ask a question—respectfully?" I blurted out.

"Na'am," he said, using the formal Arabic for "Yes."

"Everything you say about the Raïs shows he's a man with a big heart who wants to reform his country, abolish privileges and undo the injustices done to the Egyptian people—"

"Na'am," he repeated, wondering where I was going.

"Well, uh, why are Egyptian Jews not part of the Egyptian people? Why were Jews jailed or thrown out of Egypt? Most of them were never Zionists."

Ostáz Kamal remained silent for a long moment. I worried. Although he'd said I could ask him anything, I wondered if 'anything' included tough questions about his beloved leader's treatment of the Jews of Egypt.

"I'm told that most Jewish people left in 1948 because they now had their own country," said Ostáz Kamal, "and the Jews who'd remained left after the tripartite attack on Egypt."

I shook my head. "Some Jews left Egypt in '48 to join the Jewish state, but many more left because the Muslim Brothers bombed Haret el-Yahood, killing and injuring Jews and destroying their homes. And in '56, a huge number of Jews were expelled, including all my family except for my father and me."

After a long silence, Ostáz Kamal said, "I don't think we should talk about such political matters without your father's permission."

"Why? My father believes in free speech, and would never—"

"It's not about freedom of speech. It's about a teacher appearing to exercise undue influence on his student!"

"But I'm not a child!" I said. I stopped because I could hear the shrillness in my voice and tried to tone it down. "And I know the difference between debate and propaganda—"

He shushed me with a gesture. "Understand me, boy! I'm not *refusing* to discuss these issues, I'm open to it, but not behind your father's back!"

"I'm sure he won't object!"

"Then we will have an interesting series of discussions. You're a courageous boy. You're not afraid to speak your mind."

I couldn't help a burst of nervous laughter. "I'm quite afraid, actually!"

It was Ostáz Kamal's turn to laugh. "An old sheikh, my teacher and master, used to say that admitting fear is where courage begins!"

***

Pat asked me, not for the first time, "How come you never talk about your ex-girlfriends?"

"My father taught me that a gentleman never talks about a lady without her permission."

She laughed and said, "Gentleman? Lady? Good God, you sound like my grandfather! I thought all Arabians had many wives and girlfriends!"

"First, we say *Arabs* for people, not Arabians, and *Arabic* for the language. The only exceptions are the *Saudi Arabians* and *Arabian horses* for the breeds of horses that originated in the Arabian Peninsula."

"You forget *The Arabian Nights?*"

"The original title is *One Thousand and One Nights*, not *The Arabian Nights*. That's a stupid English translation!"

"Okay, I stand corrected. I still want to hear about your love stories. Do you have a harem of girlfriends?"

"We don't have harems in Egypt anymore, and I have to go now. I'll tell you everything the next time."

"Promise?"

I promised.

On the way, I brooded over what to say next. My only amorous adventures had been a few kisses stolen from Claudette, a French girl who'd stayed at the Anglo-Swiss for a few days, and my masturbatory fantasies about Alice. My record achievements were nil compared to Pat's who sounded like she's had a new boyfriend every school year. I couldn't tell the truth, especially since she thought I was sixteen years old, and Pat wouldn't believe me if I said I'd reach that age without a single romance. It was fib or perish.

The fib had to be consistent with my fake age and compelling enough to make Pat a bit jealous. Luckily, I lived in a hotel, the crossroads of destinies, a perfect setting in which I could graft a dramatic potpourri of love conquered and lost. Inspired by the romantic novels I'd read through the years, I invented several heart-wrenching amorous encounters, the saddest being of a forbidden love with the daughter of a fierce and brutal antisemitic Egyptian general.

I enjoyed imagining stories; they seemed to invent themselves; the hard part was to remember them, so I kept cryptic notes that only I could decipher. Soon those notes took on a reality of their own, and I began to flesh them out into stories. Remembering the fairy tales of my childhood, I reflected on the power of words. If, by the mere stroke of a pen, a prince could turn into a toad, and vice-versa, perhaps I could find the words that could enable an awkward and insecure thirteen-year-old boy to capture the heart of an unattainable goddess. Inspired by a smidgen of reality and heaps of imagination, I lined up plain words into sentences, memorized and rehearsed them until they became almost real in my mind.

When I was ready, I told Pat my stories with the discretion of a proper gentleman and without a whiff of braggadocio. She seemed to eat them up. The strokes of the pen were now strokes of luck. With each story of hearts broken and mended, my stature increased in her eyes, and we grew closer and more intimate.

Even after I exhausted my stash of tales and no longer needed new ones to get Patricia's attentions, I kept writing for no reason other than I enjoyed making up stories. Writing came easily to me, and it felt good to transform the long list of imagined characters that crowded my mind into protagonists of dramas. I was aware that many of my stories were not entirely original; they were tributes to the masters whose prose had delighted me for so many years—Dumas, Balzac, Hugo, Maupassant, and others—but I felt that my own voice was emerging in some of them.

When I scrawled the words "The End" on the last page of a story, I would look at my ink-stained fingers and dream of becoming a *real* writer. It was an eerie feeling. All of a sudden, the world was full of possibilities.

I often thought of Nono and his library. I had a fantasy that up there, in his home in the heavenly clouds, my grandfather and namesake would read my books and deem them worthy of a place on his big bookshelf in the sky. The books would stand in alphabetical order, close to the books of Emile

Zola, the literary god whose initials my grandfather and I proudly shared. *Insh'allah!*

***

Armed with Papa's consent, Ostáz Kamal set the basic rules of engagement for our political and cultural discussions—facts before opinion, listening before reacting, reason before emotions.

The momentous events of 1958 and the first months of 1959 provided fertile terrain for political discussions. The first topic was the UAR. A year earlier, Nasser and al-Quwatli, the presidents of Egypt and Syria, had announced a merger of their two countries into a single entity called the United Arab Republic. The Egyptian leader would be its first president. All winter the radios had played songs proclaiming that "Egypt is Syria and Syria is Egypt, one country, indivisible and invincible!"

Discussing the event with Ostáz Kamal, I learned that the creation of the UAR was enabling Nasser to pursue his dream of a Pan-Arab coalition. He had already created a confederation with the Kingdom of Yemen, creating the United Arab States, and that pact had prompted Iraq and Jordan to sign a similar agreement under the name of Arab Federation.

Under the influence of the Egyptian leader, the chessboard of Arab politics suddenly moved at a furious pace, wiping out kings, rooks and bishops, and replacing them with Nasserite zealots. A group of Iraqi army officers took pages from the Free Officer's revolution and overthrew King Faisal of Iraq but, lacking the Egyptian officers' gallantry, they executed him on the spot rather than let him drift into exile. In Lebanon, Libya, Yemen, Saudi Arabia and Turkey, Nasser-inspired groups led revolts and each coup and countercoup brought new leaders into the headlines for a spin before some of them ended up in hiding, in jail or in a coffin.

I was familiar with the current news by reading the French and American magazines left in the Anglo-Swiss reading room, and by discussing them with my father at dinner, but the discussions with Ostáz Kamal gave me the view from the other side of the political spectrum. I hadn't realized the extent to which the consequences of the Suez war, which the press now called the "Suez crisis," were reshaping the postcolonial Middle East. It had damaged the relationship between the United States and its allies, Britain, France, and Israel, and it had jeopardized the delicate balance of the Cold War by opening the door to Soviet influence in the Arab world. Under Nasser, Egypt and its allies were swinging between the East and the West and the nonaligned countries.

I had difficulty holding my own in these discussions. Although my vocabulary in Arabic had expanded considerably, it was still too limited to convey my thoughts. Wanting to be fair, Ostáz Kamal allowed me to use colloquial Arabic, and even a few words in French or English, when I couldn't find the right words. It surprised me that he relaxed his own rule. It also told me that he understood French and English, but he never spoke long enough to let me determine the extent of his fluency.

Hearing the perspective of a young educated Arab intellectual gave me insights into the affairs of the new Middle East. Ostáz Kamal's passion for the new Arab order was palpable and sometimes contagious. I learned more about the ideals of the revolution, and they resonated in my heart and mind, not without a touch of bitterness. I knew there was no place for me and my people in this dreamy world of equality and justice. And it seemed that I was changing his perspectives on the Jews of Egypt.

From his questions, I gathered that he saw Jews as capitalists who owned railroads and industries and large department stores, and he looked incredulous when I told him that the vast majority of Egyptian Jews were shopkeepers, artisans, teachers, lawyers, doctors, pharmacists, rabbis, scholars. The Jewish community counted volunteers who took care of the poor and the indigent, with donations from Jews of all social classes, especially from some millionaire philanthropists. Before the expulsions, few Jews had felt the need to uproot themselves from the land they'd inhabited since Abraham. There were even Jews who were Egyptian nationalists and opposed Zionism like my uncle Shehata Haroun.

"Interesting information," Ostáz Kamal said at the close of the session. "Our people are like cousins who know little about one another. I look forward to further discussions."

***

My time with Pat had whetted my appetite for American literature, and particularly for modern authors. On Monsieur Michel's recommendation, I started with Hemingway's *The Sun also Rises*, using its French translation *Le soleil se lève aussi*, when I needed linguistic help.

Perhaps because I felt like an expatriate in my country of birth, I felt an instant familiarity with Hemingway's story of American expatriates in Paris, then in Spain. I also had deep empathy for Jake Barnes and his impotent despair, but I was shocked by the antisemitism he unleashed on the Jewish protagonist, Robert Cohn. I had always believed that America was the only country in the world that didn't tolerate antisemitism, perhaps because I'd always been told that the Americans were the good guys, the liberators of Hitler's camps, the fearless fighters against tyranny. In their country, a Jew could become a Supreme Court Justice, a senator, a governor, a mayor, or a movie star without fear of retribution.

I wondered if Barnes stood for Hemingway's true beliefs. Whether the author was antisemitic or not, his hero's relentless Jew-hatred cast a cloud of gloom over the novel. It didn't lessen my admiration for Hemingway's prose which was so clear, so sharp, so simple that I had little need for the French translation. My solution was to ignore an author's credo and separate the creator from his creations.

To my dismay, Pat had read neither Hemingway nor Fitzgerald. They weren't on her school's reading list, she said. It was impossible to fathom what did or did not interest Pat. She had an encyclopedic knowledge of sports, movies, and television—a new contraption I'd seen on the newsreels made of a fuzzy miniature movie screen mounted atop a console radio—but she cared little for literature, history or politics. How could Pat and I be so opposite in almost everything and yet have such fun times together?

Pat sensed my muted disappointment and asked me to tell her about Hemingway's novel. She was interested in the story up to the running of the bulls in Pamplona, but the mention of the bullfighter Romero made her cringe and triggered a passionate rejection. She said it made her think of Ferdinand the Bull, and she mocked me when I confessed I knew nothing about him and wasted no time telling me the story of the cute bull. It was the death knell for Pat's interest in Hemingway.

I thought it was a funny and somewhat absurd situation: at a poolside table in a Cairo oasis, a French-educated Egyptian Jew of thirteen was working hard to introduce an American girl, three years his senior, to one of her country's literary giants, and failing at it.

Pat must've had the same realization because she whispered, "You put me to shame with all the books you read! Are you sure you're only sixteen?" I knew better than to answer that question. She pointed to my pile of books. "No wonder you know so much!" she added. "When do you have time to have fun?"

"Reading books is fun. Speaking with you is fun."

She gave me an inquisitive look. "If you have such fun with me, um, how come you never ask me out?"

I turned beet red.

Pat seemed to find my discomfort amusing and let me stew in my mortification before flashing a comforting smile. "Look, I know you people are very formal about these things. We Americans are not, so relax and take me to see a movie, will you?"

***

The next conversation session with Ostáz Kamal was particularly painful. I brought up the partition of Palestine between Arab and Jews, and the refusal of the great Arab nations to allow for the creation of an Arab Palestine. He said the UN was a puppet of the European and American colonial powers, and Israel was its beachhead. If a Palestinian state were created, who would guarantee that the Jews wouldn't keep expanding at their expense? The Arab coalition's aim was to return the Palestinians to their land and hold Israel accountable for their war crimes against the Arabs.

"War crimes? I asked, stunned by the words I'd only heard in connection to the Nazis.

"You probably don't know about this, and I don't know if I should tell you," he said.

"I want to know!" I insisted.

Ostáz Kamal relented and said these war crimes were well documented. His older brother had fought in Palestine, and he had witnessed the Israeli expulsion of the villagers of

Lydda, El-Ramlah, and Deir Yassin. He had seen first-hand the women, children and elders fleeing the massacres on trucks, buses, bicycles and on foot, all heading toward the retreating armies of Egypt to the south, Syria and Jordan to the east, and Lebanon to the north. The worst of the massacres took place in the village of Deir Yassin which spread terror in all of Palestine.

My first reaction was to reject these stories as propaganda, but the name Deir Yassin was oddly familiar. I asked Ostáz Kamal for more information, but he refused to go into more detail, suggesting instead that I do my own reading if I wanted to know more.

The name of Deir Yassin continued to buzz in my head and drive me insane—until a memory resurfaced, vague at first, then gradually emerging in my consciousness. I remembered a holiday dinner at Nona's with the entire family present, including Tante Marcelle and Shehata, her husband. Nona had retired for the evening, I'd been sent off to bed, my cousins to the family room, and the adults had adjourned to the foyer for their usual discussions. As always, I had kept my door ajar to listen in on the news of the week.

That evening, the news was that Nasser was financing groups of Palestinian fedayeen to infiltrate Israel and attack civilian targets, and their leader was a nephew of the Grand Mufti of Jerusalem. They had already attacked an Israeli school bus full of children. Shehata retorted it was a terrible thing, but it was nothing compared to the massacres committed by the Israelis in 1948. "The Zionists behave like Nazis. I have a new name for them—Nazionists. The world will remember the massacre at Deir Yassin as the symbol of the evil of Zion!"

I told Papa that I'd heard people talk about Deir Yassin in school, and I wanted to know about it. He said he didn't know much—only that it was a battle during the Palestinian war which the Arabs called a war crime and the Israelis a casualty of war. "Only the survivors of Deir Yassin know the truth!" said Papa. "On both sides!"

Deir Yassin haunted me. I couldn't believe that Jews would massacre civilians like the Cossacks and the Nazis had done to Jews. It was an absolute impossibility. Since birth I'd been taught that Judaism was not only a religion, but a philosophy of moral rectitude, unbending ethics and justice. We were the descendants of Solomon and his infinite justice, David and his defense of the oppressed, and Moses of the Ten Commandments. We'd survived massacres, expulsions, forced conversions and pogroms in all corners of the world; we'd burned at the stakes of many Inquisitions and inhaled the deadly air of gas chambers—all to keep the fires of righteousness burning. The thought of Jews violating our most fundamental beliefs was shaking the bedrock of my entire being.

***

Two days before Pat and I were to go out to dinner and a movie, I was in a tizzy. How to dress? What to say? Which restaurant to go to? Pat had told me she wanted to see *An Affair to Remember*, which she'd already seen a few times. I agreed, but I feared that I wouldn't understand enough of the dialogue to carry on a discussion with Pat. If she would compare me with her American boyfriends, I worried, she might find me wanting. I would be crushed if I made a fool of myself.

A day before the rendezvous, I asked my mother for an advance on the secret allowance she gave me to supplement my father's stipend. In the same breath, I asked her, par curiosité, about the cost of a fine restaurant and a taxi.

Maman seemed delighted to be my advisor in matters of love, and seduction was her forte. She gave me a short list of restaurants, their respective costs and the amount of tip to leave. She remembered the clothes she'd bought me, and her advice was precise to the color of my socks. "Elegance and politeness are the key. Especially with her parents. If you make a good impression on her mother, she'll feel more at ease with you."

"Okay, I'll be very polite, especially with the mother."

"I'm not done yet, darling. Listen carefully. Be very attentive to the young lady and encourage her to talk about herself. Don't talk about yourself unless and until she asks you. Don't be too cocky, and don't monopolize the conversation. If you can, make her laugh! And remember, she is the center of attention, not you!"

"That's quite a program! I'm not so sure—"

"You'll do just fine, just trust your instincts!" A tear or two rolled down Maman's cheeks, leaving a faint smudge of kohl under her eyes. "You're growing so fast, ya rohi, and I'm missing it all!" she lamented.

In the evening, all decked out in my blue blazer and my spit-polished loafers, I walked to the Semiramis, the palatial turn of the century hotel on Tahrir Square where Pat's family stayed. Mrs. O'Keefe said her daughter wasn't ready, and she excused herself after offering me a soda and a cup of almonds. Pat's father joined me and unleashed a swarm of questions that felt more like a full-fledged investigation than a chat. He asked about my parents, my father's profession, and in a way that wasn't as subtle as he thought, tried to tease out my religion without asking for it. I said I was Jewish with a touch of defiance, but he didn't flinch. I had a vague intuition that he was relieved that I wasn't an Arab, but perhaps that was just my imagination. Relief came with the return of Mrs. O'Keefe.

A few seconds later, Pat emerged. She was barely recognizable. Absent her blue jeans, her tank tops, and her sandals or tennis whites, Pat looked like a woman, not a girl. With a soupçon of makeup and her shock of blond hair falling over the light silk scarf that covered her shoulders, her tight-fitted dress and her high-heel shoes, she was a vision of beauty, elegance and poise. I had a moment of intense panic. How could she not detect that I was a fraudulent thirteen-year-old masquerading as her peer!

In the taxi on the way to the Metro cinema, Pat worried about her choice of movie. "Maybe you'll hate *An Affair to Remember!* It's a romantic movie, and boys don't like that stuff. They like movies with guns and airplanes and tanks and such!"

I assured her I didn't care for guns, tanks, or warplanes. "My favorite film is a love story that takes place in Rome, most of the time on a Vespa scooter."

"You liked *Roman Holiday! Whoa!*" she exclaimed. I nodded, and she rewarded me with a sparkling smile. "Then you will adore *An Affair to Remember!*"

When the lights dimmed down, Pat pointed to my folded pocket handkerchief and whispered, "You're going to need it, it's a tear-jerker!"

The first scenes left me cold. The encounter of a dilettante artist and a nightclub singer aboard a transatlantic liner was not *Anna Karenina*, but it didn't matter. I was more interested in Patricia. If I leaned back, I could see both the film and Patricia's profile. She was deeply immersed in the drama and didn't seem to notice my stare. A shimmering dance of light, emanating from the screen, caressed her face and bounced off her hair in an ethereal dance. I ached to hold her hand, but I only dared to brush my elbow against hers. During the couple's visit to Cary Grant's grandmother, Janou, Pat's eyes were wet long before anything tear-worthy had taken place, and the couple's final goodbye scene opened a flood of tears.

Pat gripped my forearm and only released it when the lovers were aboard the ocean liner sailing toward New York.

As I pondered my next step, Pat leaned on my shoulder and whispered, "You can kiss me if you want to. We're way past our first date." I didn't know what she meant by "date," but kiss her I did. She kissed me back with an ardor I suspected was inspired by Cary Grant and Deborah Kerr, but I savored every second of my first *real* kiss. We continued to kiss until, alerted by the soundtrack, Pat turned her full attention to Cary Grant walking dejectedly on the observation deck of the Empire State Building. Then, just before a car hit Deborah Kerr, Pat took my hand and once again squeezed it hard. Her lips moved silently, mouthing every line of the grand finale. I could feel her fingernails cutting through my flesh, but I didn't move. At the end of the film, she turned back to me, and we kissed until the theater was nearly empty.

As we walked out of the movie palace, Pat seemed to be in a trance, and so was I—but mine had nothing to do with the emotions unleashed by the film.

"Not a bad movie for a first date, eh?" Pat asked.

"What exactly is a *date*?" I asked, feeling rather dimwitted.

She stopped in her tracks. "Are you kidding me? How can you *not* know what a date is?" she exclaimed.

"I know of two kinds of dates—the month-and-day in a calendar, and the fruit of the palm tree."

"What do you think we're doing now?"

"We're on a rendezvous! A night out."

"La-di-dah! You're so French!" she giggled. "We call it a date, not a renday-voo! Boy, it's going to be hard to Americanize you!"

A puzzling statement, I thought, but first things first. I asked Pat whether she'd like to go to a cosmopolitan café or an Egyptian restaurant. "Egyptian, of course!" she answered. "I want the real McCoy!"

I didn't know who this McCoy was, but I got the word "real."

***

The fancy Egyptian restaurant Maman had recommended was closed for the night to accommodate a large party, so I took Pat to Abu Soueif, a rotisserie Papa and I patronized when we went out for Arab food. I hoped we wouldn't run into him and his paramour du jour.

Abu Soueif was a cross between a French bistro and a sultan's palace. With its walls adorned with arabesques, its floor covered with rich Turkish carpeting, and its banquettes and chairs upholstered with Arabian-style silky fabrics, it was a place out of the *Arabian Nights* of Patricia's fantasies.

The head waiter recognized me. An elegant old-fashioned gentleman in a double-breasted suit, Mr. Hisham, welcomed us like royalty. He looked at Patricia with appreciative eyes and whispered in my ear, "The khawaga has become a fine young man." After exchanging the obligatory salutations, he asked if we wanted an apéritif. Patricia wanted something "more fun" than a soda, and I ordered one of the few alcoholic beverages I'd tasted. "Two arak, please."

Mr. Hisham seemed hesitant. He knew I was not of age to drink, but I whispered in Arabic, "Please don't embarrass me." He left us with a smile of complicity and a discreet wink.

Pat took a sip of her drink, which I'd diluted with water and ice, and said, "It tastes like licorice. I love it!"

"You said something about Americanizing me." I said. "Why?"

"No reason, really," she answered sheepishly. "I thought everyone wanted to become an American—"

"Sorry, Miss America! I am like, um, how do you call a dog from a mix of races?"

"A mongrel?"

"Yes, a mongrel, I'm a Jewish-Egyptian-French-Italian mongrel, and I like it."

"So you're Jewish too? Not just Arabian?"

I had a moment of anxiety. "Very Jewish, by birth and culture, if not by practice."

"Really?" she said in disbelief.

"Really," I nodded.

Our orders arrived before she could probe further—*mahshi hammam* and *roz mea'amar*, stuffed pigeon and fragrant baked rice. Pat examined them with suspicion before taking a cautious bite, a few less cautious bites, and then devouring the rest with squeals of bliss. We talked about the movie, and I confessed that I'd found it boring until the midpoint of the story.

"Is that why you kept looking at me through the whole movie? You were bored?" she chortled.

"No, it was because, uh, you're very beautiful."

"You're making fun of me!" she said in a stern voice.

"What did I say?" I asked.

"I'm not beautiful, I'm average."

"If you're considered average, what do ugly girls look like in America?"

She smiled and said, "I know I'm not ugly, but I'm not beautiful. Kinda cute, maybe, but not beautiful! Beautiful is Marilyn Monroe, Grace Kelly, Audrey Hepburn, Ava Gardner, your mother—"

I thought she was joking at first, but she was dead serious. I couldn't imagine any woman, whether my mother or any Egyptian or French woman, rebuking a male for praising her beauty. Was that an American peculiarity?

I smiled and raised my glass, "I think you are beautiful, but if you prefer cute, then cute it is!"

It was her turn to burst out in laughter. "You're sump'n else! American boys never say things like that!"

"What do they say?" I asked.

"If they say anything, it's something like, 'You're okay!' or 'You don't look too bad!' But they usually say very little."

"Do they talk at all?"

"Sure. About sports and cars or they tell jokes. You're different. You speak about books and things. I like to listen to you, even if it makes me feel stupid sometimes—"

"Stupid?" I nearly spilled my drink on the table. "Did I ever say anything to make you feel stupid?"

"No, it's not what you say. It's, uh, I don't know how to say this—sometimes you talk with an intensity that's a little, um, intimidating—"

Me, intimidating? Really? *She* intimidated *me*! Everything about her was intimidating—her beauty, her directness, and the supreme ease with which she glided through life.

"I'm sorry. It's all coming out wrong. I guess I had too much of this stuff—" she said, taking another gulp of arak. "All I'm trying to say is that I'm kinda scared. Just a little."

"Scared of what?" I asked, a little more gobsmacked.

"Nothing and everything. You talk to me like I'm a girl with a brain, not like a dumb cheerleader. I'm not that smart or that pretty, but still you treat me like I'm the Queen of Somewhere. It's weird!"

"My father always tells me to treat a woman like a queen—"

My father's actual maxim was, *Always treat a harlot like a queen, and a queen like a harlot*, but I wasn't about to reveal the full sentence.

"I'm sorry!" she said. "I keep putting my foot in my mouth with you, and I don't mean to. Damn! What am I going to do with you?"

The question was too absurd to answer, but I did. "Nothing!" A few seconds later, I added, "Well, one thing. Sometimes you observe me like I'm some kind of exotic species in a zoo—"

She turned bright red, but I silenced her protests by saying, "It's all right. Sometimes I feel like I live in a zoo, so please, please, please, just pretend I'm normal!"

She giggled and made faces, and we stepped out into the balmy Cairo night.

A lone *a'arabeya hantoor*, a small covered carriage pulled by a tired old horse, was hobbling along. I could see the face of the *aarbagi* under the light of a lamppost. He was as old and as tired as his horse, but he was smiling at an invisible presence. I hailed him on a whim. Pat's face lit up. "Where are we going?" she asked after I gave the driver a direction.

"To the Semiramis. I promised your father I'd get you home by midnight," I said, pointing to my watch.

"Don't worry about them. They'll be asleep anyway. We have time. Show me Cairo by night! Please!"

I gave new directions to the driver, and the *a'arabeya hantoor* shuffled along the Nile. When we reached Roda Island, I called a stop at my favorite place—the point where the modern city gives way to medieval Cairo. At a distance, right above the Mamluk aqueduct, the lights of a plethora of minarets illuminated the distant Citadel as though they were fireworks etched against the purple sky.

"This is breathtaking," Pat whispered, holding my arm a little tighter.

"This is why we call Cairo 'The City of a Thousand Minarets' among other names."

"What are the other names?"

"Al-Qahira, the Victorious, Al-Nagm al-Qahir, the Star of Conquest, A'ain Shams, the Eye of the Sun, and favorite, Umm al Dunya, the Mother of the World."

"Mother of the World, huh? A little bit pretentious, maybe?" Pat asked with a giggle.

I told the *aarbagi* to take us to the Semiramis. He turned the carriage around, dangling his whip over the horse's muzzle, and made clicking sounds to cajole his old nag into a semblance of a trot. I took Pat in my arms, and we watched the city unfurl its myriads of lights. I was happy to share with her the 'love' part of my love-hate affair with Cairo. Tonight, Cairo the city is truly the Mother of the World. I looked at the magnificent girl-woman sitting by my side, and I hoped she could feel what I dared not say—I'm falling in love with you.

***

In my dinner conversations with Papa, he frequently talked about Al-Andalus, the area of Spain and France that the Arabs had occupied for seven centuries. He was fascinated by that period, particularly by the period of *convicencia*, which meant "living together." Although life for the Jews alternated between prosperity and persecution throughout the centuries, Papa described Al-Andalus as the golden age of tolerance and knowledge for all religions. In that period, the alliance of Arabs, Christians, and Jews had made remarkable scientific advances in the fields of medicine, pharmacology, astronomy, agronomy, mathematics and in philosophy, art and architecture. For the persecuted Jews all over Europe, Al-Andalus became a safe asylum.

"Ostáz Kamal says the same things about Egypt during the Nahda. They had the same kind of renaissance you described from the nineteenth century to not so long ago."

Of course! You know what the word Nahda means?"

"He told me it means Enlightenment."

"It can either mean enlightenment or awakening."

"But Ostáz Kamal didn't say a thing about Egypt as a refuge for the Jews, though. He doesn't know that much about the Jews in Egypt or anywhere."

"But it was! Egypt has been a refuge for the Jews from the time of Napoleon. Refugees came in droves from the rest of the Arab world, all of Europe, and even from African countries. Under the Mohammed Ali dynasty—which ended with King Farouk—Jews were allowed to become lawyers, journalists, novelists, and even senators and members of Parliament. Two of my cousins, both lawyers, had served as advisers to the throne and Farouk made one of them a Pasha and the other a Bey. And, something very few people know, two Jews contributed to the writing of the first Egyptian constitution which was promulgated in 1923 as a result of the revolution of 1919—a poet, Murad Bey Farag, and a senator, Yusuf 'Aslan Qattawi."

"How was it possible for Egypt to go from the inclusiveness of the 1920s to the persecutions of the 1950s in just thirty or thirty-five years?"

"I don't know the answer. Times change. Empires rise and fall. History is full of periods of progress and regress, especially for Jews. Across the world and in any century, life for Jews has been a balancing act." He moved his hands up and down like the two plates of a scale. "Prosperity here and persecution here. Killing camps here and Nobel Prize there. That's the Jewish condition, here and everywhere."

He remained pensive for a long moment, then added, "Murad Bey Farag died in '56. He was a hundred years old. I hope he never heard that all Jews are Zionists and enemies of the state. He would have shed tears of blood."

"Wow! I have to tell Ostáz Kamal! He'll pee in his pants!"

"Hey, hey, be careful. Don't gloat about it. He's a good man, but he's also an Egyptian nationalist!"

***

I couldn't wait for the conversation session with Ostáz Kamal. We resumed our discussions about the two Egyptian revolutions. I waited for the mention of King Fuad's constitution.

"Did you know that there were two Jews in the team writing the Constitution of 1923?" I asked.

He was caught off balance and he was silent for a long moment, then said, "Really? Jews?"

"Yes! A writer and a senator," I said

"Who are they?" he asked. "Do you know their names?" he asked.

"The first one was a writer, Murad Bey Farag, a great Jewish poet who wrote in Arabic. The second was a Jewish senator, Yusuf 'Aslan Qattawi, who was a member of King Fuad's Constitutional Commission."

"Where did you learn all this?"

"My father, who is a living encyclopedia of History."

"Of course! You're lucky to have that father. You know a lot for your age!"

***

Pat returned after spending two weeks with her parents in Upper Egypt.

Our first reunion was awkward. We both felt shy and self-conscious, as though we were starting all over again, and I worried that our romance might not have survived her absence. While she was away, I had found a spot at the Gezira club to shelter our romance. It was a secluded grassy area, surrounded by patches of blossoms, and it offered a sweeping view of the river and the Cairo skyline. It took some time before I felt comfortable to take her there. We walked along the Nile as Pat recounted her enchanting time in Luxor and Aswan, and I read her Shakespeare's Sonnet 18 of which I had painstakingly memorized the first nine lines.

"You're too much!" she said. "Nobody's ever read me a poem!"

Encouraged, I took her to my grassy spot. She liked it right away and called it a great hanky-panky nest. Of course, I had to ask what that meant. She planted a vigorous kiss on my lips before singing a silly song in which "doing the hokey-pokey" rhymed with "hanky-panky." We met at the nest several times a week, often past the time to be home. I loved these moments—the kisses, the caresses, the longing, the desire, and the frustration of abstaining, and I wanted to return to our hanky-panky spot minutes after leaving it.

My time with Pat came at the cost of sleepless nights which I spent catching up with my Arabic and Hebrew homework, but it was a small price to pay for the most fun I'd ever had.

Occasionally we would leave our spot and meander through the souks and alleys of Islamic Cairo. For these outings, Pat wore full-length dresses and covered her blond locks with a shawl. I thought she was more fetching in that discreet attire than in her poolside shorts and revealing tank tops. We ambled through the old city until our legs begged for mercy. There was a bittersweet taste to these walks—Pat was saying hello to Cairo, and I was saying goodbye.

In the late afternoon, when the heat subsided, we would repair to our berth and frolic on the grass, a little more daringly every day. Pat taught me the American sports vocabulary that charted the progress of sexual intimacy from *first base* to *home run*. I also learned the various forms of dating, double-dating and blind-dating—the latter being a new name for the traditional matchmaking of our elders.

On weekends, the Gezira Sporting Club held dances aptly called *thés dansants* because they started on time for high tea. Pat was eager to partake, but I was too fearful of stepping on her toes and found excuses not to go. Luckily, Pat was going on another trip with her parents, and I promised her we'd go dancing when she returned. It gave me time to learn—if I could find a teacher.

***

I was hesitant to tell my father that I wanted to learn to dance for fear he would make fun of me. He surprised me by saying it was a good idea and told me to contact his cousin Nisso, the professional dancer.

"What brings you to this place of perdition?" asked Nisso when I showed up at his academy.

"I must learn to dance, rapido presto! Or at least to *not* look ridiculous on a dance floor."

"Do I hear the violins of young love?" he chortled. I hemmed and hawed. "Okay then, please define rapido presto for me." he asked gently.

"Two weeks."

"Pas de soucis!" Nisso affirmed. "All it takes is having an ear for music and rehearsing until you drop. I've gotten couples ready to dance at their wedding in less than two weeks! My students were no Fred Astaire or Cyd Charisse, but they did well enough for the occasion."

"When do we start?"

"Now. But I must call your father first. I need his permission."

"Please don't say anything about the occasion or the girlfriend," I begged. "He'll tease me to death."

"That sounds like your father! I'll be discreet."

While Nisso was in his office making the call, I wandered through the academy. Dancers milled around in a handful of dance studios, and rumbles of music pealed out from them—ballroom, classical, Latin-American. I enjoyed observing them through the glass-paneled doors of the various rooms. A large studio housed a group class, while the smaller rooms were reserved for couples and their instructor. There were more men than women among the dancers, and they paired in every configuration—men with women, men with men, women with women. The earthy and sensuous physicality emanating from their taut bodies was both alluring and intimidating. In a flash, I understood what Nisso meant by "house of perdition," and why he needed my father's permission to teach me. Most of the dancers and their teachers were homosexual.

Why do they make such a fuss? I had a homosexual experience with Omar, and though I hated it, it didn't kill me. I'd also read novels about homosexuals, and I had particularly liked Roger Peyrefitte's story of a passionate friendship and physical intimacy between two boys in a Jesuit school. It had caused a huge uproar in Catholic France, and the religious authorities had banned it. I couldn't understand why the book had shocked so many people.

Nisso returned, interrupting my reverie. "Your father said it's about time you learned to dance! And that it's about time you had a girlfriend! Well, I'm paraphrasing. What he really said was it's about time the virgin got some action!"

"Who says I'm a virgin?"

He laughed and said, "I'm not going there! Your Papa also promised not to tease you about the girl! Make sure you hold him to it! He even offered to pay for the lessons, but I refused. Your dancing education is on me, my boy. It's the least I can do for a young cousin in love!" He winked and asked, "Does the girl have a name?"

"Patricia."

"It's a good season for a Patricia!" he exclaimed. "There are three hot tunes, all entitled 'Patricia'—a beautiful Cuban tune by Pérez Prado, an American one by Perry Como, and the French one by Mouloudji." He selected a record. "Let's start with Pérez Prado. Young love goes with fast feet."

Nisso showed me the basic mambo steps. After a half-hour, he dismissed me with a hearty tap on the shoulder. "You can be an excellent dancer, but only if you work very hard at it."

"Really? I thought I had two left feet! You're just being nice!" I said.

"I'm *never* nice when I teach dancing!" said Nisso. "I say what I see. You take after your father—he was the king of the ballroom when we were young. He made me green with envy!" He laughed at my look of utter surprise and added, "As you can see, I caught up with him, and then some! But he was good! And you will be too!"

"In two weeks?"

"If you work hard, in two weeks you'll sweep your Patricia off her feet!"

Nisso paired me with one of the academy's teachers, Mona, and they set up a schedule around my tutoring timetable. After the first few lessons, I stopped feeling like a two-legged elephant and felt at ease on the dance floor. By the tenth session, Nisso said I was ready for "some action," literally and figuratively.

It was timely. Patricia would be back by the following Saturday.

I arrived early at my first *thé dansant* with Pat and asked the bandleader if he would play all three "Patricia" songs throughout the afternoon. I offered him a banknote for his effort, but he refused. "Use your money to buy something nice for your sweetheart and have a good time!" he said with a flourish.

My first few steps leading Patricia were stiff, but the beat of the music silenced my brain, and my feet took over. I was thankful to Nisso and Mona for the long hours of practice and the self-assurance they had so generously given me.

"Where did you learn to dance like that?" asked Pat as we danced to the Pérez Prado tune.

"Here and there," I said, trying not to sound like the cat who ate the cream.

All three of her namesake songs thrilled Patricia, particularly Marcel Mouloudji's nostalgic French love song. She asked me to translate the lyrics. I asked the bandleader to play it again, and I tingled with desire as I held Pat in my arms and whispered the words of love in her ear.

"Patricia, rappelle-toi ce violon
Patricia, rappelle-toi cette musique
Apprends-moi, Patricia, cette chanson
Qu'on jouait l'an dernier sur le quai..."

***

Ostáz Kamal opened our next conversation session by saying he'd read some of the work of Murad Farag Bey. "He's a superb poet, but he puzzles me," he said. "His poem "My Homeland, Egypt, Place of My Birth" is one of the most moving love songs to Egypt I've ever read, and yet the same man wrote "Al-Qudsiyyat," a hymn to the glory of Jerusalem and Zionism. It's quite a contradiction."

"From what my father said, Murad Farag wrote that he was an Egyptian nationalist, then a Jew, in that order. He didn't see a contradiction."

"But he wanted Jews to occupy Palestine."

"He thought of it as a sharing of the Holy Land, not occupying it. There were Jews there since biblical times. All three religions look toward Jerusalem in their prayers."

"But the land is now occupied by Jews from Europe. Why should the Palestinians pay for the persecutions of the Jews of Europe? What makes that right?"

"I don't know what's right, but if you're saying that all Jews in Israel are European, you're mistaken. European Jews may be the leaders of that country, but long before these immigrants came, there were Jews in Palestine—Jews from the days of the pharaohs, Jews from Babylon, Jews from before the Arab Conquest, and now Jews from Arab lands, etc."

I caught myself preaching, and I stopped immediately. I felt I was going too far, and I doubted anything I said would change Ostáz Kamal's narrow views about our history.

"If it's true, you may have a point." said Ostáz Kamal with a smile. "I'll try to verify it, and we'll continue another time."

I was about to say something, but I reconsidered and started to pack my books.

"You looked like you were about to say something," asked Ostáz Kamal. "Go on!"

"Yes," I said. "What happened to the Palestinian Arabs is terrible, but they were not the only ones displaced by these wars. I don't know if my father told you, but since Suez, our entire paternal family has had to leave Egypt. Only my father and I stayed. They are now dispersed over the continents. Only a few went to Israel. Many moved to Europe—France, England, Italy, and Switzerland—and the others have gone wherever they could land as refugees. My father has cousins in Argentina, Brazil, Australia, South Africa, and the United States. I don't know of anyone going to India or Pakistan, but who knows?"

"Yes, war is a tragedy for us all," said Ostáz Kamal. "I'm sorry for all of you. But bear in mind that if the Zionists hadn't occupied Palestine, the Jews of Egypt would still be in Egypt, not all over the continents."

"On the other hand, my mother's family is determined not to leave Egypt. Ever. Unless there's another war. Do you think there'll be another war?"

"I hope not, but only Allah knows!"

***

Being with Patricia was a release from the hours spent on Hebrew for my Bar Mitzvah, my Arabic lessons, and the difficulty of painstakingly deciphering Naguib Mahfouz's writings. The time I spent with Pat was a whirlwind of wonder and puzzlement, fun and lightness, irritation and disbelief. Her high energy, her incessant curiosity, and her effervescence were pulling me out of my shell and challenging my solitary, bookish soul.

Pat made me realize I was living in the past and in the future, ignoring the present. Until I met her, I had considered the present as a passage in Purgatory, a gap between my Egyptian past and my European future. She made my life joyful. Was it real love or just an infatuation? It was not the obsessive, dangerous, tragic l-o-v-e of my romantic novels, but my heart thumped a little faster when I saw her bouncing up the path toward me. She wasn't always interested in my intellectual pursuits, but I loved her quick wit and her inventive humor. She chased away my sorrows, and there was no end to my desire for her.

After an outing or a dance, we would go to our lair and put our lips together. When the kisses grew longer and hungrier, we would gently wrestle in the grass, thrusting and yielding in a delicious tug of war. We quickly reached the level of what she called second base, which often ended in frustration and embarrassment. Once or twice, I'd ejaculated in my pants. If Pat had noticed it, she didn't show it.

After a moment of deep tenderness, I blurted out words of love. She blushed and barked, "You can't say things like that!" She saw my look of stupefaction and added, "We're not like the French! We don't take love so casually!"

"Wait a minute. It was a sweet moment, and I said a few sweet words. It wasn't a bloody marriage proposal!'

"It's enough to do nice things. No need to say that you love me!"

"You keep saying things like hanky-panky, making out, fooling around, but you can't use the word 'love?'" She didn't respond, so I tried to break the tension with a bit of humor. "Do you think Romeo wouldn't say to Juliet, 'I love thee!' but 'Hey, cutie, lets fool around!'?"

"Ha ha and ha! We're not Romeo and Juliet! We're two teenagers in a summer romance, not actors in some romantic stage play or adventure movie!"

"Too bad!" I exclaimed. "I want my life to be full of more adventures than you can see in any movie. I want it to be fun and exciting every day. Otherwise, what's the point of living on this earth?"

Pat gave me the look one gives a babbling child. She picked up her bag and walked away, mumbling that I was *impossible*! After a few steps, she turned around and asked, "What do you mean when you say you love me?"

"Just that I love being with you, talking with you, and yes, fooling around with you."

"What *exactly* do you like about me?" she asked in a tone short of yelling.

Her angry tone made me uncomfortable. "A lot! Everything! You make me laugh—you're smart, direct, and you're cute. Not beautiful at all, but cute! And you speak your mind. I love that!"

"Yeah, right. Yes, you like me to speak my mind, but how come you never speak yours? You're full of secrets, and you just ignore all my questions!"

"I've told you everything, except, uh, answering your nosy questions about old girlfriends. It's rude to speak about *previous* dates with *present* dates. It's not discreet—"

"Not discreet, no, Mr. La-di-dah! Well, excuse me, sir, I'm just a crude, unsophisticated American with no education, as you well know—"

"I never said that! I never *thought* that, so how could I have *said* it?"

"Not in so many words. You didn't say it, but it's what you think!" She pouted for a moment. "So, are you going to ask me what I, me, Patricia, like about you?"

"Please tell, Miss I-Never-Speak-of-Love."

"Up yours! You only care about books and sex, sex, sex!"

"Pat, stop! What did I do to make you so angry?"

"I was going to tell you something important, very important—but, since it involves a previous boyfriend, forget about it!"

"Tell me anyway!"

"I said, forget it! See you 'round! Or see you *never again*!"

She picked up her bag once again and scampered out of sight. I stood there like a pillar of salt, unable to move. How could she go from kiss-and-hug to go-to-hell in just a few minutes?

It was a long time before I could drag my low-spirited bones out of our love spot and walk home. At the Qasr-el-Nil bridge, I stopped for my usual salute to the lions of stone. They stood at attention, as always, but they too looked sad. I had the feeling they were speaking to me. This shall pass, they whispered. It shall pass because, in the life of mortals, all things must pass.

CHAPTER 13

Fall of 1959

Un seul être vous manque et tout est dépeuplé—You miss a single being, and life is barren.

My mind couldn't stop churning that verse of Alphonse de Lamartine, one of my beloved French romantic poets. I was still bruised by the inexplicable end of our love, and I wanted to excise all memories of Patricia from my thoughts. I avoided American books, music, and movies, and I found myself irresistibly drawn back to my literary roots. Searching for modern French literature in Monsieur Michel's bookstore, I stumbled upon Albert Camus's *The Stranger*. I was immediately hooked by the opening line: "Maman died today. Or maybe yesterday, I don't know. I got a telegram from the old people's home: 'Mother deceased. Funeral tomorrow. Faithfully yours.'"

I bought the book and continued to read the first chapter as I walked home. I devoured it with passion, finished it in the early morning, and read it again without a break. Camus wrote with the same limpid simplicity as F. Scott Fitzgerald. The difference was that reading Camus was akin to going back home. I could feel the scorching Algerian sun, the hot sand of the beach, the tang of the Mediterranean, and the sweet-and-sour smell of clusters of blended ethnicities. Camus's Algeria was a familiar land, torn between the centrifugal tugs of our conflicting cultural identities. I felt as though

Albert Camus was an older brother guiding me through life's treacherous shoals.

My impending Bar Mitzvah was another, less thrilling, distraction from the sadness of losing Patricia. My father was insistent that the ceremony take place before my fourteenth birthday, even though the poor quality of my reading in Hebrew was embarrassing. A year earlier, the rabbi had thought that my Hebrew reading skills were insufficient to allow me to read from the Torah, and this year my tutor reported that I still wasn't ready for the ceremony. My father argued that it would only be fair to let me "read" memorized prayers, since political circumstances had compelled me to attend a Christian school and neglect my Jewish studies. Isn't a Jew without a Hebrew education a better prospect than a lapsed Jew lost to his religion? Whether the good rabbi bought the argument or just got fed up with my father's appeals, he relented and agreed let me "read with a little memorizing." They scheduled the ceremony for the second week of August, a month before my birthday.

On the day of the ceremony, dressed in a brand-new navy-blue suit, I joined three other Bar Mitzvah boys in front of the Ark of the Torah. The prayer hall was half full, a sign of the times—before the war, people would be standing in the aisles. The once-majestic synagogue was showing signs of decay; the mahogany pews were no longer shining bright, and their upholstery was fraying in places.

My friends JP, Ike, Coco, Gil, and Momo had come back from their Alexandria vacations for the occasion. I winked at Momo, who was fidgeting with his prayer shawl and his kippa. It was good to see my gang of Muslim, Christian and Jewish brothers assembled again. In the women's gallery up in the mezzanine, Tante Marcelle and her daughters were waving at me.

The ceremony began. I had taken the last position behind the other Bar Mitzvah boys, so nobody could see me glance at the tiny cheat sheet taped under my sleeve. After an endless stream of prayers, the rabbi called the Bar Mitzvah boys to the Holy Ark. After pulling the thick red velvet curtain embroidered with a large golden Star of David to reveal the Ark, he intoned a prayer.

I felt the intensity of eyes looking at me. Papa looked worried, as though he expected me to flub my lines, and my friends seemed to struggle to keep a serious composure. I looked up again to the mezzanine, and I noticed a lone woman sitting in the last row, nearly hidden behind two other women. She wore a white and gold ensemble, and her head was covered with a golden veil. I didn't need to see her face to know that ethereal presence was my mother. Nor did I need to sit close to her to hear the muffled sobs that shook her chest almost imperceptibly. She'd said she wouldn't come to the synagogue for fear of causing tensions with my father, but I wasn't surprised that she had come after all. Unexpectedly, it felt good to have her there, even though the thought of my father and my mother in the same breathing space was unsettling.

I was the last one to read the haftarah before the cantor began to chant. I looked up to the mezzanine gallery once again, but the woman in white was gone.

Two days later, Maman threw a party with the entire Mani family, Tante Aïda and Khadr Bey. During the gathering, Maman asked me why I hadn't invited my pretty American girl. For some reason, I didn't want to tell her that the American girl was no longer *my* American girl, so I answered casually that I didn't want to give away my actual age. Maman burst out in raucous laugher.

"What's so funny?" I asked.

"My little boy's becoming a man—he can lie like the best of them!" She ruffled my hair and added, "You're learning too much too fast, my son. Reste mon petit garçon un petit peu plus longtemps! I want to enjoy my little boy a little longer."

"Don't count on it, Maman!"

"Anyway, she misses you."

"Who?"

"La mignonne petite Américaine, voyons!"

"Patricia? Did she say that?" I asked.

"Not in so many words, but a woman feels these things!" Maman said. "She asked if you were sick because she hasn't seen you at the club for a long while."

"I'm too busy. Too much homework."

"You think your old mother can't guess why you suddenly stopped doing your homework at the club? What happened? Did you two have a spat?" I gurgled a feeble denial. "Well, my son, if you're smart, I mean really smart, you'll show your face at the club. Don't waste your time on who's right and who's wrong. If you love her, let her be right, even if she is not!"

"Thank you, doctor!" I said. "I'll think about it."

"Think with your shoes, not your head! And listen to your old mother!" she repeated.

"When did you become my *old* mother?"

"It's just a manner of speech, mon chéri!" she said as she walked away to greet arriving guests.

***

I sat in my usual spot at the Lido. I'd spread my Arabic books and my notepad on the table, but my efforts to do any real homework were failing. Late on the second day, Patricia came into sight. She was walking with a girlfriend, and they both wore tennis whites. From the corner of my eyes, I saw her bid her friend goodbye and walk the long way around the swimming pool so that she could appear from behind me. I pretended not to see her.

"Reading and writing, and guess what? More damn writing and reading!" Pat said, giving me her usual punch on the shoulder. "Where have you been all this time?"

"Homework, friends, movies—you know."

"You're full of French-Italian-Egyptian baloney! You were mad at me for my little tantrum the other week!" She ignored my noncommittal pout. "I was out of line! But I was confused. There were things I wanted to say and, um, I just couldn't bring myself to say them!" She looked toward a group of boisterous youths converging toward the pool area. "Can we go someplace quiet to talk? Like go to our spot?"

I packed my book bag slowly, trying not to look too eager. When we reached our nest, Pat planted a big kiss on my lips and pulled back. "We need to talk first."

We sat on the grass. Pat's mood had suddenly changed. She suddenly looked like a sad canary flittering in a cage. She took a breath and blurted, "I haven't been honest with you. I didn't exactly lie, but I didn't come clean either. What I was trying to tell you is—" She took another deep breath and said quickly, "I have a boyfriend back home. His name is Rusty. I should've told you before!"

This scene was not in the libretto I'd composed for our make-up reunion. My emotions bounced from disbelief to betrayal, rose up to anger, and came down to icy detachment. I sneered, "Why are you telling me now?"

"Listen, when we started, it was going to be a quickie—"

"A what?"

"It means a quick summer romance. Nothing more. So, there was no point in telling you about my boyfriend at home, right?"

"Absolutely right!" I sneered.

"Please don't be mad! Pretty please?" Pat said. "Then things got a little more, uh, more *involved* with us, and then you said you loved me. And it made me feel dishonest and dirty." She saw my look of incomprehension and added, "And I couldn't keep lying—"

"Of course not! I suppose you'll lie to Dusty?"

"It's Rusty." After a lengthy silence, she asked, "Do you want me to tell him?"

"Franchement, ma chère, c'est le cadet de mes soucis!" I said.

"Come on, speak English! What did you say?"

"I said, 'Frankly, my dear, I don't give a damn!' It sounds much better in English, I must say."

Pat let out a laugh that sounded like a dry cough. "Hilarious! Well, I give a damn about *you*! I lied because I didn't want to lose you, okay?"

"So—now what?" I asked.

"Since you're asking—" she paused, "I mean, nothing's changed, except that I opened my big fat mouth. So, if I had my druthers, we'd continue like before."

I was torn between pride and lust. It was humiliating to be the minor character in Pat's stage play, but I missed her. And, if I were honest, I had no right to make a fuss. Pat had lied by omission about the boyfriend in Toledo, but I had done much worse. I had lied about everything—my age, my fake former girlfriends, and my fake travels and adventures. If two wrongs didn't make a right, could one wrong void the other?

Patricia sensed my change of mood and gave me a quizzical look. I waited, wishing she'd make the first move. She moved closer and whispered in my ear, "We both knew it would be a summer romance, but the summer's not over, right?" she said.

She smelled of sun and chlorinated water. I could no longer resist, and I pulled her toward me.

There was something different in our embrace this time—a deeper feeling of closeness and harmony, an unspoken promise of greater pleasure. Pat squeezed my hand and gently drew it toward her chest. Emboldened, I slid my hand under her halter top and the delicate skin of her womanly breast filled my hand. It was as soft and firm as a ripe summer mango, and I imagined it tasted even sweeter.

"At the end of summer, when I'm back home," she whispered, "how quickly will you'll forget me?"

"You'll forget me before I forget you," I whispered back.

"No way!" she cooed. "I'll never forget you. You're my Sheik of Araby!"

"Who's the Sheikh of Araby?" I asked.

"Shush now! I'll tell you someday," she whispered. "For now, just hold me!"

***

The summer was ending. I had more time to myself since I no longer had Hebrew studies, and my tutoring with Ostáz Kamal was winding down. In two weeks, Pat and her mother would go home. We had to find ways to spend more time together. Pat found pretexts to forgo going with her parents on more trips away from Cairo, and I took leave of my books. Rather than lament the looming end of our time together, we reveled in the present in all its seductions.

We went on a binge of camel rides in the desert, dances at the Club, and rides on rickety hantoors or walks along the Nile. Back in our corner of heaven near the Botanical Garden, our sexual intimacy grew in intensity and pleasure. Our embraces felt like we were dancing the tango, slow, slow, quick, quick, slow, a daring move forward, a gentle push back, in an infinite loop. I wanted to have sex with Pat, but she wasn't ready, and she insisted that we stop short of penetration. I didn't disagree for different reasons. I was dying to lose my virginity, but I feared that having full, unbound sex with Pat would unleash torrents of emotions that would swallow me alive.

When her parents were traveling, Pat took to sneaking me into her hotel suite at the Semiramis. I would tell my father that I was spending the night at JP's and go to her. As

Pat feared that the hotel staff might report my visits to her parents, we devised an amusing cloak-and-dagger way to get me in her room. We would meet in the hotel's tearoom for a time, then we would part with loud goodbyes. She would return to her room, and I would use the service stairway to join her. If someone was in sight, I'd go into a lavatory and wait until I could slip, unseen, into Pat's suite.

The reverse, leaving the Semiramis late at night, was less fraught with risk. It was easy to avoid the reduced staff and slip out through the service entrance. Most of the time I only ran into an old domestic who swept the service stairs. He looked amused by my illicit presence in his quarters and gave me a warm smile of complicity. I assumed he expected a baksheesh, but he refused when I proffered a handful of piasters. I grew to like the old man and missed him on the nights he wasn't at his post.

Pat's suite comprised two bedrooms separated by a large living room with a dining corner. On her own turf, Pat's behavior changed somewhat. She was more formal and acted like a perfect hostess, mixing drinks at the bar. The first time, I was embarrassed because I'd never had a mixed drink, but I remembered the Belafonte song and ordered a rum and Coca-Cola cocktail. I didn't care much for alcohol, but the tinkle of ice cubes in the glass made me feel suave and debonair. Pat would call room service, always ordering only one dish and a bunch of appetizers to make believe it was a meal for a single person, and I would hide in the bathroom when the food was delivered.

Entering the intimate sanctuary of Pat's bedroom, amidst her clothing and her cosmetics, and the scents of her femininity, was a far more erotic experience than our frolics on the grass. In her own bed, Pat was more subdued than she was in our hideaway at the Club, but on my third visit Pat's sexual ardor returned with a vengeance. I marveled at the electric jolts that went through me at the touch of Pat's skin, the tingle in my fingertips when I brushed her shoulders and her breasts, and my elation when I sensed her pleasure. Our physical closeness made it even more difficult to resist the urge to explore our bodies beyond the limits Pat had set.

Between embraces, we would talk well into the night. Pat had a slew of questions about my Egyptian childhood that were difficult to answer. I didn't want to lift the veil that separated my reality from her idealized view of Egypt. Pat's Egypt was a glorious movie of Arabian tales, projected on a silk screen in full color. My Egypt was a gritty black-and-white newsreel that told stories of fractures and dislocation. I was reluctant to spoil the memories Pat was garnering for the rest of her life.

Out of the blue, Pat asked me why I was keeping so many secrets. I didn't answer. "You can talk to me," she whispered. "I'm not the china doll you think I am. You don't have to protect me. You can tell me anything you want."

The gentleness of her tone scared me. I wanted to get up and run, but the panic went away. Then I felt like crying, and that went away too. And, finally, I entered a realm of peace, free of make-believe, free of judgment or punishment. All the masks I'd worn throughout my life fell off, and I felt free to be myself. No need to pretend to be tough, impervious to pain or to any emotion that resembled weakness. No need to blur edges or shroud the truth in shadows to avoid being judged and condemned. I could speak without censure, and I did. In my broken English, and often in French when I couldn't find the words, I let out a stream of feelings that had been long buried in my consciousness. I knew Pat could not understand much of what I said, and we both knew the words didn't matter. She held me tight, planting delicious pecks on my back and shoulders that made me shiver. For the first time in my life, I was surrendering to the love of another.

As my eyes were closing, a few gentle taps on the chest brought me back. The room was lit by a beam of moonlight. Pat's hair shone in the dark as she stroked my bare chest. "It's very late," Pat whispered. "I wish you could stay till morning, but if a servant notices and tells my father, I'm as good as dead!"

I made a grimace of displeasure. She put a kiss on my lips. "You feeling OK?"

"I feel naked," I said.

She tapped my chest and said, "You *are* kinda-sorta naked."

She moved to get up, but I held her hand and stopped her. "Pat—" I stopped for a deep breath, not quite knowing what I wanted to say. The only two words that came to me were, "Thank you."

"For what?"

"Just for being you."

"For what?" she repeated.

"For shining so bright!"

"Shut the hell up!" she breathed. "No French sweet-talking at this hour!"

I took my time arranging my clothing and taming my disheveled mane. Pat was humming a melody. I'd heard it before, but I couldn't place it. I asked Pat about the tune. She took a few dance steps. "The sun that shines above—Will light our way to love."

"What's the song?" I asked again.

She took another dance step. "You rule this world with me—You're my Sheik of Araby."

She planted a killer kiss on my lips and pushed me out the door without telling me who the hell was that damn Sheik of Araby!

***

Ostáz Kamal added two sessions to our schedule so we could finish our work on Naguib Mahfouz's novel. On the last session, he narrated a condensed version of the unread part of the entire Cairo trilogy, then asked me to talk about what I'd liked or disliked the most about the trilogy.

"It's complex. I understood the lifestyle of the al-Jawwad family. I felt at home with them. Not entirely, but most of the time. I enjoyed discovering a different Cairo than the Cairo I live in—life in the old Islamic city compared to life in the European city which people call 'the Paris of the Nile.' And I like to think that, during the long period covered by the story, my four grandparents were in the prime of their lives, my father and my aunts and uncles were children, and my mother a newborn baby."

"Excellent. What else?"

"It made me reconnect with the Egyptian part of my roots. I came from a culturally divided house—Egyptian and European. The book was about half of me."

"What do you mean by that?"

"My paternal family is steeped in European culture, and my mother's side in Egyptian culture. They spoke Arabic at home."

"You never told me that!" said Ostáz Kamal.

"You didn't ask about my mother's family."

He nodded and motioned me to carry on.

"I learned a lot about politics, the divide between the rich, the poor, and the growing educated class that led to the revolution of 1919. And about the conflict between the secular and the religious Muslims, and the communists and the military. I loved the last chapters that ended near the end of World War Two, just before I was born, when I imagine that Mohammed Naguib, Nasser and the other officers started thinking about a new revolution. Naguib Mahfouz might have entitled the series, *Between Two Revolutions* instead of *Between the Two Palaces*."

Ostáz Kamal smiled. "Well observed. Any final thoughts?"

"My only regret is that there were no Jews among Naguib Mahfouz's characters. I would have liked to read about Egyptian Jews before Israel existed."

"Maalesh," he said. "Maybe someday you'll write your own book about Jewish life in Egypt."

I resisted the temptation to reply that it was improbable. Others would probably tackle that story, historians and maybe novelists, but not me. Once we're out of Egypt, I want and need to forget all about it. If not forever, then for a very long time.

Ostáz Kamal gave me a list of the great Arab writers of the Arab Renaissance and said he hoped I'd read them someday, perhaps in the original text, if I pursued my study of Arabic. I agreed, but we both knew it would not happen. Naguib Mahfouz's trilogy would be my swan song in Arabic culture. Even though Ostáz Kamal's exercise had been rewarding, it was akin to Sisyphus carrying his mythical boulder up the steep mountain, only to see it roll down faster than he'd carried it upward. I was loath to repeat that experience. I knew my father would say, "Never say never," and perhaps someday the pain of the past would fade away, and I might want to return to my Egyptian roots. But not for a long time. I was now readying for a long and painful divorce, and divorce was a nasty old friend.

We sat for a time without uttering a word. Here we were, a Muslim teacher and a rebellious Jewish teenager, brought together by an old Catholic school principal, reaching the end of a long journey. We had started with prejudice, suspicion, mistrust, and anger that had all seemed insurmountable and we had somehow found reconciliation simply by listening to one another—and now it was time to say goodbye.

When we got up, I thanked Ostáz Kamal for the knowledge he'd imparted to me. He nodded in acceptance and said,

"You are not the only one who has learned at this table. I wish you well, wherever life takes you. You're smart, a little too precocious for your own good, but that runs in our Egyptian blood. Gamal Abdel Nasser became active in politics when he was your age."

At the elevator, after a long handshake, he said, "May our paths cross again someday—"

We both knew that it was improbable; yet, true to Egyptian tradition, we both said "Insh'Allah!" in unison.

***

My last dance with Pat was to the tune of "Autumn Leaves" sung by a duo, male and female, alternating the French and English lyrics. The French words brought back distant memories of Ras-el-Bar, the feluccas and the intertwined voices of my father and an unknown woman singing words my young mind couldn't fully comprehend. Now I understood the words of love and loss of love. Their poignancy reverberated through my entire body. I was no longer that little boy. I was days short of fourteen, a man in the Jewish tradition, and I was dancing with a beautiful girl, almost a woman, I loved and who loved me—yet in a few moments we would leave one another forever. In a few moments, we would become the disunited lovers of the song, and the sand would cover our footsteps. It sounded awfully grownup, too grownup perhaps, and I wondered whether I was ready to come of age quite that quickly.

After a few dances, we repaired to our nest. It was the start of autumn and darkness was falling earlier. I was grateful for that. It would be easier to mask my emotions. I had vowed not to get sentimental on our last night together. Our last embrace began in a subdued cuddle. Waves of tenderness overwhelmed me as I held Pat in my arms, inhaling the scent of her sunbaked skin and the light whiff of her peppery perfume. Her string of pearls and her earrings glowed in the semi-darkness, and so did her teary eyes.

Then desire eclipsed tenderness, and we were soon wriggling on the grass, kissing hungrily, reaching under our clothing for bare skin, fondling, stroking, kneading until we reached our familiar state of pleasure and aching frustration. But this time the will to restrain ourselves failed us and we gave in to a frenzied exploration of the never-seen and never-touched parts of our bodies. I slunk my fingers under Patricia's lacy lingerie and timidly touched her pubis while she unbuttoned my trousers, slid her hand through the fly of my briefs and held my penis close to her. I was about to enter her when our erotic pas de deux culminated in an unwelcome climax.

We lay quietly for a time, still clutching each other's groin, still dazed by the intensity of the moment. Then Pat let go of me. She sat up and looked at her hand full of my semen. She giggled, took a sniff of my gooey substance, and licked a drop or two before wiping it off on the grass.

"It's sweet," she said. "Sweet and tart."

I tasted her musky fragrance on my fingers. "Spicy," I chimed in.

We held each other in silence. I hoped I'd given Pat as much pleasure as she'd given me. I thought she had climaxed, but it was too subtle to be certain.

"What are you thinking?" Pat asked, a tad alarmed by my silence.

"Did you—?" I stopped in mid-sentence because I didn't know the English word for climax.

She laughed softly. "Oui, monsieur. Same time as you." Then she whispered, "It was my first time. I mean, um, with someone other than myself."

There was something oddly reassuring to learn that girls masturbated too. It brought me closer to Pat, as though I were inside her, sensing her sensations, and it aroused me again—but we had run out of time. We straightened our clothes, removing the telltale leaves of grass, then kissed a few more times before taking the path back to the Lido.

From a distance, we saw Pat's parents having drinks at a poolside table, and we stopped and hid behind a tree for a last kiss.

"Better they don't see us together," Pat whispered. "Mom will know on the spot!"

"How would she?"

"Right now, I feel like I'm made of clear glass. She'll know!" We kissed again, and she whispered, "Gotta go!"

She took a step forward, then turned back for another last kiss, and another, and several more, each "last" kiss punctuated by another whispered, "Gotta go!"

The agony of saying goodbye became unbearable. I held Patricia in my arms and whispered, "It's time for my sunny Cinderella to turn into a pumpkin." She gave me her familiar punch on the shoulder, smiled a teary smile, and walked away toward the rest of her life.

Numbness engulfed me. Hidden behind the tree, I watched her join her parents at their poolside table. She was already back in her real life. It was time for me to return to mine.

As I approached my guardians of stone at the entrance of the bridge, their eyes told me they knew how I felt better than I did. They'd seen parades of lovers—happy lovers, jilted lovers, guilty lovers, desperate lovers at the end of their rope—and they'd heard their rhapsodies of passion and their howls of sorrow. If only they could talk. I knew they would repeat what they'd already told me once—this shall pass. In the life of mortals, all things must pass.

The numbness lifted when I reached the end of the bridge and stepped onto Tahrir Square. The lights of the Semiramis shone brightly at the far end of the monumental square. I blew a kiss toward it. Somewhere in that massive edifice of luxury from another age, there was a room that had harbored moments of pleasure and tenderness, and a tidal wave of gratitude swept me away. Gratitude for the sunshine that lit up my darkness. Gratitude for all the joy, the laughter, the friendship, and the sex. Gratitude for having learned how to claim the patch of happiness I never thought I deserved. A few droplets trickled down my cheeks—dewdrops of joy, not sorrow, an offering to all the gods that had smiled upon me. I thought of Pat again and thanked her for our own affair to remember.

CHAPTER 14

Winter of 1959

In the weeks following Patricia's departure, my mood alternated between joy, nostalgia, and acceptance—an acceptance of the mind, but not of the body. My body still ached for Pat's touch.

"Le dare tiempo al Tiempo," were the words trotting around in my mind. They were Nona's response to my early childhood temper tantrums. Give Time the time it needs.

My friends were all back from their summer vacation, but I avoided them. I knew they'd heard about the pretty blond American girl from the sporting club, and I didn't want to field nosy questions or listen to their inevitable wisecracks. A few days remained before school opened, and I spent them daydreaming and brooding.

Coming out of the hotel elevator into the lobby, carrying a bagful of books from the library, I saw Papa in deep conversation with a woman. Intrigued, I moved closer and recognized the woman's voice before I got a full view of her face. She was the Greek woman who'd come to my thirteenth birthday party for a few minutes and vanished. Her name was on the tip of my tongue, but it eluded me.

"I'm sure you remember—"Papa begun.

"Of course I do!" I said. A name jumped out of my mouth, and praying it was her correct name, I said, "You're the young cousin of Mr. Giannopolous—uh, Mademoiselle Calista!"

She laughed and said, "Thank you for remembering me, and for the 'young' cousin, and especially for the 'Mademoiselle,'" she said. Her French was fluent, and she spoke with a slightly musical accent.

"Your son is quite a gentleman," she told Papa.

"Only when he wants to be!" Papa said.

We adjourned to the salon near the lobby and sat down on the plush armchairs. My bag dropped to the floor with a thud, spitting out a few books.

"Books again?" asked Papa. "The boy's an inveterate book addict," he said to Calista, then he turned to me, "May I see your new books?"

I handed him my book bag. It contained Simone de Beauvoir's *The Blood of Others*, a book of André Gide's poetry, and a French translation of John Dos Passos's *ManhattanTransfer*.

"You're reading *Manhattan Transfer* in French?" Papa asked with a touch of reproach.

"I tried reading it in English, and it's bloody hard to understand it, even in the French translation."

"Could you define the meaning of 'bloody hard' versus just 'hard' in what you just said?" asked Papa.

His priggish tone surprised me, but I quickly figured out it was just a display of paternal authority for Calista's benefit. I played along.

"Bloody is harder than not bloody," I said, then I turned toward Calista. "I apologize for my language, uh, mademoiselle, uh, madame—"

"Just Calista. I live part-time in the United States where people are very casual," she answered with a laugh. "But, again, it's quite flattering to be called mademoiselle at my age."

I said I had homework to do. As I walked away, I heard Papa say, "If you're too old to be a mademoiselle, then I already have a foot in the grave."

"Are you always prone to such exaggerations?" she chuckled.

I walked away, quickly enough to hide my laughter. So, this is how adults flirt, I thought. I should study Papa's techniques to learn how to go from flirty witticisms to seduction and sex.

At dinner, Calista was a guest of honor at the table of the owners of the Anglo-Swiss hotel, her cousins. I couldn't keep my eyes off her. She was a Venetian blonde, and her reddish-golden hair fell a touch below her neckline, her high cheekbones flanked a small turned-up nose, and her deep turquoise eyes shone with intelligence. Her body made me think of the statue of the *Venus de Milo*, with the difference that she had two lissome arms attached to her shoulders. I had a flash of embarrassment which caused me to divert my eyes from Calista. The *Venus de Milo*'s flawless breasts of marble had figured prominently in my masturbatory imagery, and I felt a twinge of shame—my father had eyes for her, and looking at her in a sexual way felt a tad incestuous.

After dinner Calista brought slices of her birthday cake to our table and joined us for coffee. Our conversation lasted until midnight when Papa sent me off to bed while he remained with Calista. I realized that I'd been so engrossed by her conversation that I was no longer paying attention to her Olympian beauty.

It was impossible not to like Calista. She was sharp-witted, well-read, beautiful, and warm—and her life was glamorous. She lived in both Paris and New York City, flying back and forth, a little too frequently for her taste. In Paris, she taught the history of music at a prestigious music school, and in New York she conducted lectures and seminars on the same topic. She was currently on a sabbatical leave from both schools to write a book on the history of music across the Mediterranean Basin from antiquity to present times.

Calista knew Cairo well. A branch of her family had emigrated from Greece to Alexandria and Cairo, and she had visited them many times before. This time, she was in Egypt for both pleasure and work. She was delighted to reunite with her family, and she would research ancient religious music and the instruments of that age.

Calista's visit was a promise that life at the Anglo-Swiss would be fun and exciting.

***

The new La Salle campus to which I was assigned stood in a neighborhood named Daher, far from home, and I had to ride the streetcars to get there. I'd seldom been on a trolley car, and never alone, but I was eager for the experience. Before school opened, fearing I might be late on the first day, I took a trial ride so I could time the trip and explore the neighborhood around the campus.

That first ride was as hair-raising as the most harrowing roller coaster in a carnival. The streetcar sped along the rails, bells ringing at the crossings, often shaking the mass of men who hung from the sides and back railings, a few inches from being mowed down by automobiles careening at full throttle and threatening the clusters of fare-dodgers huddled on the roof, perilously close to the electric wires. At the intersections, the tram drivers would ignore the traffic lights and speed ahead, missing crossing automobiles by a hair, or they would brake abruptly, shaking the entire train from side to side in a cacophony of wheels squealing, bumpers banging, old wood creaking, and passengers shrieking curses. The tram stops were more hazardous than the rides. Oncoming trams wouldn't always slow down fast enough to avoid gliding into, or colliding with, the streetcar ahead, causing men to slide off the roofs or fly off the railings. Undaunted, the men would jump back aboard when the trolley car took off again.

Inside the cars, the windows were obscured by the clusters of humanity peering in. They hung on the sides of the tram by one hand while using the other hand to push the windows open and extend their open palms, sometimes touching the faces of passengers. Hawkers pushed their way between the hard wooden benches to sell food and beverages from trays hung around their necks; petty thieves worked in tandem, one distracting a passenger while the other picked his pockets; and beggars roamed the cars using crying flea-bitten babies for their hustle. The women's cars, shielded by dark curtains, resounded with strident shrieks when a man dared to peep between the drapes.

As perilous as it was, I loved every minute of the ride. I was at one with Cairo, with its people, its smells, its sounds, and its profound humanity. When the streetcar swept beyond the Ezbekiya Gardens, the northern border of the Cairo I knew, I was plunged into another world—Nasser country. On every street, giant posters with his likeness adorned the walls and covered the storefront windows, and the street vendors' carts flew pennants and banners bearing his image. The streets boomed with the music of the legendary Om Kalthoum, who had supported the revolution with new songs celebrating the liberation of Egypt.

In these parts of Cairo, Nasser was everything to everyone—pharaoh, savior, commander, father, brother, son, and neighbor. It was easy to see why. The face on the enormous posters projected both the warmth and depth of a leader's powerful love of Egypt and its people. The masses believed he had the ambition and the strength to restore their pride and dignity and the lost glory of their country, and the Raïs's fervor was contagious. I would have loved him too, were it not for his eagerness to wipe the Jews off the maps of the Arab world.

The Daher campus had an impressive façade, dominated by a monumental, tan-colored chapel that looked like a submerged whale covered with snail-like shells. It towered above the surrounding buildings with an aura of Olympian majesty. An arch at its entrance proclaimed its identity in gold letters in French and Arabic—Collège des Frères du Daher.

The gates were open. I ventured inside a courtyard as large as the main sports arena at the Gezira Sporting Club. The entire compound dwarfed the Bab-el-Louk campus and my old lycée put together. There was not a soul in sight, but muffled chants drifted from the chapel. I retreated, intimidated by this ocean of Christianity.

I took a long walk around the neighborhood. Like much of Cairo, the district of Daher was an eclectic blend of opulent streets lined with elegant apartment houses and slum-lined unpaved alleyways in which vehicles had left deep furrows in the dirt. Walking through it aroused in me a hunger for exploration I hadn't felt since I'd roamed the Bab-el-Louk souk in what seemed like a lifetime earlier. Like all Cairenes, I knew the city was huge, but until that ride I hadn't imagined its tentacular immensity. There was no end to Cairo's lacework of streets and alleys, no end to the breathtaking beauty of its mosques and minarets, no end to the subtle variances of its neighborhoods, each with its own style of architecture, and no end to the diversity of its people. Muslims, Christians and remaining Jews, Nubians, Berbers, Armenians, Europeans from the East and the West, and crossbreeds of every combination walked its streets. Cairo was truly *Umm al Dunya*, the Mother of the World, and I wanted to explore it all before leaving it for the rest of my life.

***

On a Saturday, as I walked down the stairs on my way to the hotel kitchen, I heard piano music emanating from the dining room. Quietly, I opened the door one inch at a time, enough to peep inside without disturbing the player.

At the piano, Calista seemed to be in a trance. Her fingers rolled over the keyboard as though they had a will of their own. I didn't want to disturb her, so I pulled the door back, but its hinges shrieked like a wounded cat. Calista didn't stop playing. She looked up, smiled and made a beckoning motion of the head. I tiptoed to the table near the piano.

When she finished, the only word I could utter was, "Magic!"

"Thank you, my dear. Do you know this piece?" she asked. I shook my head. "It's the third movement of Mozart's Piano Sonata, *Alla Turca*. It's commonly translated as the Turkish March, but it literally means the Turkish way."

"Why Turkish? I thought Mozart was German! No?" I asked.

"In those days, Turkish music was all the rage in the courts of Europe. It inspired Mozart to write a first piece, *The Turkish Concerto*, before *Alla Turca*, and later an opera entitled *The Abduction from the Seraglio*, a self-explanatory title."

"Did he travel to Turkey?"

"No, Mozart never set foot in Turkey, just as he never came to Egypt, but he wrote two operas set here—*Thamos, King of Egypt* and *L'oca del Cairo* . . ."

"The Eyes of Cairo?"

"No, dear, eyes is 'occhi,'" she chortled. "'L'oca' means the goose, and the opera's title is *The Goose of Cairo*."

"Seriously? An opera about a goose?"

Calista smiled and said, "Seriously. It was a silly story about an aristocrat who used a hollow goose to seduce a girl, just like the Greeks used the Trojan horse to win their war. Mozart knew it was worthless, and he didn't bother to finish it. Do you like classical music?"

"Some. We haven't been to a concert since the Suez war. But we listen to recitals on the BBC sometimes," I said. "I liked what you played. You could be a professional pianist!"

"I *am* a professional pianist," she said with a half-suppressed laugh. "Rather, I *was* one." A flash of sadness whooshed over her eyes, then she smiled and said, "Now I teach future professional pianists."

"But you play better than the pianists on the BBC!"

Calista smiled again. "If you're still as gallant by the time you're of age to attend university, you'll be a lady-killer!"

"A what?"

"Not literally!" she chortled. "It means you'll break the heart of many a lady."

I asked why she'd stopped playing professionally. Another fleeting shadow came and went. She said a car accident had damaged her left elbow and forearm, making it too painful to play for long periods of time.

"Professional musicians must practice day and night to be good. I was not in shape for that." A second later, her mood bounced back, and she asked, "Do you want to hear a short waltz by Chopin?"

"Yes, please!"

"Chopin's original name for it was *Valse du petit chien* because its inspiration was watching a tiny dog chasing his tail," she said. "In English they call it the *Minute Waltz*, pronounced as 'my-noot,' which means tiny, miniature, not 'minit,' as it's commonly mispronounced by people who think it's a one-minute waltz," said Calista as she filled the room with Chopin's joyful little waltz.

***

The first weeks of school left me more disoriented and estranged than I'd ever been at the old Bab-el-Louk campus. A sense of darkness permeated the air in the classrooms, the hallways and the three school yards. The process of Arabization of Egyptian education that started after the revolution was nearly complete. A new crop of young French-speaking Egyptian or Lebanese Brothers had replaced the old guard. The newcomers were more overtly political than their predecessors, and many were loath to enforce the old Lasallian rule of keeping politics out of the school. As a result, the yard resounded with political arguments that, more often than not, ended with some form of vilification of the *Yahood*. When fights erupted, the courtyard supervisors were prompt to stop them, but they did little to defend the tormented from the tormentors' jeers and taunts.

It killed me to remain passive in the face of injustice, but I had vowed not to get in trouble. I would only fight back in self-defense. The bullies in the courtyard were few, but they were loud and muscular. They were self-baptized *les Duraillons*, the Toughies, and their targets were the Jews and the *tapettes*, the French word for faggot. That slur included anyone they deemed too effeminate or not tough enough to strike back at them. They liked to stand over their prey, too close for comfort, and tell them in fine details how they would slaughter them and their families, and throw their mangled corpses into the sea.

In February, the entire country celebrated the first anniversary of the merger of Egypt and Syria into the United Arab Republic. All over Cairo, crowds marched to the tunes of martial music and to voices shouting political and anti-Jewish harangues, along with the everlasting wails of Om Kalthoum's songs of love and country.

In the neighborhood of Daher, the streets were dense with women in black abayas and niqab, men in galabeyas and keffiyehs. Fewer people went out wearing occidental clothes, which confirmed the mounting influence of the Muslim

Brotherhood and other fundamentalist groups. It was odd because Gamal Abdel Nasser was virulently anticlerical and he had thrown Muslim Brothers in jail by the busloads, especially after their failed assassination attempt against him. He railed against the religious leaders for their attempts to impose a dress code for women and to restrict their education or access to work. Yet, the majority of the Brotherhood praised Nasser for his ongoing ethnic cleansing of the Jews.

The decibel levels were a shade more subdued in the elegant vicinity of Tahrir Square than in the impoverished all-Arab neighborhoods along the streetcar line, but the crowds' fervor was identical.

The euphoria found echoes in the school courtyard. It galvanized the bullies and their attacks redoubled. So far, I'd rarely been the target of the nasties, but I knew it was coming. I contained my rage by remembering Oncle Léon's teachings about Gandhi's principles of non-violence. When I was tempted to punch a bully, I would mull over the words of the Mahatma, "An eye for an eye makes the entire world blind." The mantra still made me chuckle and calmed me down, but I knew I was reaching the limits of my inner Gandhi.

***

As the romance between my father and Calista burgeoned, I was both happy for them and worried. I'd never seen my father so smitten before, and Calista seemed to reciprocate his attentions. In the past, there had always been some distance between Papa and his paramours and, except for Mrs. Wertheim, his liaisons wouldn't last long. Papa's women would take a few laps on the stage, some longer than others, but they would vanish when the curtain fell. With Calista, everything was different. Living under the same roof at the Anglo-Swiss brought us in contact every day, several times a day sometimes, but that was only one factor in their relationship—the main factor is that they had fun together, and the times I spent with them were a feast of laughter, teasing and fun.

At dinner, Calista often regaled us with stories of her education in the music schools she'd attended in Athens, Milan and Paris. Many of her classmates had reached excellence and fame in the world. Papa seemed to know their names; the only one I recognized was Maria Callas because her photographs were all over the covers of magazines and newspapers. I was more interested in learning about Calista's work during her sabbatical—which I called a 'satanical' to make her laugh.

Papa feared that my frequent questions would annoy or distract Calista, but she insisted that she enjoyed educating me on everything from the difference between a monograph and other forms of scholarly publications and the variances between musical traditions in neighboring countries.

She soon became a constant presence in our daily life. We saw her at breakfast, often at dinner, and sometimes they would go out on the town together. They kept a certain distance in public trying hard not to appear to be a twosome, but they were becoming a couple. I wished they would stay together, not only because they were happy, but because Calista was the first of my father's lovers with whom I was forging an affinity of my own. Still, I knew their time was finite. In a few weeks, Calista would take her sabbatical work to Istanbul, and she would vanish from our lives.

I was overjoyed on the day Calista invited me to observe her work when I came home from school. When she wasn't out scouring museums and archives, she worked by the piano in the hotel dining room. Between meals, the room was hers. On one table, she would place a pile of large volumes with rich pictures, and several notebooks and folders of various colors. On another table, she would set a microphone by the piano and play her transcriptions into it. The music was recorded into a heavy machine with a ribbon running between two reels. Calista introduced the machine as 'the thief of sounds' and showed me how it worked. I'd never seen a tape-recording machine, and I marveled that it played music without the scratching sound of a needle dancing along the grooves of a vinyl record.

***

At La Salle, it was all I could do to avoid being sucked into disputes, political, racial or otherwise, and resist provocation. It came at the cost of being called a coward and a faggot. I ignored the insults because I didn't want to engage in a cycle of permanent fighting.

The first challenge to my vow of non-violence came when a pack of bullies mocked and mistreated a younger boy, calling him a faggot in disguise. The boy ran away in tears to the end of the yard, sat on a bench, and curled up in a fetal position, trying to shrink himself and become invisible. I sat next to him and whispered words of comfort in his ear. The leader of the pack, a strapping lad named Christopher, noticed my move and came running.

"Hey, Jew!" he yelled. "What do you think you are doing? This is not your business, it's my business!"

"Fine business, scaring little boys!"

"Little and big Jew boys! I don't discriminate!" He looked me in the eye. "Someday we'll shoot every one of you like ducks in a pond."

"How very sporting of you! Big fat guy shooting helpless ducks in a pond! It's so manly!"

"Get up and I'll show you manly!"

"I don't fight with thugs," I said. "I believe in non-violence."

"Non-violence, that's the new word for being a coward and a faggot Jew! A khawal hiding under his own shadow!"

The bell rang, ending the recess. Christopher spit on the ground. "I'll get you, Jew! Maybe not today, not tomorrow, but I'll give you a taste of this!" he said, grabbing his genitals.

On the following day, Christopher and his buddies jeered and taunted me with insults, hoping to start a fight, but I ignored them. They grew angry and redoubled their provocations, but I stood still. One of my classmates, Mario Schiaparelli, came to me and said, "If you hang out with me, these assholes will leave you alone."

I was surprised. Mario and I were not friends. We were far too different for that. Mario was easygoing and companionable while I was inhibited and kept to myself. We'd had only a few brief and inconsequential conversations, so I didn't know why he was protecting me, but I was grateful for it. At recess, if the bullies would come near me and try to provoke me, he would nonchalantly join me and engage me in conversations about books and films. He seemed to scare the toughies because they ceased to bother me.

Mario stood out at La Salle. He was tall, intelligent, and he had a good sense of humor. Everyone liked him. It helped that he had an illustrious last name. He liked to boast that he was the great-nephew of Giovanni Schiaparelli, the celebrated Italian astronomer who'd studied the solar system and mapped the surface of Mars. He had another celebrated relative, the designer Elsa Schiaparelli. When he dropped their names, just in case I didn't know about his famous relations, he was visibly surprised that I didn't look impressed. I thought it would turn him off, but it had the opposite effect. It made me more interesting in his eyes, perhaps because I wasn't a sycophant like some of his classmates. I was as well-read as he was and could hold my own in our literary conversations which he approached with the killer instinct of a duelist.

Although our tastes were as opposite as could be, literature became our primary bond.

Mario loved science-fiction with a passion. I hated the genre, but his enthusiasm made me want to learn about it. He revered his great-uncle, Giovanni Schiaparelli, whom he called "the Master of the Celestial Universe," not only for his discovery of asteroids but also for his studies of the planet Mars. Mario claimed that Giovanni's books *The Falling Stars* and *Life on Mars* had inspired the likes of H. G. Wells, Edgar Rice Burroughs, and many other masters of science-fiction.

Mario was horribly disappointed when I told him I had not read H. G. Wells or Burroughs's futuristic novels. I was only familiar with Burroughs's Tarzan books, which I'd read years before.

"How could you not like sci-fi?"

"I have no affinity with sci-fi, as you call it. Pure and simple!"

"If you read a single Jules Verne novel, I bet you will become a sci-fi fanatic on the spot. How much do you want to bet?"

I refused the bet, but I agreed to read one Jules Verne novel. He handed me a two-for-one volume that contained both *From the Earth to the Moon* and *Journey to the Center of the Earth*.

"If you read both books, you'll become an addict," he predicted.

I was skeptical about that, but a friendship was born.

***

Wednesday afternoons were time off in the French school system. It was a pause intended to give the students an afternoon for outdoor activities, but it was not compulsory. We could use that time at our discretion. Usually, I spent these afternoons in my room, reading, writing, daydreaming, or masturbating, but that changed when Calista issued an open invitation to visit her at her makeshift studio in my free time.

I loved listening to Calista's exotic recordings. Her huge collection of eclectic tapes included ancient music played on primitive instruments; old songs that only very old people could remember; religious chants recorded in churches, mosques and synagogues across the Mediterranean basin; and interviews with all kinds of musicians, composers, and teachers. Calista had also amassed a treasure trove of ancient music sheets of all eras, photographs from ancient manuscripts and handwritten musical notes on lined paper. She would annotate them and rehearse them on her piano before recording them on her 'thief of sounds.'

"These precious recordings allow us to isolate and define the common threads that tied together the countries around the Mediterranean basin."

"How can you detect which country influenced which other country?"

"It's not an exact science. It's more like assembling pieces of an enormous puzzle using solid scholarship and a lot of guesswork that will later be put to the test by scientific research."

Calista took a dog-eared atlas with several bookmarks of paper or cloth embroidered with Arab calligraphy and opened it on a double-paged map of the Mediterranean. She then covered it with a sheet of tracing paper annotated with multicolored arrows and marks.

"All these countries in the Mediterranean basin were parts of vast empires at certain times in their history. Too many to enumerate, but I'm sure you're familiar with the Greek, Roman, Arab, and Ottoman empires. These devastating wars of conquest and annexation caused wide migrations of populations within the expanded empire."

"What that's gotta do with music?"

"A lot. Migrants don't leave their culture behind. They carry their knowledge with them—their traditions, their songs and dances, their oral histories, and even their clothing styles and culinary customs. They also take on the customs of their new surroundings. Just imagine the prodigious consequences of such a rich exchange of cultures! It affects their lives, their laws, their spirituality, and their values. It's the silver lining in the clouds of pain and turmoil of the wars of conquest."

Calista opened another page of her atlas and once again covered it with tracing paper full of annotations. Her index finger drew a sweeping circle on the map from Western Asia to the edge of the Soviet Union. "That's the Ottoman Empire under Suleiman the Magnificent," she said. "At its height, the empire comprised a sizable chunk of the world, from what is now the Greater Middle East, which covered the Arab world and western Asia, the Levant, and North Africa—"

Calista moved her fingers across the map, softly caressing each country as she enumerated them. "All that, plus Cyprus, Iran, Pakistan, up to Afghanistan. And through the Balkans all the way to present-day Hungary and Ukraine, now part of the Soviet Union. Can you imagine?"

"Not really."

"Do you think it's a coincidence that countries as different as Greece, Turkey, Spain, the entire Middle East, and even Bosnia, show so many similarities in their music, their poetry, their food, their architecture, and other cultural traits? What do they have in common?"

"Obvious! Just being a part of the Ottoman empire! Whoa!" I exclaimed. "And you're studying all that?"

"Yes, I said it earlier, it's worse than a Chinese puzzle, but that's where all the fun is!"

Listening to Calista made me aware of my abysmal ignorance, especially in the realm of music. Of classical music, all I knew were a few pieces by Mozart and Beethoven, which I had listened to on Nona's scratchy gramophone. Of Arab music, I only knew the songs of Om Kalthoum and Farid el Attrash that poured out of shops and cafés along the streets. I was more familiar with modern music from French ballads to rock 'n' roll.

After a few hours Calista would look at her watch and exclaim, "Time to stop! Your father will be furious with me if I interfere with your homework!"

"Nah, he never gets mad at you. He likes you too much for that!"

"Did he tell you that?"

"I've known my father for almost fourteen years. I don't need words, I just read his mind."

Calista let out an amused titter and wave me away.

***

Another attack on a vulnerable younger boy made a showdown with the bullies inevitable. Christopher's latest prey was a half-Jewish and half-Maronite Catholic Lebanese boy named Anatole Tabet. The boy was dressed with fastidious care, and he sported a flaxen pompadour, which Christopher called faggot hair. Anatole swore that he only liked girls, but Christopher ordered him to bare his ass so he could see if there were traces of buggery. Getting only tears for a response, Christopher grabbed the terrified boy by the waist, yanked his belt open and pulled his pants down as his mates chanted, "Pants down, faggot!"

A spike of anger rocked my gut and, without thinking, I yelled at Christopher, "It takes a perverted moron to say he can tell if a boy has been fucked by looking at his naked ass. If there is a faggot here, it's you!"

A rumble rose in the courtyard, and I realized the extent of my foolishness. Christopher was a member of a boxing team, and a single punch would probably flatten me—but it was too late to stand down even if I wanted to. And even though I was terrified I wanted an eye for an eye and a tooth for a tooth.

Christopher's first three punches left me breathless and staggering against a wall. I thought he would finish me with another few punches, but Christopher lifted his arms in victory, flexing his bulging biceps, and told me to get ready for the coup de grâce. While he was prancing, I seized the moment to lunge at him and kick him in the balls with all my strength. He fell to his knees, then down to the ground, howling like a wounded animal. I fell on my butt, overwhelmed by dueling feelings of guilt for the pain I'd caused and relief for my fortuitous victory over the low-rent Goliath.

Two schoolyard supervisors rushed to lug Christopher to the infirmary. The third overseer looked at my roughed-up face, declared that I didn't need medical help, and dragged me to the office of Brother Karim, his superior.

I tried to explain to Brother Karim the reason for the fight and the urgency to defend Anatole against a vicious aggressor, but he wasn't impressed. No matter what I said, his response was that I should have called for help, not handled things myself.

"So it's wrong to rescue the meek who shall inherit the earth?" I asked.

The Brother looked surprised. "A Jew quoting Matthew 5:5? That's a first! Well, I commend you for your knowledge, but you're not in charge of defending the meek! Who do you think you are, boy?"

Later that day, I asked Anatole about the outcome of the deal. He said that Brother Karim had scolded him for keeping company with "rabble-rousers" like me—and that the Brother had ordered him to keep quiet for his own good.

Later, Mario told me that the fathers of both Christopher and Anatole were generous contributors to Catholic charities. If one rich donor knew that his vicious son had assaulted and humiliated another rich donor's son in front of his classmates, the donations would stop flowing.

***

Mario's father had an extensive collection of modern sculptures throughout the house. His cavernous home study housed a vast library of novels and books on all forms of art. On his shelves, the volumes were interspersed with portraits of Salvador Dalí, Picasso, Juan Miró and Max Ernst, and many others I didn't recognize. Entire rows contained slim volumes by surrealist poets. I felt nostalgic for my grandfather's study. The Schiaparelli library was larger and more varied than my grandfather's, but the office of both men reflected the same spirit of devotion to great minds.

On our walks through the Daher neighborhood after school, Mario and I would discuss ad nauseam the fine points of art and literature. We'd both read books about the Dada art movement, and we could argue forever on whether it was true Art or just anti-art created by cheeky artists to provoke the bourgeoisie. While I didn't share Mario's passion for all things avant-garde, I was delighted to discover new writers and artists, and forms of art I didn't know existed. We seemed to differ on almost every subject, but our debates were inventive and stimulating.

On Mario's birthday, his parents gifted him with a shiny green Raleigh bicycle. I was both happy for Mario and choked with envy. A bicycle was just what I needed to roam the areas of Old Cairo I wanted to explore. Mario would often lend me his new bike and ride his brother Salvatore's red Raleigh. Sal was studying art in Florence and had authorized Mario to ride the Raleigh just enough to keep it running.

It was easier to negotiate the traffic of Cairo on bicycles than I had expected. Mario had equipped both bikes with battery-operated horns that were almost as loud as the klaxons of cars and buses. We used them liberally to stave off careless motorists and pedestrians and to avoid collisions. Riding fast in the hot wind gave me a sense of total freedom, and every minute on the saddle was pure joy. The streets of Cairo were all mine, at last.

***

It was the last week Calista would be in Cairo. Neither she nor my father were displaying sorrow or emotions about their impending separation. I was on pins and needles.

How did they feel? Did they have plans for the future? I couldn't resist broaching the subject, and I asked Papa, "Calista will leave in a couple of days. What are you going to do?"

"What is there to do? I'll drive her to the airport and wish her bon voyage."

"That's it? No marriage proposal, no engagement, no nothing?"

Papa shook his head. I was surprised by his nonchalance. Incredulous, I insisted. "But you love her, don't you?"

"That's neither here nor there," he answered after a long moment. "Marriage is not possible."

"Why?" I asked.

"Isn't it obvious? Her middle name is Christina and her last name is Christakos. That's a lot of *Christ* compressed into a single name!"

"So what? I bet you she's as practicing a Christian as you are a Jew!" I said, forming a zero with my fingers. Anticipating his response, I added, "You don't have to tell Nona she's a different kind of infidel!"

"Funny! Since when do you give a hoot about my marital status?"

"Since you found a smart one to fool around with!"

He gave a weak smile and said, "Look, hijico, I know you like her and you mean well, but it's not just about her religion. Calista is much younger than I am, she's a brilliant and independent woman. We traveled together for a while and made each other happy, and that means you too—" I nodded. "But some things aren't meant to happen. Calista has her own life, and I know she'll go far in the world. Her very own world—not my world. It'll never work!"

"How can you know for sure?"

"Neither Calista nor I want to marry again, and that's that!"

"*Again*? What do you mean, *again*?"

"Calista is a widow, son." Papa was surprised by my bewilderment. "I thought you knew. Calista said she told you about her accident—"

"Yes, she told me about the accident," I said. "But not that she was married."

"She was. That accident didn't just take her career. It also took her husband's life."

I wanted to cry for Calista. I would have never suspected that such a happy and vital person could have suffered such adversity. Where did she find the strength to overcome such hardship? Not only had she survived the loss of her husband and her career in one fatal moment, but she hadn't allowed grief or recent handicap to destroy her passions and her love of life. She continued to pursue her musical career, albeit in a different way than she had imagined. My admiration for Calista turned to pure awe, and it made the prospect of losing her unbearable.

The rest of the week went by fast. We continued to ignore the sword of Damocles that hung over our heads by a thread. I understood that both Calista and Papa had made a mutual decision to spend their last time together in gratitude rather than in sorrow.

The night before Calista's departure, her relatives organized a goodbye party. It was a bittersweet affair. There was much sadness beneath the conviviality of the evening. I could see it in the eyes of both Papa and Calista, and I could barely keep my eyes dry.

After the last guests had retired, it was my time to say goodbye. I knew Papa and Calista would leave at dawn for the airport, and I might not see her.

Calista and I hugged for a long time. I was determined not to say anything sad or sorrowful, but I couldn't help whispering, "I wish you could stay with us forever." Calista mouthed her answer, "Me too!" There was nothing more to say. A last long hug, and I walked away, holding my tears. As I climbed the stairs to my room, I reflected that much of my life had consisted of serial goodbyes.

When I entered my room, there was a gift package on my bed, accompanied by a card. No words, a drawing etched in bright red lipstick of two lips forming a large smile. I smiled back.

Calista's gift was a rare album of flamenco music from her collection. When we had listened to it together, a song, a *canto hondo* had pulled at my heartstrings, and I had asked Calista to play it again. Not only had Calista remembered, but she had given up one of her precious possessions as a token of her love. It moved me deeply.

I played the record throughout the night. The *canto hondo* resembled the chant of a muezzin resonating from the top of a minaret. Calista had taught me that the Roma language was a blend of Spanish and Arabic dialects, and the more I played the *canto hondo*, the more words I could decipher with the help of my dormant Ladino. The *cantaor* chanted his words in elongated syllables that sounded like long laments, much as Om Kalthoum did in her love songs. Flamenco was the sound of home.

That *canto hondo* was the chant of the exiles longing to see their homeland. It conjured up visions of a home I'd never seen but which I imagined had been the home of my ancestors in medieval Spain. I remembered my father's stories of the golden centuries of *conviviencia* in Islamic Iberia, the time of coexistence between religions, before the Inquisition turned the new Garden of Eden into a river of blood. I'd always wondered whether the legendary Al-Andalus was myth or history, but either way the rich guttural voice of the *cantaor* gave me an otherworldly sense of déjà vu.

Wavering between heartbreak, wrath, nostalgia and hope, the song spoke of *añoranza*—another word Calista had taught me—the yearning for a home real or imagined but forever lost. As I listened to the lament, its raw poignancy made its way into my soul, reviving along its path atavistic memories of times and places that were, truth or legend, the core of my heritage.

CHAPTER 15

Winter of 1960

Mario's brother, Salvatore, had come back to Cairo for the Christmas holidays, so I could no longer borrow his bicycle. It was time to get one of my own. Papa still refused to buy me a bike because he thought the Cairo traffic was too dangerous, so I decided to buy one in secret and set out to raise the money for it.

I went to the Bab-el-Louk souk and sold the old winter clothes Maman had bought me a year or two earlier, and Monsieur Michel was kind enough to buy back many of my books for his used book section. I told my mother that I needed new textbooks and asked for money—but it wasn't enough to pay for a used bicycle. I turned to my maternal uncles, Jacques and Maurice, who owned a sports store in Heliopolis.

Before I could ask for money, Oncle Maurice said, "You're not yourself today. What's going on?"

"Nothing," I said.

He gave me a knowing look. "Girl trouble?" I shook my heard. "Fellous trouble?" he said, rubbing his fingers to indicate money. I shook my head again. He insisted. After extracting a promise that he wouldn't tell my mother, I vented my frustration about Papa's refusal to let me have a bicycle. Without a word, Oncle Maurice opened his wallet and proffered a twenty-pound banknote. It was such a generous gift that I felt too embarrassed to accept it.

"I didn't confide in you to get your fellows," I protested.

""Nonsense!" he said as he shoved the bill in my shirt pocket.

"Il faut que ça reste entre hommes. Let's keep this between men, all right? Your mother would kill me if she knew!" At the bus stop, he almost dislocated my shoulder with a powerful goodbye slap on the back. "Ma'al salama! Go in safety and in good health! It's good to follow your passions, but don't be reckless, my son."

When I found my dream two-wheeler, I was short by eight pounds. I didn't look for a cheaper vehicle. My mind was set on that burgundy-colored 1951 Raleigh Sports equipped with a three-speed Sturmey-Archer shifter that had seen better days but still worked. Even after hard bargaining in true Egyptian fashion, the shortage was only lowered to six pounds. I begged the seller to hold the Raleigh for me. I would return shortly with the full price.

And once again I became a thief.

I lifted three pounds from my father's wallet and six pounds from my mother's purse, one pound at a time in the hope that they wouldn't notice that the money was missing. Stealing filled me with guilt and self-loathing, but my obsession won over my moral sense. Riding my new, glorious machine, I was king of the road.

I'd stolen more than the selling price so I could pay a shopkeeper near La Salle to store the bicycle during school hours, and I promised the *bawab* at the Anglo-Swiss Hotel that my mother would give him a larger backsheesh if he would let me park my contraband bicycle in a storage room behind the elevator. Secretly, of course.

Riding to school the next morning, I felt both exhilarated and a little guilty—but I was still king of the road.

***

My favorite explorations took me deep into the core of Naguib Mahfouz's Cairo Trilogy. When I was studying the Mahfouz's work, Ostáz Kamal had deployed maps of the area that had two names—Old Cairo and Medieval Cairo—and was divided into religious quarters such as Islamic Cairo, Coptic Cairo, and the Jews' Alley or Haret el-Yahood.

The old city was fascinating. Its core was immutable, frozen in time, but its adjoining neighborhoods were being gentrified by the new elite. I was particularly moved by the areas that were once predominantly Jewish. Those streets and alleyways had seen successive generations of Jews throughout the ages—old pharaonic Jews descended from Joseph; Karaite Jews who'd come from Iraq during the Caliphates; Spanish Jews expelled by the Inquisition; Ashkenazi Jews who'd fled Eastern Europe ahead of Hitler's drums of war; and Arab Jews who'd left Syria, Libya, or Yemen to seek a better life in this land of plenty. Now dozens of jackhammers and steamrollers were used to renovate old dwellings and bring the modern world to the old grounds.

During Salvatore's Christmas visit, he had sung the praises of the brothels of the Shubra and Faggala districts, and Mario was determined to find one or two of them. At a *baladi* café, in a souk, among the noise of men smoking *sheeshas* and playing *shesh-besh*, we overheard a conversation between two young men, probably university students. They were boasting of sexual feats at their respective bordellos. The older one was describing his new discovery in the Mouski, *Sett* Latifah's bordello, going over the fine points of each lady's charms while bringing his five fingers to his lips and kissing them to state his utter delight. As the young man gave his friend the address, Mario pulled a notebook out of his pocket and wrote it down. The young man noticed it and seemed to find that very funny. He turned to us and gave us the names of the two best girls. I asked awkwardly about the price of a turn with them. He gave us a range which went from the affordable to the heights of extravagance, explaining that the most expensive ones were known to take men to the highest peaks of *mazag*, which rendered them unable to enjoy sex with their wives and concubines. "Tell Sett Latifah that Samir Ashraf sent you. Maybe you'll get a discount and I'll get a free pass!"

Mario wanted to go immediately. I was more reluctant. I hated the notion of sex for sale, but I couldn't resist the call of my hormones. I needed sex with a woman of flesh and blood, not with a glossy picture and a lubricated hand. Friday being the Muslim day of rest—as was Saturday for the Jews and Sunday for the Christians—we chose a Saturday night because, since many couples and families would be out on the town, going to shows and restaurants, the cathouses would be less crowded and therefore more likely to let teenagers in.

I didn't worry much about Papa staying home and cramping my style. Since Calista had left us, he had resumed his Cairo-by-night escapades, although there were still shadows of sadness and loneliness in his eyes. I knew he missed Calista as much as I did.

***

At sunset on the following Saturday, Mario and I chained our bicycles to a palm tree and walked toward the brothel. It was surprisingly lodged in a large elegant house on a tree-lined street. We first thought we had the wrong address, but the flow of men walking toward the house told us otherwise. A few yards from the front door, under a sheer canopy, a tall and muscular Nubian in a bright white galabeya and a large red waistband checked the visitors before letting them in.

When I mentioned Samir Ashraf's name, the Nubian told another servant to replace him and motioned to follow him. He left us at the front door and went inside. From the open door, we could see him whispering in the ear of a woman who smoked a flat Turkish cigarette in a long holder. Her queenly demeanor made it obvious she was the madam, Sett Latifah.

When the Nubian let us in, the woman took a long look at us with an air of amusement, then she broke out in laughter.

"My young friend Samir has a sense of humor," she said in French with a heavy accent, "Does he think I run a kindergarten?" Sett Latifa's entourage mirrored her laughter. "The school for babies is down the street."

Ignoring the sarcasm, I said, "I don't think we'll find Zeinab and Khalila down the street."

Sett Latifah laughed again. "Can you babies afford them?"

"Of course!" I said, pretending to be offended. I proffered a few banknotes in the exact amount Samir had suggested. "My friend here has the same amount."

Again, Sett Latifah burst out in a raucous laughter. "All right, boys. Khalila and Zeinab will see you. On one condition, and that is—" She took her time, prolonging the suspense, and laughed again, "When you babies grow up and make lots of money, you will remember it was me, Latifah, who helped you two get laid for the first time!" She barked an order to a servant girl and walked away in a puff of smoke.

In contrast to the house's elegant facade, its salons were garish. The entire decor was a discordant symphony in red and gold, and its furniture was a bricolage of Arabian-style ottomans and fake antique French furniture that smelled of fresh wood and paint. Men and women in tuxedos and long dresses mingled with people in galabeyas and headgear. The air was thick with the scent of incense, cigarette smoke, and a medley of perfumes that was a little nauseating. I whispered to Mario, "What do we do if we like the same girl!?" The women appeared before we found an answer.

Zeinab and Khalila did not bother to ask for our preferences. Zeinab took my arm and Khalila took Mario's. Coincidence or professional instinct, their choice would have been ours. Zeinab was dark-skinned, petite, wide-eyed, and her makeup was bare. She wore a white abaya and a sheer hijab that revealed a shock of long henna-reddened hair, but her modest attire belied the promise of naughtiness in her eyes and mocking smile. Mario's girl, Khalila, was her opposite. She wore a tight Western-style dress with a plunging neckline that revealed an ample cleavage, and her hair had been bleached to a platinum blond hue that made her look like an Arab Marilyn Monroe.

In the pink bedroom, Zeinab sensed my discomfort and took charge. She sat me on the bed, removed my shirt, and caressed my chest with an occasional light scratch of her fingernails as she disrobed. Her odor of cheap perfume, dried henna and earthy sweat were inhibiting, and I was only mildly aroused. Zeinab ignored my reticence; she guided my hands to her breasts and fondled my genitals, playfully at first, then with a harder touch. When I reached full hardness, she took my full erection into her mouth. Her unrelenting tongue, and the sight and touch of her bouncing breasts made me shake with lust. I said I wanted to be inside her, but she ignored me and brought me to climax, swallowing my semen with groans of pleasure as though she were drinking a sweet nectar.

"Tammam! Perfect!" she exclaimed. "Mabrouk, ya habibi! For a first time, you were a real tiger!"

I knew she was faking it, but it didn't diminish my pleasure. "What makes you think it's my first—?"

Zeinab smiled and said, "Women know these things."

She got up and got dressed. I wanted to talk a little longer, but Zeinab was ready to go.

"Yalla! You'll get me in trouble with Sett Latifah!"

Zeinab brushed her lips over mine. "Come back and see me again, ya habibi!" she said, rubbing my crotch. She smiled and walked out.

Mario was downstairs and had already paid *Sett* Latifah. I paid my money and added a large tip for Zeinab. The madam smiled and said, "See you, boys!"

When I got home, I took a long shower, using half a bar of soap to wash away the reek of sweat, incense and cheap perfume. In bed, I reviewed the experience with mixed feelings. Zeinab has taken me to the highest level of pleasure I'd known, but something was missing. I was not fulfilled. I wanted sex with a bit more meaning. I missed the way I felt with Patricia, even after having partial sex—overwhelmed by feelings of joy and peace that lingered on for days.

***

The inevitable happened. As I was wheeling my bike through the lobby to park it in the back, my father came out of the elevator, dressed to the nines. Before I could utter a word, Papa barked, "Put that thing away and meet me in my room! Now!" I took the bike to the storage room and walked the eight flights up, trying to figure out a way to handle the blow.

"Where did you get that two-wheeled disaster?"

"It's mine. I bought it."

"You bought this thing without telling me?" he yelled. "*Against* my specific orders?"

"Your orders are unfair! And, once upon a time, I had a father who taught me it was our duty to disobey unjust orders!" I countered.

"We were talking about war crimes—not buying bicycles behind your father's back!" He was growing angrier by the minute. "How did you pay for it? Did your mother buy it for you?"

I laughed. "No, dear father, when it comes to suppressing my freedom, you and my mother form a perfect union. No! I sold my books and my Bar Mitzvah gifts, and I bought the cheapest bike I could afford!"

He looked at his watch. Knowing Papa hated to be late, especially for his romantic assignations, I thought of a gambit and played my hand. "All right, you win! It's not fair, but I give up!" I said, tossing my keys on the table. "Do whatever you want with the bike. I won't be here to find out."

"What do you mean by that?" Papa asked.

"I mean that I'm on strike as of this moment. No more school, no more studies."

"Over my dead body!"

I remained cool and said, "That's a cliché, dear father. Go to your rendezvous, and leave me alone! I'll go out too!"

He was taken aback by my cold and detached stance rather than my usual tantrums, and I could tell he didn't know quite how to handle it.

"And, pray tell, where will you go?" he asked, visibly worried despite his flippant tone.

"Why would you care? Just know that I won't go and live with my mother. She's worse than you are!"

"What the hell is going on with you?" he asked with growing alarm.

"What's going on, dear father, is that I'm fed up! Fed up with everything—my school, this country, Jews, Arabs, everything! And now you're taking one of the few things that gives me solace in this vie de merde! That's what is going on!"

"You're always so dramatic!" Papa said. "It will make your life very difficult in the real world."

"I don't care for your real world. That world is mean and ugly. It's a puke festival!"

"Calm down and tell me what's bothering you, will you?"

"Look, Papa, I don't want to be ungrateful. I know you've worked hard to keep me educated, fed and clothed—but for what? What's the point of my life? I'm locked up in a place that hates me! My school is a nightmare of insults and constant fights! My whole life is on hold! Please, Papa, tell me what's the point of this shitty life!"

"That's a whole other discussion. First tell me, is owning a bicycle the remedy for these painful things?"

"No, but it helps me forget. It makes me feel free! Riding around and discovering places takes my mind off this shit. I can breathe! And I've been riding for weeks without a single accident. I'm not a bloody baby! I'm fifteen years old—"

"Sorry, son, your math is still lousy. Fourteen years and two months do not make fifteen!"

I knew he was trying to bring humor into our confrontation, but I wasn't ready to calm down.

"Okay, but I'm still not a baby!" I said. "I feel older than Methuselah. If I had to choose between this shitty life and being hit by a bus, I'd go for the bus!"

Papa's face was suddenly ashen, and I felt deep pangs of guilt. "I'm sorry, Papa, I didn't mean to say these stupid things—"

"I'm the one who is sorry, hijico." Papa said. "It's all my mistake and I'm sorry. I should have listened to Nona and Rebecca, and we should have left this godforsaken place with them. I should have anticipated all the things that could go wrong, especially the toll it would take on you. I'm sorry, and I hope you'll forgive me."

That was not the reaction I expected. It was heartbreaking to see my father on the verge of tears, but it was comforting to feel heard and loved. "I've forgiven you a long time ago!" was all I could say.

We hugged for the longest time. Then I felt a need to change the mood and lighten things up. "Hey, Papa, you're beyond late for your rendezvous. Somebody taught me to never keep a lady waiting. Who was that?"

Papa let out a burst of sad laughter. "Okay, smart ass, I'm going! We'll talk about your infernal machine tomorrow, all right?"

"You mean, you'll let me keep it?"

"With a few conditions, like a complete safety check of your machine, and a few talks about traffic rules and other safety things a reckless boy might overlook."

"Fair enough!"

"You know you're the worst pain-in-the-butt son a man could have, right?"

"Do I have to answer that?"

After Papa left, my relief gave way to new pangs of anxiety. I sensed that this quarrel had been about more than the contraband bicycle. We'd been on the verge of a break. We had stopped at a fork in the road, a point where our paths could have diverged. There was no break this time, but what if it had happened?

Until that moment, I'd never seriously thought about a life without my father. He'd always been the main protagonist in my private playhouse—with my mother in the lead supporting role, and the rest of the family as the chorus. Since my earliest years, he'd been the headspring of my life, the headmaster of my knowledge, and as much as I craved to break away from the shackles of childhood, I feared a life away from the protective cocoon my father had woven around me.

***

At the end of Ramadan, a spectacular couple came to live at the Anglo-Swiss Hotel. Nazeem Al'a'Din Nazari Bey cut quite a figure with his waving mane of white hair, his Savile Row suits, and his monogrammed shirts. Everyone addressed him by his aristocratic title, Nazeem Bey, even though the revolution had abolished the titles of nobility. Traditions died hard in Egypt. Nazeem Bey was accompanied by a beautiful young lady named Gamila whom he introduced as his niece. She only spoke Arabic.

The Oxford-educated aristocrat was fluent in a quintet of languages. Beyond his native Arabic and his Oxonian English, he was fluent in French, Italian, and Greek. He had been an ambassador to several countries under King Farouk, but he had survived the purges of the revolution and was now active again, this time as a diplomatic envoy. He traveled frequently, usually without Gamila, and on rare occasions with her. When he was in town, two aides would come to the hotel every morning, share a cup of Turkish coffee, and have long conversations. Then the trio would leave in the Bey's chauffeur-driven shiny black Cadillac.

Nazeem Bey's niece was shy and avoided talking to strangers. After dinner, she would often retire to their suite, and Nazeem Bey would join our table and chat with my father while enjoying a snifter or two of Armagnac. He and Papa got on well. They liked to speak about contemporary issues as well as reminisce about bygone times. I loved to listen to their exchanges. They worried about the growing influence of the two new empires, the USA and the USSR, and the Cold War they were waging. Papa was convinced that the American Empire would win that Cold War because its policies were more in tune with the needs of the postwar world. Unlike the British and French empires, America's dominance would not be territorial but economic, strategic and cultural. I felt privileged to be a witness to their debates. It was like entering Plato's cave and listening to the discourse of giants.

Like all the monarchy's nobility, Nazeem Bey had seen his estate redistributed after the revolution, but the loss of land

and treasure had dented his fortune without reducing his lifestyle noticeably. He and his niece were staying at the Anglo-Swiss while his house was being remodeled, but I wondered why he'd chosen a modest hotel rather than one of the grand hotels near Tahrir Square. I also wondered why he presented Gamila as his niece when he was visibly enamored with her. Did he have another wife? Multiple wives? Muslim men were allowed four wives and many concubines, so why the need to hide Gamila from sight?

When Nazeem Bey was abroad, which was often, Gamila took her meals in her suite. She would only appear in the dining room when a girlfriend joined her for lunch or dinner. I enjoyed watching them chat and laugh together. In repose, Gamila had the serene facial expression of the figures on the bas-reliefs of ancient monuments, but when she laughed, the placid perfection of her traits would shatter, making her look like an impish girl rather than a pretty young woman. When I first saw her, she was hiding behind a colorless dress with no adornments and a headscarf that covered her hair and part of her face. Her face would light up when she removed her scarf and revealed big violet eyes full of vitality and mischief. It was all I could do not to stare at her when she came into the dining room.

"This is one smitten boy!" Papa said. I shrugged, but he continued, "Love or lust? That is the question!"

"My dear, dear father, didn't you tell me that life is better when everyone minds his own business—not once, not twice, but a thousand times?"

"My dear, dear son, your dear, dear father got the message," he said. "But I think this girl likes you."

"No way! What makes you think she likes me?"

"While she's talking with her friend, she darts looks at you, just like you stare at her when you think she's not paying attention."

"No way!"

After dinner, I fetched a magazine from the lobby and went back to my table. I sat and pretended to read while Gamila and her friend, engaged in a lively conversation, lingered at their table. To my surprise, my father wasn't wrong. Every now and then, Gamila would cast a furtive glance at me as she and her friends laughed. I felt pangs of desire, followed by fits of anxiety, hoping they weren't laughing at me, and again desire and an unwelcome erection. I couldn't get up for fear Gamila would notice my arousal. I was puzzled. Not only did she have a man in her life, uncle or lover or both, but why would such a pretty Arab woman be interested in a European schoolboy—and a Jewish one to boot?

***

A week or two later, I ran into Nazeem Bey by the pool at the Gezira Sporting Club. He ordered beverages and a plate of mezzes and asked questions about my academic interests and plans for university studies in the future. Then he said in a whisper, "You're an intelligent young man. Maybe you can help me."

"Me, help you? How?"

"Gamila is an extremely bright young woman, and she needs to perfect her education. I already have two tutors working with her, one on language and the other on arts and culture. Would you like to teach her French?"

I was flabbergasted. "I'd like to," I said, "but I don't know the first thing about teaching."

"I don't mean formal teaching—that will come later. For now, she needs basic conversation, just to get a taste of French culture. An appetizer. She's already learned the Latin alphabet, so you can read easy things with her."

The offer was appealing, but the prospect of working with Gamila filled me with anxiety. I feared that daily proximity to her would exacerbate my attraction to her, making it difficult if not impossible to focus on anything else. How could I resist the call of the forbidden fruit?

"I'm not sure I can do it," I said to Nazeem Bey. "I need to check my school schedule. May I answer in a day or two?"

After a long silence, Nazeem Bey told me "in strict confidence" that Gamila was not his niece but his protégée. After her parents died, Gamila became the ward of an uncle who worked for Nazeem Bey, and like all his employees and their families she came under his protection. Gamila's intelligence and beauty hadn't gone unnoticed by Nazeem Bey. He paid for her education, watched her progress, and waited for her to be old enough to become his third wife.

That was another surprise. Muslim customs allowed girls to marry at the age of puberty, so why the wait? Nazeem Bey answered my unspoken question. "Times are changing, and traditions need to change—that's why we had a revolution. In this new world, no woman or girl should be a man's property. I want Gamila to be mature and educated, and to marry by choice, not to please me or her guardian."

Before leaving, he gave a tap on the shoulder and added, "Needless to say, you would be well compensated for your efforts. Think about it."

I was burning to accept his offer, but it was fraught with danger. In the Machiavellian part of my mind, it was a double-edge sword. If I were to offend Gamila inadvertently, my father and I would be exposed to the wrath of a powerful man and that could jeopardize our exit from Egypt. On the flip side, if Gamila's progress satisfied Nazeem Bey, his influence could help secure exit visas for us. In either case, I would have to curb my lust for Gamila.

The next morning, I told Nazeem Bey that my answer was a resounding "Yes!"

***

Nazeem Bey opened the door to his suite and introduced me to Gamila. When I extended my hand, she hesitated before putting her hand in mine and shook it with a slight look of distaste.

After Nazeem Bey left the room, I felt awkward. Gamila and I hadn't exchanged a word before, and I wasn't sure how to address her. She took the lead and started quizzing me in an assertive staccato voice.

Why did Nazeem Bey pick me as a tutor? Why was it important for her to learn French? Why did everyone consider France the cultural beacon in the world? Why did they call French the diplomatic language?

Although my conversational Arabic had improved considerably after my summer of study with Ostáz Kamal, it was still awkward, and I had to pause to find the right words to answer her incessant questions. Gamila gloated when I asked her to speak more slowly. I didn't think it boded well for our work, but I soldiered on.

As we spoke, my eyes wandered around the sitting room. Vases of cut flowers, a few potted plants, and colorful shawls and veils covering the hotel furniture gave it a homey feeling. A hallway led further inside the suite, and I could see two doors which I surmised led to separate accommodations. Did that mean that Gamila and Nazeem Bey slept in separate bedrooms? I hoped they did, but I chased the thought away. I wasn't going to let my libido drag me into perilous territory.

At the end of our first session, it was clear that Gamila was of two minds about learning French. I asked her how she felt about the task. She said she had qualms about studying the language of Egypt's aggressors, France and Britain, but she was eager to please Nazeem Bey.

I said I understood and offered to stop the tutoring. "There's no point in wasting my time or yours," I said. "I'll let Nazeem Bey know in the evening."

Gamila looked contrite and repeated that she wanted to honor the Bey's wishes. She would do her best to overcome her resistance and work as hard as she could.

It took several lessons for Gamila to open up to my teaching. Emulating Ostáz Kamal's method, I started us by reading illustrated children's books. She was a fast learner, and she took to French with remarkable speed, but tutoring her was a difficult task. Gamila was given to mood swings, and from one session to the next I didn't know whether to expect an earnest student or a petulant child.

Whenever I threatened to quit, Gamila would instantly turn on the charm and beg me to stay for Nazeem Bey's sake. I truly wanted to quit every day because it was getting harder to hide my attraction to Gamila. She did nothing to help. When she would catch me staring at her, she would stare right back until I backed off. If she was aware of my feelings, she never let on, either because it offended her or because Arab women were expected to be demure, or both.

***

In spite of our ups and downs, Gamila's conversational skills improved. She spoke in halting language but with surprising clarity of mind. Nazeem Bey said he was pleased with Gamila's progress and asked me if I could take on other duties. He was arranging for tennis lessons with a former champion at the Gezira Sporting Club, and he wanted me to chaperone her on my days off school. "You can use that time as additional conversation classes."

"Shouldn't her chaperone be a female?"

"She has very few friends in Cairo, and she doesn't want a hired hand."

"But I *am* a hired hand, and I'm a male. What will people think?"

"They'll think of you as family. She trusts you now, and she speaks highly of you," he smiled. "And I'll tell my driver to spread the rumor that you're her European-educated cousin! You look like us anyway, so why not?"

I wanted to say that many people at the club knew that I was Jewish, but I let it go. It was puzzling to hear that Gamila "spoke highly" of me. We were like cats and dogs during our tutoring sessions. Did she like me more than she let on?

On tennis lesson days, Nazeem Bey's chauffeur would take us to the Club, and I would read while Gamila played. She disliked her tennis instructor, who had a knack for being both obsequious and condescending at the same time. She didn't like the Gezira Sporting Club; she took a scant view of its unbridled luxury, the subtle snobbery of its staff, and the colonial atmosphere that continued to reign so many years after the revolution.

After Gamila's tennis lesson, we would devote an hour to conversational French, then the black Cadillac would whisk us back to the hotel. Now and then, I would stay at the Club to meet my mother for lunch.

Inevitably, the time came when Maman came to the Club earlier than planned. She came to our table while I was still working with Gamila. Maman took an instant liking to my student and invited her to join us for lunch. I was mortified, but once again my mother did wonders. She was perfect with Gamila. She treated her like a long-lost daughter and sprinkled many *baladi* expressions in her perfect Arabic to make Gamila feel at home. It was good to see Gamila enjoying herself. In the short span of a lunch, my mother had broken down many of the barriers that Gamila had built between us.

Over my school holiday, Gamila and I spent more time at the Club after her tennis lessons. We would walk in the gardens or sit by the pool and talk. I wanted to know about her life, her village, and her family. She had grown up in a small village between Ismailia and the Great Bitter Lake. During the Suez war, the British had launched airstrikes on military installations in the Canal Zone, and explosives had fallen on her village, killing both her parents and her two brothers. She'd gone to live with her maternal uncle who worked in Nazeem Bey's farm in the Fayyoum. It surprised me to hear about the devastation sustained by Egyptian civilians during the war. The radios had only reported Nasser's military triumphs against the tripartite aggressors.

I wondered if she was in love with Nazeem Bey or if she was just grateful to him. After her parents died, he had taken her under his wing. It sounded medieval to me, but I understood that in some parts of Egypt, some traditions from the Middle Ages were still alive in the twentieth century. On large agricultural properties like Nazeem Bey's, the landowners took care of the fellahin who gave him their labor and their allegiance. In Gamila's eyes, Nazeem Bey was the most generous and compassionate lord who took care of every one of his fellahin, including their families and their livestock.

Everyone in Nazeem Bey's domain believed that he was educating her to make her a concubine when she came of age, but he surprised them. When Gamila was fifteen, Nazeem Bey went to her uncle and guardian and asked for the girl's hand in marriage. He could have married her at any age, but Nazeem Bey wanted to wait until Gamila's twentieth birthday, and he encouraged her to continue her education until then. He also gave her permission to reconsider the nuptials if she felt he was too old for her.

It sounded like a fairy tale, but she swore it was true. How could I possibly compete with such an admirable man?

***

My friends knew I was tutoring someone named Gamila, but they hadn't met her. I hadn't said much about her, and I had deliberately made no mention of her beauty because I knew it would unleash torrents of irritating ribbing and crude jokes. I knew that an encounter was bound to happen, but I tried to delay it by avoiding their usual spots.

The encounter I dreaded took place as Gamila was coming out of the tennis court after her lesson. I saw the gang—JP, Gil, Mono and the two Isaacs—heading toward us and I quickly told Gamila that it was time to make a quick getaway, but she didn't move. Ignoring my irritation, Gamila asked me to make the introductions, then invited the group to join us for tea. "I want to be polite to your friends," she whispered. We exchanged angry looks, then we both looked away.

As I'd expected, the boys jockeyed for Gamila's attention. It was not the first time our group had competed for a girl's attention; we'd had numerous silly cockfights when we had nothing better to do than chase girls. It was fun more often than not—but not this time. I was tense and distant, especially with Gamila whom I treated with the strict decorum of a tutor engaging with a tutee. For the first time, I saw my buddies as a threat, and myself at a disadvantage. I envied Gil's movie-star looks, JP's suave worldliness, and Momo's quick-witted sense of humor—which was even sharper in his native Arabic than in French.

A shadow of melancholy descended over me. I knew I had no claim on Gamila's affections, but I wanted to keep her to myself, to own her body and soul. It was insane and ridiculous. She was promised to another man—a man who adored her, not a boy with raw desires and a well-developed erotic imagination. I was small and insignificant in her eyes—and now in my own. I had to end this nonsense and stop tutoring her.

We barely spoke during the drive home. Once in the hotel, I asked Gamila to postpone the remaining lesson to the following day, excused myself, and repaired to my room.

A light tap scratched the door. Gamila came in, closed the door behind her and took my hand. "I don't like to see you sad," she said. "You're smarter than all those boys at the club put together and much better-looking too!" she added with a titter that was oddly provocative. I thought of taking her in my arms, but she put a hand on my forearm as if to forestall the move. She stepped back toward the door and said, "Why don't we study this evening? I'll have the kitchen bring up food."

Her fragrance of rosewater and orange blossom lingered in the room long after she'd left.

***

At the agreed-upon time, I tapped discreetly on Gamila's door. It opened by an invisible hand and shut as soon as I had crossed the threshold. I turned and saw a woman dressed in a pharaonic costume. Her brows and eyelashes were highlighted with mascara and kohl, her eyes shadowed by green malachite, and her skin covered with a chalk-like substance that gave her a pale cast. She made a pirouette to show off her attire—a long bright-white dress, part toga and part sheath, with a low-cut front tightly wrapped around her body and held by a belt with a large turquoise scarab. A simple headdress with another scarab rested on her forehead.

I thought I was hallucinating. This is what Cleopatra must've looked like. It's only when she smiled that I recognized Gamila.

"I am a little obsessed with Ancient Egypt," she said by way of excuse. "Maybe I can teach you something for a change!" she added with a giggle. "I have all kinds of pharaonic dresses and jewelry. Do you want to see them?"

She was going on about her attire—her dress replicated the garments worn by women servants of the Middle Kingdom, hence the headwear, and she knew the names and properties of each gem. Many of them, she said, were genuine pharaonic gems that Nazeem Bey's forebears had bought long ago, probably from grave robbers.

"Does he know about this little ... obsession?"

"Of course. It's our little game."

She led me to a low coffee table made of inlaid mother-of-pearl, and we sat on large leather ottomans. I'd brought a workbook with me, but I couldn't focus on anything other than Gamila's fetching attire. I was mesmerized.

"Gamila, I can't concentrate on our work with you dressed like this."

"Really? I thought you'd like it, especially after we read the article about Cleopatra and Julius Cesar."

I thought I had walked into an erotic dream. I wanted to touch her, take her in my arms, caress every part of her body, and get lost inside her. My hormones were raging. I had a fleeting thought for Nazeem Bey, and I held on to the few strands of loyalty left in my consciousness to abstain.

"Look, Gamila, your outfit is more beautiful that anything I've ever seen, but it's too distracting. I can't think. Maybe we should do our work some other time."

Pouting, Gamila said, "All right, I'll change my dress!"

We both got up at the same time and bumped into each other. Instinctively I took Gamila in my arms, but she pushed me back. "No," she said. "You're just a boy!"

"I love you," I whispered.

She laughed gently and repeated, "You're just a boy! What do you know about love?"

"I'm not a boy, I'm a man! In my faith, a boy becomes a man at the age of thirteen—we even have a ceremony for that!"

She laughed, then she saw my look of hurt and smiled softly, but she continued to rebuff me. "Look, this is not good. I'm engaged to marry, it's not good for us!"

Stop or carry on? I didn't know what to do. In romantic movies, there was a ritual of seduction that varied little from one picture to the next—the man would try to kiss a woman, but her honor demanded that she resist his advances several times before yielding and kissing him back with passion. I wanted to play that game no matter the consequences. Gamila resisted. I persisted gently and she continued to resist. After what seemed like hours of jousting, my arousal growing and her resistance weakening, we fell on a pile of pillows holding each other and kissing hungrily.

We struggled to remove our garments while still holding onto each other, clumsily, haltingly, until most of our clothes fell away and we made love. I had to pinch myself to confirm that I wasn't having an erotic dream but an erotic encounter. Gamila's body and mine were truly intertwined. It was no longer a fantasy.

Our lovemaking was powerful, passionate, and desperately short. I was awash in ecstasy, awed by the plenitude of my pleasure and by the bottomless closeness I felt holding Gamila in my arms. I was the luckiest man-child in the world.

Gamila broke the silence with a giggle and whispered, "You were right, you're a man, not just a boy!"

The tenderness in her voice aroused me again.

"Not now, ya habibi!" she tittered. "I'm going to change my clothes." She got up, wrapped herself in her toga-like dress, and opened the door to her bedroom.

I quickly put my trousers on and followed her into the room. She was already sitting at her makeup table, using creams from small jars to remove the layers of paint that covered her face. She tried to shoo me away, but I didn't budge. I was fascinated by her ritual. This woman was a far cry from the self-effacing girl I'd known until now. I looked at her with wonder, and once again I felt as though it was all a dream, and I prayed to all the gods in the sky to prevent me from waking up.

After restoring her face to its natural state, she rubbed a few smears of cosmetics off my face. Her touch aroused me, but I sensed the timing was wrong. Gamila looked ill at ease, perhaps regretful, and I didn't want to give her a chance to reject me.

"Let's eat," she said.

A feast was laid out in the sitting room. On a low table surrounded by huge floor pillows, a shiny brass chafing-dish presented a variety of kebabs with rice and vegetables; under a glass dome, a smaller tray contained an array of pastries, and two large pitchers offered mango and apricot nectars. Neither Gamila nor I were hungry. We picked at the food and looked at each other in silence.

"What's going on, Gamila?" I asked, softly. "Are you sorry?"

She shook her head. "Not for this, no."

"Then for what?"

"I wanted to tell you before Nazeem Bey. He's coming tomorrow and he will speak to you, but I wanted to tell you first."

"About what?" I asked, fearing the worst.

"We're leaving for Alexandria in two days."

"For how long?" Since Gamila and Nazeem Bey often took trips together, I didn't understand why she seemed so disturbed.

"For a very long time. I'm going to marry Nazeem Bey. Next month. And we'll live in London."

"I thought Nazeem Bey wanted to wait until you're twenty years old."

"How do you know that?" she asked.

"He told me. That's how he convinced me to tutor you—he wanted his future wife to learn French. I wasn't that keen on it."

She laughed. "Why?"

"Because I knew you were trouble the minute I saw you," I said with a fake smile in an attempt to make light of the situation.

"You're right. I am trouble. And I'm sorry." She ate a few grapes and poured me a glass of sugarcane juice. "I'll be twenty in two months." She fell silent, and I followed suit. I felt as though a bucket of iced water had fallen on my head. "Nazeem didn't ask me. I asked him. I knew he'd wanted to marry me for years, and it was time. He never tried to force me, never tried to sleep with me. When I turned eighteen, I gave myself to him. We've been lovers for two years."

Gamila looked at me with visible anxiety as though she awaited my reaction. In the typical Egyptian gesture of bowing to fatality, I extended my palms upward, pointing to the sky—the sign of submitting to the fates, of acceptance of one's destiny. "Maktoub!" I said. "It is written."

Gamila's face showed both relief and a speck of hurt at my lack of protest. I sat still, although I wanted to scream. Losing Gamila on the very day we'd come together was painful to bear—but it wasn't a complete surprise. Just a few hours earlier, as I was dressing up to meet Gamila, I'd had a blinding flash of a premonition that tonight would be the last time I would see Gamila. The thought was too absurd to be taken seriously, but it had lingered on until I knocked on Gamila's door.

Gamila came to my side and sat close to me. "Thank you for not being angry with me."

"I'm not angry, but I don't understand. If you knew, why did you sleep with me tonight?"

"I don't know. It happened so fast. I'm a crazy woman, and I don't always know what I'm doing or why I'm doing it," she said. "I hadn't planned anything. I thought you'd enjoy my little disguise and have fun before I told you that Nazeem was posted to the embassy in London and all that."

She was speaking so fast that I could barely understand her. I stopped her with putting my hand on her lips, and said, "Please speak more slowly."

She repeated what she'd said in slow motion, and added, I don't know what happened, I must have lost my head, and—"

"So did I," I said gently.

"Maybe I felt bad because we were very close these last months, and maybe it was my way of thanking you for everything—"

"Gamila, you gave me the most wonderful goodbye gift in the world—the best gift ever given to me. Ever!"

"So, you liked my goodbye gift, bad boy!" she said with a teary smile. She came into my arms and whispered, "You're tough, as a man should be. I'm a woman and I just want to cry."

We made love, this time gently and slowly and tenderly. Gamila had a way of making the most daring gestures feel natural, and she elicited instinctive caresses and motions I'd never imagined my body could give. My arms and hands and lips were discovering a life of their own. It was a ritual dance that went back to the dawn of time—a dance where the dancers die in ecstasy and are reborn with renewed desire, over and again until they collapse in exhaustion.

We held each other in total appeasement until dawn—the longest, sweetest goodbye.

***

When school resumed after Spring break, Mario and I resumed our bicycle rides through old Cairo. I still enjoyed them, but they had become routine. I needed fresh places to explore. I had dreams of escaping on a flying carpet across the Mediterranean and landing atop the Eiffel Tower as free man.

To get out of my doldrums, I wrote. Random thoughts, bad poetry, fragments of dreams, cries of freedom, tirades against zealotry and fanaticism, anything that came to mind. As a common theme emerged, the oppression of zealotry, I fashioned my notes into a playful and humorous satirical poem à la Voltaire. It was not very good—poetry was not my forte—but writing it had been an exorcism of sorts. It was an explosion of rage and longing, and it spoke of religion and fanaticism and love and sex, and my profound hatred of all forms of oppression and repression. I gave the poem the title "Ode to the Zealots," copied its four pages in legible handwriting, and gave it to Mario to critique when I returned to school.

Anatole overheard my conversation with Mario and asked to read it too. I answered playfully that one had to lose his virginity to understand the poem. He looked pained and walked away without a word.

When Mario got home, the poem was not in his satchel. The next day, he confronted Anatole, the only other person who knew of the poem's existence. Anatole denied having touched Mario's bag. I didn't believe him, but there was nothing I could do about it.

A cloud of doom descended on me. If my poem got into the Brothers' hands, I would be in deep trouble. It was unlikely because Anatole had often expressed gratitude for defending him against the bullies, and he had no reason to harm me.

I was wrong. The unlikely happened, and a few days later I was summoned to the Brother Principal's office.

The Brother Principal was not in his office when I arrived. An assistant led me to a conference room where three men in black cassocks awaited me. One was standing, the two others were sitting, all three erect like gargoyles and wrapped in ominous silence. I wondered why the Brother Principal was not among them.

They didn't introduce themselves. They stared at me in total silence. Then the standing priest verified my name and turned to the oldest priest with an inviting gesture. The latter picked up my four-page poem with an air of contempt and said in an icy voice "'Ode to the Zealots.' Is this your handwriting? Did you, uh, commit this . . . trash to paper?"

"Yes, Brother!" I said.

"Father!" the three priests yelled in unison.

"Father!" I repeated. "I wrote this poem."

They all looked at me with utter disgust.

"Poem?" one of them said. "You call this trash a poem?"

I wondered why they'd brought in three ordained priests instead of clerical Brothers for this inquisition. Did it mean anything? Since I didn't know their names, I thought I would baptize them with names of my choice. They'd never know they'd been re-christened by a Jew!

The older priest had an impressive leonine mane of the whitest shade of hair. He was extremely thin and stood tall in his impeccably pressed cassock. I named him Father Quixote. Sitting behind him, the second priest was fat, short and bald, and he became Father Sancho. I named the third priest Father Gargoyle because his face was frozen in a grimace of contempt and scorn.

The trio continued to stare at me in ominous silence. Then Father Quixote took the lead. He looked at my poem once again and repeated its title with a contemptuous look. "'Ode to the Zealots.' Did you write it yourself, or did someone help you?"

"I didn't need any help, Father."

The three priests took turns as they unleashed a barrage of questions. They affected an amiable tone, but there was steel and cold rage underneath their words.

"Do you believe in good and evil, my boy?" asked Father Gargoyle.

"Yes, Father."

"Can you give an example?"

"Peace is good. War is evil."

"Another example, please!"

"Tolerance is good. Persecution is evil."

The barrage of questions continued—a blur of animated gargoyles blending in a surrealistic dream, their voices indistinguishable from one another.

"Is lust evil?"

"It depends." I answered. "Not when it's accompanied by love, I suppose!"

"No suppositions here! Is lust evil, yes or no?"

"No!"

"You wrote about carnal love. What do you know about carnal love?" asked Father Gargoyle.

"Not enough yet!" I answered.

"Have you known a woman?" he insisted.

"Many—my cousins, my aunts, my mother's friends—"

"Don't play dumb!" barked Father Sancho Panza. "It's a yes or no question. Did you have carnal knowledge of a woman?"

I hesitated before answering, "Yes, Father."

There was a chilling silence before the next question, "Was the woman a prostitute?"

"No, Father."

"What kind of woman would let a boy desecrate her body?" Father Quixote asked.

"The body of a woman is a sacred temple. It is God's creation. Love cannot possibly desecrate it!"

I was just as stunned as the good priests by the words that had sprung out spontaneously from my mouth. They were vaguely familiar, but I couldn't remember where I'd heard them.

"That's quite enough!" said Father Gargoyle and left the room, followed by his fellow priests.

I didn't know what to think. Too many thoughts buzzed around in my head, and I could hear the beats of my heart. I closed my eyes and tried to still my mind.

The door creaked open, and I heard footsteps walking back into the room. I opened my eyes and waited for the verdict. Father Quixote was alone. He uttered some words with a muffled voice, as though he spoke from behind a shroud.

"Here is where our paths separate, mon petit. You are beyond our powers of salvation. We cannot keep you in this establishment. We'll notify your father."

In these last words of repudiation, I heard sadness, resignation, pity, and compassion. I wondered what made him transition from wrath and contempt to sympathy for the sinner.

"May I ask for a favor, Father?"

He remained silent. Was it incredulity at my insolence? Fearing he would deny me, I spit out my request.

"Before you call my father, would you give me time to give him the bad news myself?"

"Yes, my boy." He smiled the kindest of smiles and patted my hair gently as though he were blessing me. "May you find God on your way."

As I walked through the portal of the Collège des Frères for the last time, I suddenly remembered the source of my fateful response to the priests. It came from a film about Francisco Goya in which the Inquisition attacks the painter for his nude portrait of a maja. A furious Goya responds that the nakedness of woman was the work of God, and the shame about it was the work of Satan. The rest of the film was a blur, but these lines had remained hidden in a back alley of my memory for years—until the poor excuse of an inquisition I'd just experienced brought them back to my memory.

I rode home, torn between relief and guilt, rehearsing the speech in which I would tell my father that, once again, I'd been kicked out of a school for brash insubordination.

As I approached Tahrir Square, I felt once again the urge to challenge myself. I knew it would be perilous, but I ignored my resolution to stay out of harm's way. Once again, I wanted to ride my bicycle around the circle without touching the handlebars. I'd done it several times before, but I'd never been able to ride beyond the halfway mark without having to brake and grab the handlebars.

Once again, I braved the insane whirlpool of traffic on Tahrir Square, and I pedaled with all the strength I could muster, but I only made it to the three-quarter mark before a bus broke my stride. It was progress but not victory. I was disappointed but my flirt with danger had lifted much of my anxiety.

CHAPTER 16

Spring of 1960

Papa burst into my room and threw a folded piece of beige card stock paper on the bed. I looked at his beaming face and I knew instantly what that paper was. I was too anxious to even touch it.

"Go ahead, read it!" said Papa.

My heart beat a little faster when I unfolded the card. The front cover was inscribed "Ministry of the Interior" in Arabic and French. The two inside pages contained multiple stamps and signatures, and lines of identification filled out in thick green ink stating my name, birthdate and birthplace. At the very top were two fateful lines, one in Arabic and the other in French: *Feuille de route valable pour un seul voyage et sans retour*. It was a warrant to travel, valid for a single journey without return. At the bottom, two entries were empty: 'Date of Departure' and 'Reasons for Departure'. Papa said they would be filled in at the airport. A huge letter "Y" in red color was stamped over the entire right page—"Y" for *Yahoodi*. The word "Jew" was printed in large letters like a badge of infamy.

Even though neither my father nor I would ever want to return to Egypt, the words *Bidoon Reg'oo*—"No Return" in Arabic—cut to the quick and sent shivers down my spine. They were words of hatred and ostracism, the ultimate kick in the teeth, and they foreshadowed the complete extinction of all things Jewish in Egypt.

That exit visa, just a flimsy piece of folded beige card stock, made me want to howl and wail all at once—wails of anger and frustration for the years it took to obtain it, and howls of joy because it was *efta'h ya semsem*, the open sesame that would open the cave and let us out into the sunshine.

Papa gently pried the card out of my hands, refolded it and put it in his front pocket, along with his own exit visa.

"How did you make it happen this time?" I asked.

"Luck. After bribing a lot of dishonest crooks, I finally found an honest crook! This one delivered!"

"When are we leaving?" I asked.

"Two weeks, ten days maybe."

I could barely control my joy. "By air or by sea?"

"By air. It's about six hours to Paris."

He turned to leave. In my excitement, I'd almost forgotten that I had just been kicked out of school.

"Wait, Papa, I have something to tell you."

"School trouble?" he asked. I nodded. "Sacked again?" I nodded again. "Can't say I'm surprised," he said with a sigh. "Give me *your* facts before I speak to the Brothers."

Papa listened to my new misdeeds and simply laughed, "Nothing new under the sun!"

"You're not mad?" I asked.

"I don't have the time to get mad. What is done is done! You are a stubborn, rebellious, nonconformist, insufferable boy—and you may always be—but maybe when we're in a safer and more welcoming world—"

"I'm with you, Papa. I'm tired of being me."

"Well, I hate to say it, but I like what you told them about love and women. What was it again?"

"Something like 'The body of a women is God's creation so it can't be desecrated' and blah-blah-blah!"

"I'm impressed even though I can't condone your constant rebellions. On this famous note, let's celebrate!"

"Don't you have a hot rendezvous?"

"Yes, but I will cancel it."

I shook my head. "No, Papa," I said. "You go and have a good time. Right now, I want to collect my thoughts about all this. Go and have a good time, and we'll celebrate tomorrow."

"All right, but before I go—will you tell me who's the lucky lady of the 'carnal-knowledge' question?" He gave me a teasing smile. "Was it the lovely Gamila?"

"Sorry, dear father. You taught me how gentlemen should be discrete, et cetera, et cetera!"

"Fair enough! Well, consider it the first act of manhood after your Bar Mitzvah!"

I lay in the dark and reflected on the unpredictability of my life and its randomness in the alternation of joy and misery. My fantasies were coming true just as I had abandoned all hope. Love was given and taken without warning. If God or the djinn were watching over me, why did they play such perverse games?

As I drifted into a state that was neither wakefulness nor sleep, I dreamt of Gamila. They were not memories of the past, but perhaps a glimpse of the future, real or imagined. I was walking on a beach somewhere in France or Italy, when I saw Gamila walking toward me, a baby in her arms; a step behind, a smiling Nazeem Bey was waving at me. As we came closer, I noticed that Gamila wore a large ring made of two intertwined ankhs with a teardrop-shaped diamond in each loop. Her baby was a miniature copy of Nazeem Bey. When we came close, she whispered, "I told you, all your dreams will come true!"

That last line jolted me back into full wakefulness, and an eerie thought flooded my mind—*did Gamila have anything to do with the granting of our exit visas? So suddenly, after so many denials?*

I remembered the letter Nazeem Bey sent me shortly after they left the Anglo-Swiss Hotel. It was an effusive letter in which he expressed gratitude for my tutoring of Gamila, and he'd ended it with assurances that my father and I could count on him for whatever we might need. I also remembered confiding to Gamila my intense frustration about the continuous denials of our exit visas. Now I wondered if Gamila might have asked Nazeem Bey to open the dungeon and let us go.

Was it wishful imagining, pure nonsense, or the truth? I'd never know, but I loved the thought that I might owe our freedom, not to the greased palms of a civil servant, but rather to a glorious night of tender love and sex with a pharaonic princess aptly named Gamila, the Beautiful. It would be sheer poetry.

***

When I went to my mother's and gave her the news, she froze in place and stood still. Then, in the traditional Arab women's expression of grief, she slapped her face several times and let out a wail that pierced me to the core. I'd never seen such raw pain. Her wail was the wail of a lioness whose heart was being torn from her breast.

I took her in my arms and let her cry until her tears ran out. It was a cruel irony that my good news was deadly news for my mother.

After our long embrace, Maman composed herself and said, "It's freezing in Europe. Even in the summer. I must make sure we get you all you need."

We'd done these buying sprees in older times when Papa thought that migration was imminent, but it was different this time. The Jewish department stores, which had been temples of elegance and beauty in their heydays, had gone the way of the British Empire. They were sad and desolate. But my mother bought enough sweaters, jackets and blankets to fill several suitcases, even though she knew the law limited us to twenty kilograms of luggage. I let her binge; it was her way of showing her love and keeping her pain at bay, and the clothes would once again benefit the children of Abdu and Mayasoon.

I asked Maman whether she and Uncle Albert would ever leave Egypt. "I don't know, ya rohi," she answered, letting out a few contained sobs. "For me, your news changes everything! All I want is to be with you!" A new fit of tears shook her. "Albert will be very sad that you're leaving, but will think your father made the right decision. We all thought things would get better, but it doesn't look like it's going in that direction."

"You mean you *might* leave Egypt soon?"

She nodded. "Not just now. We'll wait until Khadr Bey warns us that it's time to go. We'll be sending money to Europe so we're not destitute if and when we have to leave Egypt." Crying again, she repeated, "All I want is for my son to be with me!"

I felt guilty for not experiencing the same intensity of pain she did. I didn't know what to feel about my mother. In the past year, I'd gotten to know her better than I ever had, and my love for her had grown, but her dramatic ways still left traces of mistrust about her sincerity. This time, though, her wails told me that, theatrics or no theatrics, her love was true.

On the way home, Maman asked me for the third or fourth time to confirm the date of my departure. She said she was relieved that I would soon be living in a safer place but that losing me was a sudden and terrible shock. I'd never seen her look so vulnerable. The veneer of beauty, elegance, popularity, and pride that had always protected her was cracking, and she was now humble and defeated and forlorn.

It hurt deeply to see her in such agony, and I felt guilty for all the times I'd kept her at bay. I was also realizing, perhaps too late, that I loved her more than I'd allowed myself to feel.

***

I was no longer a schoolboy, but for my friends who still went to school it was Easter break. JP, Ike, Coco, and Gil were in Alexandria, and I had to see them one last time.

As expected, Papa wouldn't let me go by myself, so I came up with a complex trompe-l'oeil scheme with Mario, who was spending the Easter break at a resort in Helwan, a suburb of Cairo. Mario would invite me to go with him to a bicycle race and spend a couple of days with him. Mario and his cousin Nicoletta would monitor the phone in case my father called, and they would devise some excuse to explain my absence.

I needed money for the train ticket and for expenses while in Alexandria. Once again I went to the souk and sold most of clothes Maman had bought for me. Papa gave me several pounds to buy snacks and beverages at the bicycle race. I felt bad for taking Papa's money while lying to his face, but my compulsion was greater than my conscience.

At dawn on Friday, I got up early and took the bus to Cairo's central train station. The man at the booth gave me a funny look when I asked for a third-class ticket and he made me confirm twice that I *really* wanted to travel in third class before handing me a ticket.

Once I boarded the train, I understood the clerk's qualms. The third-class compartment was a world apart from the wagons I'd traveled in before. It was a bare wooden boxcar with no seats other than long benches along its sides. I'd seen those trains in *Bab el-Hadid*, Youssef Chahine's film, but I'd thought they were relics of bygone days. Most people sat on the floor surrounded by their crying babies, their baskets of food, and their live chickens and small livestock. A baby goat dominated one end of the car. The smells were repulsive, and I thought of jumping out of the train, but I decided to heed the call for adventure. When the train moved, I remained standing and leaned against the gangway doors.

Everyone was looking at me. They'd probably never seen a khawaga in third class. A man got up and offered me his spot on the floor by a window. He was my father's age, perhaps a bit younger, and wore a clean white galabeya. I shook my head and declined with a respectful bow. He responded with a wide smile and said something to his immediate neighbor who moved a little farther to make room for me. He spoke to me in French, introducing himself as Abdel-Hakim Mansour. He was traveling with his mother, the very old woman sitting next to him. I gave him my name, but he continued to address me as "Ya khawaga." I surmised that he was or had been a domestic in a francophone household and was taught to defer to Europeans. Old habits die hard, I thought with sadness and discomfort.

The train was painfully slow, and it stopped at stations that were only a few miles apart. Each time people got out, others came in, making the stench of food, sweat, and manure increasingly strong. I told Abdel-Hakim that my usuals trips to Alexandria with Papa took some three hours without stopping and asked why this train was taking so long.

"With your father, you were probably traveling on a first-class train. Here, we're on the third-class omnibus that stops at almost every village along the track and takes eight hours to get to Alex. How come you took this train?"

"I didn't know."

He gave me a quizzical look and changed the subject. "I take my mother on this third-class line because the first-class express train doesn't stop at her village."

It was good have someone to talk to, but my acquaintance with Abdel-Hakim Mansour didn't last long. A few stations later, the train entered their village, and he bid me goodbye. His mother put her hand on my head and muttered a blessing.

At the following stop, I ran to the ticket booth and asked how I could catch the express train, but the attendant said that I'd have to change trains twice, and that wouldn't make the trip much shorter. I returned to the swarm, determined to bite the bullet and enjoy the ride somehow.

The ticket man had said that insh'allah, with God's help, I would arrive in Alexandria around four in the afternoon. I'd planned on meeting Ike, Coco and Gil, for lunch and an afternoon on the beach, then having an early dinner with JP, and returning to Cairo on the late-night train. With my railway mishap, I'd have to fall back on the contingency plan, go directly to JP's place and spend the night in Alexandria.

I dozed on and off during the slow ride and woke up hungry. I asked my traveling companions about the next stop, and they said it would be at least an hour ahead. The food could wait that long, but I was parched, and I was too bashful to ask anyone for water. A man sitting a foot away saw that I was wetting my lips with my tongue and handed me his earthen jug with a gesture urging me to drink. Then a woman gave me a generous chunk of *baladi* bread and a large slice of onion. Once again, I marveled at the infinite generosity and the profound kindness of the poorest Egyptians. They were the Egypt I missed already.

I closed my eyes and let myself be cradled by the sounds and the scents of my early childhood. The stench of the animals faded away, replaced by the earthy aromas of food, the fragrances of henna and the pastries of the Koubbeh house, the laughter of the women, the games with Mayasoon's children, the smell of red-hot asphalt and the burnt summer air on the rooftop of Nona's house. Soon the clickety-clack of the railcar lulled me to sleep like a gentle lullaby.

***

I arrived in Alexandria in the late afternoon and took a bus to meet JP. We walked along Montazah Beach and through the gardens of the royal palace, which had been shuttered since the revolution and had recently reopened to the public. From afar, we admired the elegant silhouette of the Al-Haramlik wing of the royal abode, a blend of Ottoman and Italian Renaissance architecture. It was a perfect reflection of the Muhammad Ali dynasty's cultural universality—an era upon which the curtain had fallen.

Alexandria was pulsating with energy. We ate kebabs at an open-air restaurant. I wanted to have my fill of the tastes of Egypt. I told JP I doubted I'd find a Parisian restaurant that served my favorite Egyptian foods.

"You won't," said JP. "In Paris most Arab restaurants are Algerian, Tunisian, or Moroccan, and a few from Lebanon, but I have yet to see an Egyptian restaurant there. You're probably having your last fūl-medammas and ta'ameyas."

We spent the rest of the night talking about the future, near and far. JP's father was liquidating his holdings in Egypt and planning a move to France in a year or two. After the lycée, JP expected to go to university, then business school in France or go to the London School of Economics. His goal was to help his father salvage his family business from the claws of Nasser's regime and rebuild it in Europe."

My own plans and dreams were to study at the Sorbonne, become a journalist and discover the world, and someday when I was ready, write novels—lots of them, I hoped. And of course I would live in Paris, the literary Mecca, and hopefully in Saint-Germain-des-Prés, the Mecca within the Mecca.

"Not everybody can make a living from writing," said JP. "You could be a teacher if it doesn't work."

"That's what my father says. If I think of failing, I *will* fail. I'd rather live in a garret, starve and all that, and keep at it until I succeed. A safety net would only weaken my resolve," I affirmed.

"It sounds romantic and all, but it's a dream," he said. "You're setting yourself up for disappointment."

"Possible, maybe even probable, but it's a risk I'm willing to take. If I fall on my ass, I'll try again, until I succeed."

We knew our paths would diverge, and we wondered whether our friendship would survive the seismic changes that awaited us. We made a pact to preserve it. We wouldn't allow political differences to break our friendship, even if we espoused opposing political views or lived in different countries. Friendship was sacred. I promised JP to keep him informed of my whereabouts so he could find me when his time came to jump across the Mediterranean.

We continued our conversation until JP's parents came home. JP's mother set me up in their guest room. Too excited to sleep, I stood on the balcony overlooking the beach, my shoulders wrapped in a light blanket, breathing the salty air, and listening to the sounds of the Mediterranean. The near-full moon shone over the crest of the waves, and the surf dying on the sand below sounded like a whispered bittersweet goodbye song.

The Mediterranean—the Great Sea for the ancient Hebrews, Mare Nostrum for the Romans, the Pure White Sea for the Turks, the Middle Sea for the Greeks, among many other names—held the key to my identity. To the northeast was Israel, the thrice-promised land, a land conquered, liberated, and recaptured fifty-odd times and still fought over, and now home to a large part of my family. Straight north was Turkey, the first refuge of the Spanish Jews, including my ancestors, after their expulsion from Spain. Farther west was Greece, where Nona was born; then Italy, where my paternal forebears had lived before landing in Egypt. At the farthest western end of the Mediterranean, just above Spain, was France, my cultural home. There was a fragment of my soul in each of these places.

In the morning, JP's mother served a breakfast of eggs and caviar with a drop of champagne to celebrate my journey. When JP told his mother about my adventures on the third-class train, she roared with laughter and offered to buy me a first-class ticket back to Cairo as a goodbye gift.

"If your father finds out and gets upset, have him call me," said JP's mother. "Boys must be boys."

I envied JP for having such an open-minded mother.

Gil, Coco and Ike joined us for a final goodbye, and they all accompanied me to the train which I boarded with a first class ticket.

***

Two days before the Day, I woke up before the alarm clock rang, in a high state of agitation. My next-to-last day in Egypt and so much to do! I had to finish packing, say goodbye to Momo, take a last bicycle ride along the Nile with Mario, and attend a small goodbye party at the Anglo-Swiss. And perhaps sleep a wink.

First, the packing. Where do I begin? I knew how to pack for summer camp or a trimester in boarding school, but what do I pack for an uncertain final destination, for climates unknown, and for forever? Papa said, "One book for the plane, two sets of clothes for summer and spring, and winter garments to fill the rest of the case. Twenty kilos, total, as you know. We'll buy what we need when I get a job and we can settle down!"

"I want to get a job too," I said.

"Your job is to finish high school, then university, then you can get a job and support your old father in style! In the meantime, we'll get some help from American and European agencies for refugees."

The word "refugees" resounded in my ears like a shriek. I'd never equated our situation with the poignant newsreels images of refugees amassed in the camps of Europe or Palestine.

"Are we really refugees?" I asked. "Are we going to live in a refugee camp in France?"

"Yes, we are refugees, and no, we won't live in a refugee camp. The word 'refugee' means someone who leaves a country to escape persecution, and that's our case. We'll be spared the camps because we have family in France and Israel—and universal fraternity is probably the only good thing about being a Jew in this world."

***

Momo came back from vacationing in Ras-el-Bar to bid me goodbye. Over the years, we had grown to be close friends. I would miss his wit, his multilingual jokes and the political conversations in which he tried to explain Nasser's love-hate relationship with the Muslim Brotherhood. Although we'd gone to different schools after the lycée, Momo had been a substantial source of comfort during my travails in an increasingly sectarian Arab nation. We both knew we were living the last years in which a Muslim and a Jew could be brothers.

Momo was despondent over the political changes in Egypt. Under Nasser, it had become a far more brutal dictatorship than it had been under the king's rule. Nasser wasn't just jailing the so-called enemies of the nation, like the Jews, the communists, and the Europeans. He was now locking up many of the intellectuals who had welcomed the revolution with open arms and now disagreed with his policies.

"You're leaving Egypt at the right time!" said Momo.

There wasn't much I could say to ease his sorrow, but I listened to him until he was talked out. We took the tram to Central Station together.

"Maybe you should come and study in France," I said. "We could go to university together!"

"Only when France is ready to vote for a president named Mohammed!" he said.

"Before or after they vote for Moshe ben Cohen?"

"Bokra fel meshmesh!" he said, using the colorful Egyptian expression 'tomorrow in the apricot season,' a euphemism for 'impossible or 'never.'

As the train bound for Damietta was about to leave, we shared a hearty hug.

"Damn you, dirty Jew, I'll miss you," he said in French.

"I'll miss you too, Muslim ebn el kalb!"

We hugged again, and he climbed aboard. I turned back, mouthing, "Goodbye, brother!"

As I walked out of Bab el-Hadid, I also waved to the statue of Ramses the Great. One more goodbye.

The last friend to see was Mario. We took our last spin along the Corniche. At Tahrir Square, I challenged Mario to ride all the way around the midan without ever touching the handlebars. He said he wasn't crazy enough. It was indeed a crazy thing to do, but I had to try again. Maybe this time I would succeed where I had always failed in the past.

"You're completely nuts! You're leaving in two days. Don't risk your stupid life!"

"I'll make it safe and sound. Bet you five pounds!"

"Make it ten pounds," he grinned. "Hell, if you must kick the bucket, I might as well make a little money from it, right?"

It felt like the longest ride ever. The traffic was fierce, and the sight of my arms held up in the air seemed to provoke the wrath of many a driver. A few drove too close for comfort, honking to distract me, and some made gestures of applause. One driver, deliberately moving from side to side, tried a dangerous fishtail action, then he would brake to let me get ahead and try again. Waving my hand like a deranged automaton, I escaped his reach without hitting the brakes, which would have forced me to touch the handlebars. Another driver attempted to hit my front wheel with his rear fender, but I evaded him and charged forward until I reached the curb on the other side of Tahrir Square. Full circle, at long last!

"Bravo!" yelled Mario when I got off the bicycle. He fished in his pocket for money.

"Your money's useless in France," I laughed. "Keep it and use it to get laid at Sett Latifah's!"

After Mario left, I pondered my obsession with the ride around the *midan*. Was there a meaning behind that insane act? Or was it just madness? I felt more foolish than victorious.

***

My last day in Cairo was for my mother, and she insisted that we go to Abu Labib, her one-eyed seer, for a last visit. It would also be my last walk in Old Cairo.

The courtyard and the house no longer held the blend of attraction and fear it had evoked in my childhood. The same maid, Aïsha, opened the door. Only her sweet smile reminded me of the young woman whose breasts had sent delicious electric shocks through my body. Aïsha was now a corpulent matron, and her belly was so distended I feared she'd give birth on the spot, yet her radiance shone through more beautifully than ever.

The venerable Abu Labib's face hadn't aged one bit, but his body had. He moved his arms with greater effort and his voice had softened to a whisper. When the coffee grounds dried, Maman asked the seer to read my cup first. He examined the grounds for a long time and turned the cup my way so I could look at it. I could make out a thin trail traced between clumps of dried coffee grounds. It extended upward toward the mouth of the cup, crossed a large circle of white unsullied porcelain and ended in another thick buildup of dark grounds. It was uncanny. The blank area's shape was vaguely reminiscent of a sea between continents.

The old man brought the cup back to the orbit of his eye, searching the grains for clues. At last, he said, "You will leave this country, cross the Big Sea, and go far away. Later, years later, you will cross another Big Sea and go live at the edge of yet another sea."

My mother was crestfallen. She was a firm believer in the occult, and she took Abu Labib's predictions as truth foretold. I saw them as intuitive interpretations of one's mind at the time of the reading. It was not rubbish, but it wasn't a reliable map of the future either.

"You will walk a meandering path full of great pain and great happiness," Abu Labib continued, drawing with his hand a sinuous road with sharp zigzags. "I see riches and I see indigence, high mountains and deep pits, a castle built, a castle destroyed, and a castle rebuilt."

"Allah yestor!" Maman exclaimed. May God protect us!

Abu Labib turned his seeing eye toward Maman and gave her a half-smile of reassurance, then returned to the reading. "We all shed tears of joy and tears of sorrow, ya ebni, and Allah gave you a rockier road to travel than many, but he also gave you a powerful sword and the strength to wield it."

He closed his seeing eye, leaving his porcelain eye eerily open. "It's in your power to reach the end of that road safely, Insh'Allah! If you do, you will meet the destiny Allah has written for you." He lifted his hand as if to bless me and repeated, "Insh'Allah."

After the customary litany of salaams, Maman kissed Abu Labib's hand, and we left the cottage. At the gate, Maman gave Aïsha a hefty sum for her impending newborn, along with a litany of good wishes. The woman kissed my mother's hand and gave me a broad smile.

Back in the alleyway, anticipating my reactions to the reading, Maman said, "I swear I didn't tell him a thing about you leaving Egypt!"

"But he knew we were waiting for an exit visa."

"Maybe, maybe not, but either way, I couldn't have told him. In my last visit to Abu Labib—" Her voice was breaking, and she paused for a long moment, "then I didn't know you'd be leaving me so soon!"

"I'm not leaving *you*, Maman. I'm leaving a place that's bad for us," I said, taking her hand.

We talked again about Abu Labib. She was anxious about the second sea he'd mentioned. I didn't tell her that my father had been corresponding with his cousins and exploring the possibility of joining them in Brazil.

"He *did* say that you will meet a great destiny at the end," Maman said. "This reading is a warning to be cautious, whatever you do or wherever you go!"

We had lunch in the Khan el Khalili. I had no wish to shop, but Maman begged for five minutes at Hadj Bashir's store.

The elder Bashir had died, but his throne-like chair had remained in its place, reupholstered with the same rich black fabric with shades of Nubian blue. A large portrait of the patriarch stood upright on the seat, giving the illusion that the holy man was once again sitting on his throne. Nabil and Mounir greeted us warmly, and after a few reminiscences about their blessed father, Nabil handed Maman a tiny box and we left the store.

Aa'm Mustafa was standing by the trusty Studebaker, ready to open the door. He was crying unabashedly. On the way home, my mother couldn't hold her tears. Her makeup was running down the corners of her eyes, but she didn't seem to care. Something broke inside me and I let out a few tears—the tears unshed for years. It was one of the few times I'd allowed myself to cry for my mother.

Yet, in my grief, a flash of intuition buzzed like a mosquito—the intuition that it would be easier to love my mother from afar. Perhaps time and distance would heal the wounds inflicted throughout our rocky history, making room for harmony in the future. It was an odd thought, but one to ponder. For now, I just wanted Maman to know that I no longer rejected her love, that I accepted the visceral bonds that united us, and I realized it was no longer difficult to tell my mother that I loved her.

As we drove back to the Anglo-Swiss Hotel, Maman opened the tiny box she'd picked up at the goldsmith's shop. It contained a gold chain with two small golden amulets—a *khamsa*, the five fingers of Fatima's hand, and an ankh, the cross with a loop, the pharaonic symbol of life.

She didn't need to explain their meaning. The *khamsa* would protect me from the evil eye, and the ankh would nourish the breath of life in me.

"Hide them in your socks at the airport," she whispered. "Those Customs officers steal everything. Wear them when you're safely out of Egypt, insh'Allah, and wear them all the time. They will protect you and remind you that your mother loves you. Now go with God, ya rohi. I will pray and burn boukhour every day until God reunites us, insh'Allah."

FINALE

Adieu

It was my last night in Cairo. I was too excited to sleep. I rode around Tahrir Square, slowly, cautiously, hugging the edge of the sidewalk, away from cars and buses. This time it was not a marathon. It was a dance.

I dismounted at the Qasr-el-Nil Bridge, leaned my bicycle on the parapet and took a long, all-embracing look at the cityscape of Cairo, *Umm al Dunya*, the Mother of the World. So many of its landmarks held so many memories. I thought of the places I might never see again—the long flowing Nile, its Corniche and its *a'arabeya hantoors*, Haret el-Yahood, Islamic Cairo, and all the streets I'd roamed—and above all, the jewels that sparkled before my eyes, the Qasr-el-Nil bridge and its four lions. They were the fraternal buddies that had accompanied me through the ebbs and flows of love and love's end.

Standing between the two lions on my end of the bridge, I turned toward Tahrir Square for my last long goodbye. Like the lions, it had witnessed the happiest and the most miserable days of my life.

I had given nicknames to many of the square's buildings. The Hall of Misery was the Mogamma'a, the stodgy government building where I'd seen my father endure hours of administrative red tape in his quest to leave Egypt—the Hall of Beauty was the museum across the square where I'd fallen in love with the bust of Queen Nefertiti—and Hall of Love was the Semiramis Hotel that had sheltered the most tender moments I'd known. The Tahrir Square roundabout had been the midpoint that separated my schizoid life between the dwellings of my father and my mother. It was only a mile of asphalt but crossing it had often felt like walking the Long March of China.

Goodbye to it all.

An ancient legend asserts that whoever has drunk the waters of the Nile will always return to Egypt, but I doubted I'd ever see the Nile again. Tomorrow, I would be watching the flow of the river Seine.

Another wave of anxiety descended on me. How would I fit into that new world? Who would I be? A refugee for a while, but afterward, what? An émigré? An expatriate? An exile?

None of these words would be accurate. They all assumed having a homeland to which one could return if circumstances changed. As far as I knew, there were no words to define people whose native country had written them out of its history books.

What would I remember of my native country in five years, in ten years, in thirty years? Would I speak of it with affection, hatred, disdain, indifference? Or would I simply not think of it at all?

I couldn't see that far into the future. Perhaps if we had left Egypt when the persecutions began, if I hadn't seen my world disintegrate, I might have remembered the safer and kinder Egypt of my childhood, the times of greater joy than sorrow. But the memories of that time had been superseded by those images of the years of destruction, the years of transit, the years of vacuum, the years of unfulfilled hopes and utter despair. For years, I had lived in a no-man's-land in which my past was erased, my future hijacked, and my present frozen.

Perhaps those feelings explained the reasons for my insane daredevil ride around the Tahrir Square. Perhaps it was my affirmation that adversity and discrimination had not vanquished my spirits, and it would be good to bid Egypt adieu with a victory lap.

Other thoughts came into my my mind. "Le dare tiempo al Tiempo!" Perhaps, in the fullness of time, I would remember with gratitude the place where I had learned to overcome loss and grief, where I had explored new worlds of literature, history and art, and discovered the wonders of love and sex. Would I ever want to revisit the city where I had miraculously come of age in the rubble of my vanishing world? I had knots in my stomach as I said sotto voce, in Arabic, "Yalla salaam, Umm al Dunya!"—Goodbye, Mother of the World!"

Just before riding away, I stopped for a last look. Midan el-Tahrir was as majestic as ever in the twilight. I scanned the expansive skyline of the tentacular city for the last time and heard myself whisper again, "Adieu, Tahrir Square!"

End